FEMININE RISING

FEMININE RISING

Voices of POWER & INVISIBILITY

EDITED BY **ANDREA FEKETE & LARA LILLIBRIDGE**
WITH A FOREWORD BY **AMY HUDOCK, PhD**

CYNREN

PUBLISHED BY Cynren Press
101 Lindenwood Drive, Suite 225
Malvern, PA 19355 USA
http://www.cynren.com/

For information about special discounts for bulk purchases, please contact Cynren Press Sales at
(484) 875–3113 or sales.media@cynren.com

Printed in the United States of America on acid-free paper

ISBN-13: 978-1-947976-08-5 (pbk)
ISBN-13: 978-1-947976-09-2 (ebk)

Library of Congress Control Number: 2018944487

COVER DESIGN BY Emma Christine Hall
COVER PHOTO BY Allef Vinicius

Contents

Foreword **xiii**
Amy Hudock, PhD

Editor's Introduction: Giving Story to the Light **xvii**
Andrea Fekete

Editor's Introduction: Do You Really Think I Can't Stand for Thirty Minutes? **xxiii**
Lara Lillibridge

ON RESISTANCE & ROLES 1

Lynda Levy
The Tear **3**

Carol Gloor
Working **5**

Shobhana Kumar
Keel **6**

Sarah Sadie
Each Jar Tied with Bright Red Ribbon **7**

Estela González
Open Triangle 2012 **8**

Sarah Sadie
Without Mirrors and Minus a Gravity of Love **11**

Müesser Yeniay
Now Don't Tell Me of Men! **12**

CONTENTS

Nicole Hospital-Medina
DR (la Republica Dominicana) **13**

Ellen Cantarow
Harvard in the Sixties: (Un)Speakable Memories **15**

Cheryl Denise
God (According to Pastor Smucker) **21**

Gina Valdés
Acts of Protest **23**

Ann Pancake
Ice Fight **24**

Nicole Hospital-Medina
A Poem for the Waitress on First Street: April 18, 2011 **38**

Boutheina Laarif
Fe-Male **40**

Marianne Worthington
Failed Meal **41**

Gina Valdés
Butterfly Woman **42**

Terry Ann Thaxton
Stains **43**

ON THE BODY & SEX 53

Lisa Minney
Mental-Pause **55**

Sarah Sadie
Stretch Marks **58**

Katharyn Howd Machan
Journey through the Door into Always-Always Land: 1966 **60**

Mary Imo-Stike
The Stain **62**

Bonnie J. Morris
Puberty's Enchiladas **64**

Kali Lightfoot
Puberty, 1956 **67**

Beatriz F. Fernandez
Reunion **68**

Jessica Spruill
After Years of Being Told I Have the Body of a 12-Year-Old Boy **69**

Renée Olander
Dear Torso, Stone-Carved **71**

Anne Harding Woodworth
Sex at Six **73**

Rachel A. Hicks
The Biopsy **74**

Linda Flaherty Haltmaier
Cloaking Magic **75**

Elizabeth Johnston
Tackle Box **77**

Boutheina Laarif
A Woman's Body **86**

Michele K. Johnson Huffman
Natalie Land-Locked **88**
Natalie in the Dirt **89**
Natalie on Men **90**

Jane Chance
Spit **91**

Tuesday Taylor
Lipstick and Earrings **92**

ON LOVE & LEAVING 95

Meridian Johnson
Somewhere with Cows 97

Ruth Sabath Rosenthal
A Box, Full 99
For Want of Red 100

Cathy Cultice Lentes
After All These Years of Marriage 101

Rachel Squires Bloom
Problem Solving 102

Marged Dudek
The Anniversary Cake 104

Lauren Brimmer
Recurring Dreams 107
I Have This Dream 108

Marianne S. Johnson
Today at the Gynecologist 109

Rashida Murphy
Maybe 110

Betsy Cornwell
The Search for One Thing 111

ON FAMILY & HEIRLOOMS 117

Andrena Zawinski
After My Mother's Death 119
Rosie Times 121

Maggie Thach Morshed
Land and Water 123

Liz Dolan
For Once I Am Able to Save Her **133**

Ellen Bass
The Orange-and-White High-Heeled Shoes **134**

Barbara Ungar
Call Me Medusa **135**

Pauletta Hansel
Pentimento **136**

Melissa Helton
The Women's Gown **141**

Jamie Wendt
Pins, Ropes, and Wooden Stakes **142**

Liz Dolan
Sepia Photo: One-Room Schoolhouse, 1917 **143**

Michelle Elvy
Moments in Sand: Fragments between Sea and Sky **144**

Liz Dolan
A Secret of Long Life **152**

Jennifer L. Freed
You Believed **153**

Renée Olander
The Apparatus of the Dark **155**

Michele Tracy Berger
The Poison Our Mothers and Grandmothers Drank **157**

Marianne Worthington
Porcelain **161**
1888–1988 **162**

Frances Nicholson
On Motherhood **163**
My Grandmother's Favorite Book: On Discovering a Copy of the Selected Works of Edna St. Vincent Millay **164**

ON VIOLENCE & SURVIVAL 167

Eileen McDermott
The Angry Girl at the Funeral **169**

Penny Perkins
A Girl's Mouth **171**

Mary Heather Noble
Things I (Shouldn't) Have to Tell My Daughters **173**

Gail C. DiMaggio
Foundation **176**

Cade Leebron
Fuck Us Harder **177**

Katharyn Howd Machan
My Brother **185**

Siobhan Harvey
When My Best Friend Came to Stay; or, Corporeal Minimalism: Composition in Twelve Parts, Inspired by Philip Glass **187**

Katharyn Howd Machan
Les-Salles-du-Gardon **193**

ON SILENCE & SUBVERSION 195

Lois Roma-Deeley
Apologizing for the Rain **197**

Cheryl Denise
Swallowing **198**

Shloka Shankar
Invasion **200**

Annette Snyckers
Clipped **202**
The Final No **203**

~dreama pritt
eggshells **204**

Pauletta Hansel
Girl Villanelle **205**

Shobhana Kumar
Brown **206**

Llewellyn McKernan
Getting Out of Bed at Dawn **207**

Rachel A. Hicks
Paper-Thin Girls **209**

Mary Hutchins Harris
Postscript **210**

Pauletta Hansel
On Faith **211**

ON PREGNANCY & BIRTH 213

M. J. Iuppa
Between Worlds **215**

Melissa Helton
Gravidity **217**

Susan Richardson
Mother and Child **218**

Martha Clarkson
She Decides about the Baby **220**

Lucy Palmer
Post-Natal **221**

Wendy Besel Hahn
Where the Sexual Meets the Sacred **223**

ON LATE LIFE & DEATH 231

Jacqueline Doyle
Mirrors and Reflections **233**

Mary Imo-Stike
Old Women **235**

Jessica Lawrence
I've Spent My Life **237**

Carol Gloor
Your End **238**

Pauletta Hansel
All I Know of Death **239**

Gina Valdés
Between Worlds **240**

About the Contributors **243**
About the Editors **257**
Publication History **259**

Foreword

Amy Hudock, PhD

I was once invisible and silenced. My interior and exterior lives grew far apart, and I stopped recognizing myself in the mirror. The woman I was expected to be and the woman I was inside didn't match. In that time of disconnect, I started reading stories and poems written by women who made their inner lives visible, and suddenly, I wasn't alone. I met a community of women who claimed their power through refusing to make others comfortable by making themselves uncomfortable, and they spoke their truths despite all that would keep them silent. *Feminine Rising: Voices of Power and Invisibility* introduces us to such women.

Feminine Rising reveals a revolution in the making that is taking place online, in boardrooms, in voting booths, and on the streets. This anthology gives a platform for writers from many cultural positions who refuse to stay silent and invisible about the ways they as women have experienced patriarchal culture and thus reflects an important moment in women's history. This book offers us voices that are queer, intersectional, international, and intergenerational, voices that challenge rape and harassment culture, work to redefine both masculinity and femininity, and promote a sex-positive vision. It challenges us to read beyond the text on the page and the lives of the women who have spoken—to those who still remain silent. This book couldn't have come at a better time. We need these women's stories to energize us, to move us forward, to help more of us use our voices. This book teaches us we need be silent no more.

The turn of the century changed women's relationship to publishing forever. The traditional gatekeepers that had kept women's voices from being heard were no longer relevant. As one of the early women bloggers, I saw the rise of a blogging culture that allowed women to write for wide audiences about their personal lives without the self- or imposed censorship of the past. Women quickly took over the blogging world, so much so that it became uncool for men to blog. Sharing the personal moved from being risky to being required, and the memoir genre took off. As women built large platforms, traditional publishing houses took note, offered these women contracts, and promoted their work. The mainstream media were quick to note the dominance of women's voices, proclaiming, obviously, that all the work of feminism had been completed.

In the early years of the twenty-first century, young women tended to believe that the hard battles of feminism had been won and that hard-core misogyny was limited to the radical fringe. Women came to women's and gender studies classes I taught feeling exasperated with what they decried as a focus on victimization. They believed that their male classmates saw them as equals and that they could achieve anything they chose to pursue. They refused the label of "feminist" because they saw it as too limited. Anti-feminist feminists took up a great deal of linguistic and cultural space, and *feminism* became a dirty word. Those who did embrace feminism tended to focus on individual emancipation.

Heading into the Obama years, the media talked about a post-feminist, post-racial society. The defeat of the woman presidential candidate Hillary Clinton in the 2008 Democratic primary was said to serve a greater purpose: to elect an African American man. Her time was coming, people said, as men from the Left flocked to support the male candidate. The cause of racial justice seemed more important than gender justice—because, really, weren't women equal now? Clinton did gain the presidential nomination in 2016, the same year Beyoncé did her show in front of a huge, lit-up sign that read "Feminist," and the president said of himself, "This is what a feminist looks like." Feminism seemed to have arrived. Unfortunately, the 2016 presidential election proved that wrong.

A presidential candidate with numerous charges of sexual assault and harassment against him, who was caught on tape talking about grabbing women "by the pussy," gained the Republican nomination not despite his record against women but because of it. Other more experienced and more qualified male Republicans stepped out of the race when they saw the groundswell of support for a man whose racist and sexist statements had people across the country celebrating because he was saying what they only said when hiding behind a username. Now, they could say it as themselves. And as the internet lit up with even more trolls, ranks of real-world hate groups swelled, and people of color and women suffered more physical and sexual violence. His winning the race seemed to his followers the revenge they had been looking for—against women, against people of color, against LGBTQ people, against anyone they felt had taken away their privilege. Some men of the Left also celebrated, the ones who waved dollar bills at Clinton campaign events and who became online trolls who attacked the femaleness of women members of their own party. In the race, the man beat the woman. And that's all they wanted to know.

Many women—from many different races, religions, and sexual orientations—saw the election differently. No longer could they believe the lie that women were now equal, that the radical misogyny was on the fringe, that they couldn't expect even liberal men to have their backs. The con of "her time will come" no longer worked. The day after the election, I put a call out to women in my city, any women, to meet with me so we could vent about the election. More than fifty women I have never met before showed up. And this happened across the country. So, we took to the streets, like our mothers and grandmothers before us, with the older generations carrying signs that read, "I can't believe I'm protesting this crap again." The Women's March stood as the largest demonstration in the history of the United States and spread around the world, and it was a turning point for women regaining the will to use their collective voices to effect public awareness.

Since then, the #MeToo movement, led by what *Time* called "The Silence Breakers" on the cover of its "Person of the Year" issue, began a conversation about sexual harassment in the workplace that moved into the real world through protests and legal action against perpetrators. Women entered political races in unprecedented numbers, especially young women and women of color, using social media platforms to support their campaigns. Women of color have taken a lead in voting, organizing, and shaping social justice movements across various interests and approaches. Open members of the LGBTQ community have been elected to office, not despite who they are, but because of it. Young women like Emma González, one of the Parkland shooting survivors, spoke their truths, and their voices kick-started antiviolence campaigns. The 2016 election woke a sleeping giant, and that giant is female.

This anthology comes at a time when it is most needed. It is as if the women who posted with #YesAllWomen, #WhyIStayed, #WhyILeft, #MeToo, or #WhyIDidntReportIt, demanded more linguistic space than 140 characters to develop their stories. The works in this anthology reverberate with energy and fire and fury, proving that we will no longer be ignored. We need this book to empower us as we work to be the authentic people we know we should be, with our outsides and insides matching, because the world needs us whole, and strong, and loud. I will not go back to that silent place—and books like this make sure that we don't.

Editor's Introduction

Giving Story to the Light

Andrea Fekete

I was born in a socioeconomically disadvantaged region: the West Virginia coalfields. Growing up, I witnessed devastating injustices related to women and the poor. I didn't have language to describe my feelings and ideas surrounding my life as a girl from a hollow where if you didn't have a car, you couldn't get a job, because no public transit existed and nothing was in proximity but necessities. Although I was one of the lucky kids born to parents who went to college, the first generation in their families to do so, I still lived in an atmosphere of oppression, underprivilege, and suffering, especially among women.

Instinctively, I understood then-wordless concepts: sexism, empowerment, disenfranchisement, misogyny, feminism, justice, income inequality, and multigenerational poverty. I didn't have these words as tools to describe my experience. I was a poet from the age of seven because I needed words I did not have. That year, I developed difficulty controlling my emotions and expressing myself after a bout of childhood bacterial meningitis. I set out to speak to the world about these intense mood swings and feelings of overwhelm. But because of my background, growing up, I never thought anyone was listening or would want to. Women and girls who feel voiceless or invisible because of disability, underprivilege, abusive environments, or some other cause need *story*. To me, story is the telling of whatever ways of knowing a woman has at her disposal. As a child of the coalfields, my ways of knowing were instinctual, also set by example by the incredibly strong women in my family and the women in my neighbors' families who lived in the coal camp where I was raised.

As a teenage writer growing up in the coalfields of rural Appalachia, I felt alone in my dreams to be an author. I didn't know any writers who looked or sounded like me. But then, I'd only stepped foot in one bookstore before I went away to university. As a curious teen, I didn't have luxuries like fully stocked bookstores, playhouses, theaters, live music venues (for under twenty-one), or public transit to take me to those wells of knowledge and experience.

In high school, I was taught white ladies like Emily Dickinson and Sylvia Plath. My skin, while white as well, wasn't "the right kind" of white. I was *white trash,* and I knew from watching television that we weren't exactly the kids on shows like *Melrose Place* or *90210.* I hated those shows, just pictures of a world where I knew I didn't belong. Who acted out my stories?

There were no granddaughters to Mexican and Hungarian immigrants like me—black-headed, Catholic holler girls from the West Virginia coalfields, not on TV or in my high school literature books. I hung out in the library with Fannie Waller, a black woman with a master's degree who taught college English on the side. I was thirsty for story, my own and others'.

Unfortunately, the books in our library were old, as were the handful of computers. It was 1995 when I read *How to Talk with Practically Anyone about Practically Anything,* a book written in 1971 by Barbara Walters. I read books from the 1980s by Gloria Steinem, which I recall not understanding well. I wanted to know what smart women thought and how they saw the world. I didn't have access to much, unlike the kids on *Melrose Place* or the characters on *Friends.* Writing sustained me. Talking to Ms. Waller endlessly about life sustained me. Hearing her stories and telling her my own sustained me.

As a teenager, on late summer nights on porch swings and around tables on my parents' deck, I read my horror stories and poems to my friend Jimmy, to my best friends next door too. My friends' moms borrowed my novel-in-progress in high school. I never felt so *seen* as when one said, "Tell Andrea to hurry up and write more. I want to know what's going to happen next!"

Growing up in Buffalo Creek, West Virginia, we kids weren't hard-core consumers like your typical American teenager because of lack of access, so we made things rather than consuming them. Nothing much happened up the hollow (I say "holler") except art. All of us made things: jokes, music, songs, poetry, and dance routines at slumber parties. Maybe nothing much happened up the holler, but things *happened* in those stories and songs. *Story* happened. We were our most alive then.

We sang in our garages with our buddies. My uncles and cousins played on somebody's porch. All of us who partook in creation, the creators and the audience, came to life through the power of story. When my friends listened, I felt *seen. I mattered.* These are early lessons on story. Story would save my life many times in adulthood.

At eighteen, I left rural Appalachia for a small urban area to attend Marshall University. There, I studied English and writing. By 2014, I would have a BA, MA, and MFA. But first, at the tender age of nineteen, I was an intern in the women's studies department. Dr. Amy Hudock was one of my first mentors. Dr. Hudock juggled multiple projects preserving diaries, literature, and poetry of women. She instilled their importance in the minds of young students, protected special collections libraries like that of long-dead southern women, walls and walls of their diaries that would've mattered to not one soul back when they were written.

Her literature courses and those like hers were where I first learned words I lacked for the experiences I grew up unable to name. I was exposed to women writers of every color, sexual orientation, and religion, from every corner of the globe. The most amazing surprise of all? Working-class women from Appalachia wrote books! Imagine my surprise and joy! Readers actually *listened to what they had to say.* And these were *strangers* reading their books, not only their friends on porch swings who, let's face it, probably listened out of some measure of kindness as well as curiosity.

I finally saw myself in the women I read. I saw my story in their novels and poetry. Suddenly, my stories mattered outside of my region. That same year, in 1998, I took Appalachian Literature, marveling at the existence of this kind of literature of which I'd never heard before. I learned the poetry of Dr. Irene McKinney, former poet laureate of West Virginia. I was in awe. She talked about coal mining. Death. Love. She talked about my West Virginia. I saw my story. I was transformed.

Fate would intervene and, in 2011, I would be accepted to a new MFA program at West Virginia Wesleyan College, founded by none other than Dr. McKinney, who would become my mentor and friend. In the 2003 book *Listen Here: Women Writing in Appalachia,* a book I used as course material as an adjunct professor in 2008, Dr. McKinney is quoted as saying, "I'm a hillbilly, a woman, and a poet, and I understood early on that nobody was going to listen to anything I had to say anyway, so I might as well just say what I want to." These words could've been my own when I was a teenager. They were my mantra as an adult; I'll say what I want to. She passed away after my only knowing her one year. But her influence, both in 1998 and 2011, changed me and my relationship with story, my relationship with myself.

A specific event led to the inspiration for this book. I experienced a traumatic event in 2014, another one related to my gender. I felt silenced. Angry. I worked with a West Virginia delegate attempting to pass a bill to protect women in domestic violence situations. As an undergrad, I'd cofounded the Women's Studies Student Association under Dr. Hudock's advisory. I had a modest list of achievements related to serving or bringing justice to women and girls. Each achievement helped heal.

But this time, I was fed up. I obsessed for a month, wondering where I could put this specific anger. How could I use it to serve women and girls? Service heals. I remembered how growing up, the only time I felt heard, the only time I felt like I mattered, was when I was sharing a story. But I felt my voice was too small, by itself, to liberate me this time.

What if, I asked myself, I helped women all over the nation, maybe even the world, share their own stories? If I give them a platform, will the giver and receiver of the story be empowered? Yes. What a lofty goal.

I went to the internet, like many women frustrated with sexism, misogyny, or injustice—a quality of fourth-wave feminism, I learned. Women take to the internet to vent their frustrations surrounding life as women—often girls new to feminism and concepts of injustice, women who don't yet have words for these concepts, just as I once didn't.

This book started out as just a late-night pipe dream as I sat alone in my kitchen in the town of Barboursville, West Virginia. Not exactly glamorous, and it wasn't so realistic either. I started posting on social media, asking women to send me their work. At first, no one did. I even earned some hostile reactions from men. I kept at it. Women I knew personally told me no. I was discouraged, but I had faith I wasn't alone in my need to speak. I kept at it. The submissions finally began rolling in. Word of mouth or beginner's luck? I still don't know.

Soon, I was buried in work and needed help. I reached out to Lara Lillibridge, a writer and former classmate I barely knew who I recalled as edgy and unique. In 2014, she didn't yet have her impressive list of publications or her first book, Girl*ish: Growing Up in a Lesbian Home*, a memoir that was released in 2018.

I chose Lara because of her talent, her voice, and the bravery in her work. I couldn't even promise her anything, not even that it would be published. I had nothing but an idea and some email submissions in my inbox. Lara shared my excitement and worked hard with no reward in sight, fueled by nothing but passion for our vision. During our work these past four years, we became best friends. This collected work is a *genuine* labor of love.

I have always approached my work as a feminist, a term I have married, divorced, and reclaimed, more than once, on the individual level, which is more third-wave feminism, although I am only forty. I believe in working toward justice for women and girls, but I believe in a "boots on the ground" approach. Sharing story isn't only introducing legislation or leading a march, but it is transformative of the culture, one individual reader at a time. Have readers ever been represented in print? Is a little teenage holler girl who fears she has no chances in life reading this book, and if she is, what interior landscape transforms in this one girl? And what will she do with her life, if so?

We didn't set out with structure in mind or themes for the collection; these developed organically and over time, which sets this collection apart from many. We produced this book backward. Most anthologies start with a concept from the publisher, often a somewhat narrow one, who then hires editors who set out to make the vision become reality.

We asked women to tell us what this book would be, and they did. Our questions were broad. We wanted contributors to decide which topics were relevant to their lives, not assign relevance. Our website asked contributors to answer these questions: *Are there moments in your life when your femaleness was a source of power or hardship? When does your voice ring its clearest? When have you been silenced?* We asked for work from women of all ages, races, nationalities, and religions.

The manuscript includes seventy-five poems and twenty-three essays. Topics include women's "rites of passage," sexuality, birth stories, woman as a heroine/

protector, survival of oppression and violence, the female body, gender roles, women in the workplace, ethnicity, and ancestry. The book is broken into sections by theme. Many pieces are by women whose second language is English. We have a few who write in "broken" English, which reminded me of how my own Mexican grandfather spoke. We embraced this beauty and diversity.

The collection suits a variety of both mainstream adult readers' interests and professors' purposes. The essays and poems range from humorous to serious, frightening to inspiring, sensual to intellectual, and experimental to traditional. Professors could easily use this collection for classes in creative writing, poetry, creative nonfiction, and women's studies. Best of all, people who just love true stories will love this book. Included here are new and award-winning English-speaking women writers from around the world—no easy feat for two youngish writers with no budget, relying on the internet and a prayer.

We didn't have an idea for structure or categorization when we set out but decided we wanted to hold the reader's interest more than anything. The manuscript alternates between poems and essays, shorter forms and longer forms. The shorter forms, both poetry and flash essays, deliver the more immediate "punchline" the reader craves in just a page or less. The longer forms allow for more meditative immersion into a chosen topic.

The categorization allows readers to flip quickly to topics of greatest interest to them. We have sections on family, late life and death, pregnancy and birth, sex and the body, and more. This is what women sent us. We marveled as themes rose organically from the pages. It was easy to see what women felt needed to be said the most.

We started the table of contents with the category "Resistance & Roles" because to us, putting a woman's story in the world is itself an act of resistance.

Once it was complete, I left this work with a profound feeling of healing from silencing in my own life. Receiving and putting forth these stories provided a measure of retrograde relief from my bitterness, anger, and despair over each of my own silencing due to both my gender and my regional identity as Appalachian with severely limited access and privilege as a child residing in a holler, miles from even modern texts.

My purpose was to receive stories and give them forward to men, women, and girls who need them. I especially thought of women and girls often forgotten in the "middle-class white" feminism, the girls left out of the cast of the TV shows, the girls who can't take a day off work for A Day without Women marches—the girls in the holler, the projects, and the lands where women aren't supposed to read or where they can barely write.

We unearthed exciting new women writers. Our award-winning authors from the United States include Ellen Bass, Pauletta Hansel, Ann Pancake, and many more. Our international authors include award winners such as Shloka Shankar,

Maggie Thach Morshed, and Müesser Yeniay. Our contributors hail from Turkey, Tunisia, South Africa, New Zealand, Ireland, India, Mexico, the Dominican Republic, England, Canada, Vietnam, Israel, and all corners of the United States.

This book exists. Now what? Possibilities. Individuals transforming, both the writers and readers. Boots-on-the-ground feminism promising tangible change, although small at first, incremental and limitless. It is my fervent prayer girls and women learn from these poems and essays that voicing anger, joy, fear, love, and power isn't only acceptable but necessary, even expected.

As a seven-year-old girl struggling with mood swings and communication of my feelings after surviving a lethal brain infection, I wrote poetry and was saved by story. Then, my story was painfully suppressed by a world where I thought a voice like mine had no place. I'm so glad women like the ones who raised me encouraged me to seek out that place. Now, I'm passing on stories of others, and through them, I find healing, solace, and renewed strength to continue my work to leave the world slightly more just than I found it, as my mentors taught me to do—those mentors of my childhood and those of adulthood: the powerful women of the coal camps where I was raised and the inspiring women of my adulthood and academe.

My feelings of silencing and powerlessness seem erased for now, as I give this book, as I give story—more than I ever could've contributed with only my voice—to the light.

Editor's Introduction

Do You Really Think I Can't Stand for Thirty Minutes?

Lara Lillibridge

I didn't have any use for feminism when I was a teenager. I didn't think gender had ever closed doors or restricted my life in any way. *Of course* girls could do anything boys could do. *Obviously* females were just as good as males. Granted, I was raised by two feminist lesbians, so it wasn't exactly the normal environment. I didn't realize that I was standing on the shoulders of my mothers, grandmothers, aunts, and many unnamed women who had fought to afford me the rights I took for granted. Still, when I grew up, I didn't mind deferring to the man I married—he was older and more sure of himself. He made more money than I did, but that was to be expected—I hadn't finished college. Besides, all I wanted was to be a stay-at-home mother. I wasn't a "career girl."

I didn't really appreciate the differences in gender until I had my first child. As a pregnant woman, I was suddenly aware of my vulnerability—my doctor wouldn't even let me walk the dog, lest I fall. Then came childbirth. I was in more physical pain than I had ever experienced, and my husband couldn't do anything to help. He was willing, mind you, but nothing he did lessened the pain. It was up to me and my body to bring this baby into the world. Once our son was born, my husband couldn't keep up with the frequent night awakenings. We had planned on doing everything together, but within a few days, it was up to me alone to figure out what to do with this squirming, crying infant. I walked him up and down the hallway, hour after hour, but my feet had broadened during pregnancy, and I was sure-footed, firmly rooted to the ground. My breasts produced milk, my voice sang off-key songs that soothed him finally to sleep. Everything my child needed, my body provided.

Three months after my son was born, I returned to work, and a twentysomething man offered me his seat in a meeting.

"Do you really think I can't stand for thirty minutes?" I asked him. "I created life and kept it alive with no other nutrition than what my body produced for the past twelve weeks. What have you done in your lifetime that's comparable?" It was the first time I saw myself as strong and capable—an actual grown-up. Only then did I find myself uncomfortable in a submissive, weaker role. I started seeing how much I deferred to others, and I no longer wanted any part of that behavior, but more than that, I saw it as detrimental to my parenting.

I had a second son, but that didn't lessen my feminism. I was responsible not only for my boys' physical safety but for their emotional well-being also. The way I interacted with other people was setting the stage for how my sons would come to view women. I wanted to raise decent human beings. I wanted my two boys to be sensitive, caring people, and of course that included seeing women as equals. I had to constantly fight against sexist language and societal norms.

"Are you his little brother or his little sister?" my now ex-husband asked our youngest child on a bike ride when he struggled to keep up.

"You don't want the pink sleeping bag, it's for girls," my stepmother told my eldest boy.

I won't go into the comments I received over painting my sons' toenails or letting them play with dolls—it didn't matter that they also played with robots, footballs, and train sets. I started to see how ingrained sexism still is in our culture, and it made me steam. I had borne these children, fed them, wiped their noses and bottoms, taught them first sign language and then to speak. I was the one who answered their questions about how the world worked. I got up every few hours night after night, year after year, and still functioned at work and at home. I didn't get sick days either place. I was learning how strong I was, and I wasn't about to let anyone teach my children that women were somehow weak or less than men.

Part of being strong and capable was finally finishing my education, so I could be the person I wanted to be, as well as make adequate money to support the kids and myself—and to be honest, to prove to my ex-husband that I was as smart as he was. In college, I was exposed to women writers: Adrienne Rich, Audre Lorde, Mary Karr, and Lidia Yuknavitch. All these women had lived lives very different from mine, yet I saw myself in their words. Their writing helped me understand both my own gender identity and the world I lived in. As I found commonalities in works by women of color, queer women, and women from other countries and religious backgrounds, I started to appreciate the tribe to which I had always belonged, and my responsibility as a member of the greater feminine collective. I wanted to give a microphone to those who had never had a chance to have their voices heard. When Andrea Fekete asked for a partner in bringing this anthology into this world, I jumped at the opportunity.

Working on this collection allowed me to focus my attention on the female experience not from an academic, distanced perspective but by listening to female voices in their own words. Some of the essays are humorous, some heartbreaking. Each speaks to an aspect of femininity in an authentic and unique way. Some of the writers have published extensively. For others, this is their first published essay or poem. Placed together in one grouping, their power is unmistakable.

On Resistance & Roles

LYNDA LEVY

The Tear

"Does your weakness show as your strength?" Rivka leans toward me from behind a scratched wooden desk in her office at Neve Yerushalayim Girls' Seminary. The thin metal folding chair I'm sitting on creaks as I cross and uncross my nylon-covered legs under my long blue skirt. It's October, but the Jerusalem sun pouring through the open window feels as hot as it did in July. Sweat gathers on my forehead, under my armpits, even on the soles of my feet, sliding around in the cheap sandals I bought only a few weeks ago in a local shop.

It's 1972 and I'm seventeen years old. I'm three months into what's supposed to be a one-year stay at a religious seminary for girls who want to immerse themselves in Orthodox Judaism in the heart of the Jewish homeland. Jerusalem, the most sacred, the most holy, the most healing of Jewish cities—a city that is like a loving mother holding out arms of unconditional love for her lost children. That's how I thought about it back in Chicago. At least, that's how I would have thought about it if I could have put it into words. Back in Chicago, I helped prepare sumptuous Sabbath dinners at the home of the local synagogue youth leader every Friday evening. I chanted psalms on the sandy Lake Michigan shore just below the synagogue grounds. I jumped out of bed at 5 A.M. every Thursday morning during my senior year in high school to study the Talmud before homeroom with my equally fervent suburban friends. My teenage rebellion morphed into a search for salvation in a hippie dress. I believed in a God who responded to three-part harmony and the chords of the acoustic guitar.

Now I stare at the leather-bound Bibles and Talmudic tractates stacked on Rivka's desk and spilling out of the bookshelf on the wall behind her. I've studied these books. I've pored over their Hebrew and Aramaic phrases, learned rabbis guiding me through the nuances of the 613 religious commandments every Jew was supposed to follow. But what did I actually learn? And how did I miss the crucial laws of modesty that governed so much of what religious girls could do and say and be?

"You could get married, you know," Rivka says. "There's no commandment for girls to study Torah. Rabbi Goldstein would be happy to make a match for you." And so he would. That's the promise of the religious life. Follow these strictures and you will never be alone. You will live in community, you will never go hungry. If you are a woman, though, you will relinquish a part of yourself, just as I reluctantly relinquished the faded blue jeans I naively shipped to Israel in a battered Kmart trunk. Was that only three months ago? Since then I'd learned more Jewish law pertaining to women than I'd ever learned in those Talmud classes back in Chicago. Now I knew to dress in long skirts and long sleeves so as not to attract male eyes; to pin up my seductive long hair; to sing my psalms only in the company of other females, because a woman's voice tempts men to sin.

How does Rivka know I am weak? Why does she think I am strong? The powerful aroma of chicken soup wafts into the office from the kitchen down the hall. The other girls have been busy cooking for tonight's Sabbath dinner, and the scent of their labor fills the room. I can picture the thick, white Sabbath candles we'll be lighting in just a few hours and the colorful embroidered tablecloth on which we'll set an array of homemade delicacies. I can hear the folktales we'll tell around the table of mystics in search of God and feel the haunting pull of the Hebrew melodies we'll sing before and after the meal, our girls' voices clear and strong, free to soar in a girl-only space. My weakness is my longing to be part of this transcendent world, but where once I believed in an invisible but loving God, now all I have are the real forms of the Orthodox men I see every day on the street, with their bushy beards and black hats, averting their eyes from my woman form as they pass me on the sidewalk. The only thing I know for certain is that I can't breathe in this restricted air. One teardrop escapes my left eye, slides down my sweaty cheek. I turn my head just slightly to the side, hoping Rivka won't see.

"Are you sure you want to leave?" Rivka asks.

"Yes, I'm sure."

CAROL GLOOR

Working

I started illegally, at 14, selling toys at Woolworth's
while the manager told me not to hold the boxes too tight
or I'd squeeze the milk from my titties.
So what, I thought, *I'll get a better job,* and I did.

All I ever wanted was a paycheck every other Friday,
that brief abundant moment when you buy
the sweater you've been watching all week,
a lipstick you don't really need.
All I ever wanted was to get the jokes,
bring a casserole to the baby shower,
say *hi* to the receptionist using her first name.

All I ever wanted was

to watch the narrow light of morning
widen to yellow noon through my office window,
while I do something people are willing to pay for,

to return after a lunch bought with my own money,
then work all afternoon while the light turns rose,
then silver gray, and finally a million windows
twinkling in all the other towers,
each one a woman working.

SHOBHANA KUMAR

Keel

one day,
there were no mango trees
to climb,
no uncles to pillion with.

hopscotch became
a banished game
and with it, father's lap,
that once welcomed
tears and smiles
and dreams
that stretched longer
than mother's colorful *sarees.*

clothes were
longer, looser
and evening outings, shorter.

walking meant
watching the ground
lest the stars above
made a bait of me.

suddenly,
the family's love
had a new name.
what is it that
they call flightless birds?

SARAH SADIE

Each Jar Tied with Bright Red Ribbon

Why, turning, does my life
small itself so readily, restricting
its contours to the idea of making
homemade peanut butter with my daughter,

which leads my son to declare he will not
make anything for anybody, that he
dislikes Christmas in general and won't
even eat the cookies this year in protest.

Meanwhile I wonder if *daughter* rhymes
with *peanut butter,* once again my attention
riveted to the fleeting fascinations of my children:
the color wheel, weather, dinosaurs.

These become my metaphors but before
I've written anything they've moved on
to Greek myth, carnation pink.
Any of these worth an epic, a large canvas,

and I see how I could fit a few
naked women around the edges,
but my mind trends to handwork, the dropped
stitch no one else will notice.

ESTELA GONZÁLEZ

Open Triangle 2012

I held hands with Rosa Chávez Taylor every Friday morning. Sister Ana led my third-grade class across the field stretching between our school and church. Thirty-three gala-uniformed girls in alphabetically ordered pairs bathed in sunlight. I felt bad for Susana Zambrano, who, as the last on the line, had to hold hands with Sister Ana, whereas my name paired me with Rosa—freckled, long-haired, kind, articulate Rosa. When the breeze blew my way, I caught whiffs of her clean skin combined with the anise and chamomile growing around us. On hot mornings, our palms sealed together. We chatted softly. For those twenty minutes, she was mine.

Once, after church, Rosa fell quiet, and I feared she was mad at me. She stopped, opened her mouth, and pointed inside—the Holy Host was stuck to the roof of her mouth. The line of girls behind us backed up in disorder. Sister Ana clasped her hands and ranted about desecrating God while Pilar Merino tried to reach in and dislodge the wafer.

I peeked at Rosa's mouth. I saw a quiet *O*, pink and fragrant like the flower of her name. Within, the cushion of her tender tongue.

Rosa closed her mouth. "It's gone." When we resumed our walk, she asked if I was cold—my fingers trembled in her hand.

That was Rosa. Later years brought me Ilsa's lush brown skin. And later, Nina's Mapuche eyes. Her sass. Oh, was she sassy. She liked to smell her own skin. "Backs are sexy," she said once as we shared a towel on the beach. "If only we could see our own backs." She loved herself.

I loved her, too, and other girls. They loved me back—just not that way.

At age ten I was a tomboy—a fact everyone attributed to my having three brothers, no sisters, and a somewhat lonesome disposition.

I loved girls, but no one knew. I reveled in the intimacy girls enjoy in Mexico—sleepovers and homework dates and makeover sessions. Sharing beds and couches, braiding each other's hair, stroking each other's lips with cherry-flavored lip gloss brushes.

Why did I never kiss those lips, touch that knee one tad longer?

I wanted to be loved as much as my brothers. I was an A student and doting daughter. At age fifteen, I swapped my sneakers for high heels. I grew my pixie out into feminine locks. At twenty-three I was a full-fledged señorita with the good boyfriend and the bright future.

I worked hard for that future. I went to grad school, traveled abroad. I claimed my right to pursue my dreams. When a boyfriend threatened to stifle my freedom, I dropped him. I was a confident woman who fought for what she wanted.

Why not?

That, until I met Nina in 1989—the sassy one with the Mapuche eyes.

We were grad students on Long Island, in a country foreign to both of us. Nina's Chile had just ousted its dictator of seventeen years. "No," voters wrote on the ballots, and Pinochet was gone. Nina had done her part, and had the scars to prove it. During my teenage years, I had organized sundown-to-sunup dance parties—a sweaty exercise in sentimental education. Four thousand miles away, Nina faced water cannons on the street, and spent an occasional night in jail. My heart glowed with pride and love as she told me.

Nina had a poster on her wall of the *No* campaign showing twenty smiling naked children, their sunny faces reflecting Chileans' willingness to face fire for a greater good. Nina was a brave working-class girl getting an education on the force of smarts and scholarships. I, too, had the scholarships and the scarce cash. My upper-class family had lost everything to Mexico's 1982 monetary crisis. Nina and I met at the crossroads of Latin America's upward and downward mobility.

She was open to things I was not in the habit of considering. She knew that cops would be aggressive. I questioned the sense of attending such demonstrations. Her answer: *Why not?* She doted on a potted plant on her windowsill. One Wednesday night while our housemates slumbered, she proposed to smoke some. I sat on the carpet, my back against the wall; she in her bed. In the glow of her rice-paper lamp, we smoked. Soon everything swayed, her clock flashing orange meteors. I sat folded onto myself, crushed under a burden I did not understand.

My heart beat loudly. My words were warped. "You could easily hurt me."

"Why would I? You don't trust me. Why are you here?"

If only we had the subtitles from *Annie Hall.* Nina would know what I meant: I am weak when you are near. You can play with my body. Touch.

In a parallel universe, she would have done just that. *Why not?*

I filled the silence with nonsense. "If I were gay, I would climb into that bed, with you."

In literature, sometimes characters lie outrageously, revealing their truths.

"Right. You are not a lesbian, and nor am I."

After a fitful sleep in my narrow bed, I showered and headed to campus. *If only I could force the clock's hands back,* I thought while standing at the bus stop.

Indeed—I erased the night in Nina's room in three simple words.

Now what?
Nothing.
Those words haunt me to this day.

SARAH SADIE

Without Mirrors and Minus a Gravity of Love

One year ago, I wrote *without mirrors and minus*
a gravity of love along with a drawer-full
of fragments,

indigestible bits, sea glass and shell,
that's all I was, voices out of
sequence, static,

may morning give me thread and a bone
needle to stitch a self
from wreck.

There is no hero to this story. Maybe there is no
Hero. Rather—*spill. eddy. drift. pool.*
Could be

I'm Joseph Campbell's nightmare—equal parts
exchange and ravel, wave and particle, *hide a*
bit, sweet,

with me, inchoate jetsam stuffed in a drawer,
like any mortal, loose envelope
of prayer.

MÜESSER YENİAY

Now Don't Tell Me of Men!

My soul hurts so much that
I awaken the stones under the earth

my womanhood
a moneybox filled with stones
a home to worms, woodpeckers
a cave to the wolves climbing down my body
on my arms, new seeds are sprinkled
the man of your life is searched
that's quite a serious matter

my womanhood, my cold snack
and my pubic, a home for nothingness,
the world stands here
and yourself! live with the rubbish thrown into you

when he's gone, tell him that flesh leaves nails
that you live with the science of the break
tell him of that serious illness

like a lamb skin, I'm cold in your gaze
I'm not in debt to your mother's womb, sir!
my womanhood, my invaded continent

neither am I a cultivated land . . .
scratch off the organ that's not mine
like a snake skin, I wish I could drop it
it's not reasonable to be a mother to murder

it's not homeland that's divided
but the body of woman
now, don't tell me of men!

NICOLE HOSPITAL-MEDINA

DR
(la Republica Dominicana)

I grew up in paradise.

I.

Mami, in her underwear, climbs up a rock wall like a native lizard to slide down the waterfall. Boys and the girl watch. Small eyes on skin. In green rocks, *Mami* explodes, gone in mists.

The flies orbit the tired horse's ear.

II.

Lobo, the horse, does not listen to six-year-old commands. Squeezing hard, pulling, rope peels tiny palms pink. He chews saw grass like she slurps purple popsicles. She smiles at his lips. Pause. They pause for a snack on the trail. Chewing. Noises.

He must stop when *el hombre* comes, "*Dale*! Move his big ass! Remember you have spurs now." Those spurs—
small urchins.

III.

The sand, black, from dead volcanoes, causes her knees to swell. Thighs, too, sore inside from saddles at six. The only girl for miles collects hazardous sea urchins. Piles. Pricks. Reds. Blues. One boy is eight. He loves her: the ropes of gold, the salt crystals on her arm feathers, the heat on her shoulders, on the precarious collection of critters.

Knobby knees, scabbed, thighs of leather. She plays only with boys. Her mother doesn't look closely.

He surpasses grown-ups. They can't catch him. Before bed, he curses. With pleasure, sings, *pinga! pinga!* His favorite bad word. He sees her in the corner of his eyes.

Here, in the pile of urchins. In the dead sand. The boat ride. The drunk grown-ups. Thighs of leather. He insists on a boat ride.

She does not like his floppy float. The way he drags it behind like a broken doll. She will not go to sea with him. The way her dog doesn't like men.

He tows, persisting, "Just us in the sea!" One time he told her to close her eyes while the grown-ups were inside. On the grass, the poor lawn, "Just open them!" He was peeing in front of her. A golden arch surprise. "Remember when I saw your *teticas* in the bathroom last summer."

She remembers.

The float. Panic. Piles. Piles. Pricks. Perhaps a sea urchin will puncture it for her. The death of the dog at the vet.

IV.

At night, she sleeps on his air mattress. She is the small girl on the floor. *Papi* and *Mami* party. *Mami* borrows the polka dot dress. At night.

V.

Men play chess. Boys try. She pulls her dress crooked to show a sunny burnt shoulder. Fluffing the blonde power on her trivial head.

Forgetting what they are, he and she catch a frog to save the dogs. The dogs that follow us through the cattle. Large ranch hands with and without mustaches stain the cows with smoke.

The scent of burnt hair will haunt her blow-dryer in the future.

ELLEN CANTAROW

Harvard in the Sixties
(Un)Speakable Memories

At present, pregnancy and parturition are made by the profession to seem somehow shameful, unbefitting professional dignity. The imposition of "quasi-masculine" standards on women takes a grave psychological toll. . . . Many women professionals must think more than twice not only about when to have children, but about whether to have them at all: under present conditions, childbearing means either five years of arduous work at two full-time jobs, or the lamentable "option" of suspending one's career. The alternatives are thus very few. Many women professionals who have succeeded in their careers have in fact chosen to lop off a whole area of their lives, as men are never forced to do.

—Excerpt from an explanatory postscript to one of six resolutions on women's lives in the Academy, brought by Ellen Cantarow and Lillian Robinson for The New University Conference's women's caucus to the 1969 MLA Business Meeting.

One day in 1965, early in my progress toward a PhD in comparative literature at Harvard, I was asked to serve tea at a department function. I'd just returned after two years of "real-world" jobs. I'd served time as a secretary at Harper & Row, where "manuscript-reader," an editorial apprenticeship, was a position given only to men, and as a file clerk at the *Providence Journal,* where all first-time reporters were male. Surely at Harvard I would be an intellect; surely at Harvard people wouldn't automatically regard me as a workplace housewife!

I remember my shock when I was asked to do that little thing: pour the tea. I hadn't yet grasped that being an angry young woman amounted to insubordination, since I still held the touching belief that academia was above gender prejudice. So, I refused, saying something acid about women always being asked to do "that sort of thing." My face has always been a dead giveaway for my emotions, which means, on the plus side, that deviousness isn't among my vices, but on the minus side, that I've tended in life to be my own worst enemy. In this case I don't recall that I made any decorous ("I'll be out of town") excuse, and I must have shown my anger, because the graduate student deputized to ask me to pour the tea made his irritation with me very plain. Into the breach leaped my graduate colleague, Roger H.: *he* would pour the tea! Roger was effusively commended for his humility, goodwill, and generosity. And it was made very clear that I was being unreasonable, mean-spirited, and ungracious.

I begin with the tea-pouring incident because it's one of those "trivial" moments when wake-up bells sound: You're a woman, and don't you forget it! The sexism inherent in it—mute, potent—was more common than that of my undergraduate French professor who hissed one day, when too many of us flubbed an answer, "But why am I teaching all of you anyway? You're all nice young ladies who are only going to meet nice young men and have babies!" But I ran into enough of both sorts of prejudice to have acquired, some years before the women's movement began, a gut understanding of the implications of my womanhood in academia, how much of my sexuality was at once inferred and curtailed, and at what peril I walked the halls of the academy. I teetered on an emotional high wire, trying to be a mind (gender, masculine) in a body that bled every month, had breasts, and suggested sex, if not maternity, to all onlookers. On the one hand, I'd been raised to believe that beauty was at the core of self for women. I loved being pretty. I favored tight ski slacks, jeans, high boots, clinging turtlenecks, dangling earrings. On the other, I felt my physical presence a distressing eruption among my male colleagues with their scholarly slouches and furrowed, earnest brows. It was clear that I was meant to be womanly, but not sexual. Daughterly, never maternal.

Harvard did not tolerate mothers unless they were those ancillary persons: faculty wives. By 1965, I'd already met the man I would marry. Twelve years older than me, he already had tenure. Of his colleagues' wives, one was a concert pianist; none of the others was a professional. Two of the younger women already had children. There was a deep divide between the wives and mothers, on the one hand, and, on the other, the men and a few childless women academics and grad students.

My mother was a faculty wife with (unusual in her day) a master's degree in psychology. When I was born she left full-time work for good. It's telling that I don't know precisely how many days a week she actually worked while I was growing up. Was it two, or three? And how much did either of my parents actually talk about my mother's work, her successes or her problems on the job? On the other hand, I heard from my mother, my parents' families, and all their friends about my father's work. A renowned biochemist and cancer researcher, he went to international conferences. His textbooks had been translated into many languages, including (exotic for me in the fifties and sixties) Japanese.

My mother supported him energetically and with self-effacement. Her own rearing by a beautiful, spoiled, self-involved mother had ravaged her self-confidence.

In later life, she suffered from severe depressions. These no doubt owed to biology and upbringing, but "the feminine mystique" of the postwar period certainly didn't help.

In 1969 The New University Conference charged Lillian Robinson and me with writing feminist resolutions to the MLA business meeting. I was thinking of my mother when I wrote: "As Alice Rossi has pointed out, 'For the first time in the history of any known society, motherhood . . . has become a full-time occupation for the adult woman.' . . . The result is that mothers are often the strongest opponents of measures that might at once free them for work outside the home and free their children from a frequently debilitating dependency." In my mother, I saw the latter-day experiences of the heroine of Charlotte Perkins Gilman's *The Yellow Wallpaper*. In her life, I perceived what a writer on motherhood would observe nearly thirty years later: "Once she attains motherhood, a woman must hand in her point of view."[1]

The 1960s were still boom years in the United States. Upper-middle-class young women entering the professions didn't confront the issues of economic survival their daughters would in the eighties and nineties. We had time and leisure to drop out of school, as I did between 1963 and 1965. We could drop out, return, and then choose from a variety of options. We could become part-time or volunteer workers like our mothers and raise families, or we could be what our parents and their friends called "career women." Or we could marry and have children, *and* carry on careers if we had the courage and stamina. We had a Hobson's choice. We could "lop off a whole area of our lives," in the words of my postscript to the resolution on full- and part-time work, or we could be mothers, taking care to keep that a private affair while flogging ourselves through our comps and dissertations.

There were no older role models either at Wellesley or at Harvard to help me fight clear of my schizoid notions about gender and sexuality (at the time of the tea-pouring incident the word *gender* was something I associated only with language-learning, and *sexuality* was a fancy word for having sex). There may have been women faculty members who had children, but we never heard about their lives outside the classroom. There was no such thing as women's studies: senior faculty members like Alice Rossi and Florence Howe, and junior faculty and grad students like Lillian and me, invented the courses that launched that discipline.

At Harvard, I became an activist. In the antiwar and women's movements, I gained self-confidence as an intellectual and began to get a lot of encouragement for my writing. It was a new life, one I feared compromising, especially for that permanent obligation, a child. Perhaps, I thought, I wouldn't have children at all. At the very least, I'd wait until I'd established my career.

A few women graduate students at Harvard—very few—took the path I rejected. Martha (not her real name) studied romance languages and looked like a figure out

1. Sharil Thurer, *The Myths of Motherhood: How Culture Reinvents the Good Mother* (Boston: Houghton Mifflin, 1994), xvii.

of French classical painting—dark hair smoothed back with a center part; a lush, gleaming bun; sleek, flowing clothes. I knew her in the mid-sixties. She was married to a Nobel Prize–seeking scientist. She had an infant. When I visited her at home, she seemed very romantic, wistful about her ever-absent husband, roguish about her sexual attraction to another man. With all this, she carried on with her classes. I'd just read *Madame Bovary*; Martha seemed to me her latter-day incarnation.

At some point in our friendship, Martha confided to me that a distinguished member of the Harvard faculty had seized her in his office and embraced her while he pressed his erection against her. What should she do? Should she drop his class? How could she face him the next time she saw him? Long after we'd gotten our degrees, the faculty member in question was charged with sexual harassment of other students. But at the time he accosted her, Martha and I had no words to describe what he'd done. And I had a sense, which I articulate only today and which was then more feeling than thought, that she was more a candidate for the professor's advances, given her choice to exercise her full sexuality, than I, given my choice to restrict mine to an after-hours sport.

Susan, another friend at Harvard, also married an academic scientist. She carried on her graduate studies in French *and* motherhood *and* wifehood (her husband took no responsibility for either housework or childcare, and not long after, they divorced). She was central in activism at Harvard, agitating for a teaching fellows' union and against the university's involvement in the Vietnam War.

At some point Susan told the then-dean of the graduate school, John Elder, that she was going to have a baby. "I was a teaching fellow," she told me recently, "and in some way or other part of those funds provided for some of my health care. He said in a very hostile way that he wouldn't let my teaching funds pay for a private or even semiprivate room. He would let them go only for a room of the sort used by people on welfare. And what I remember was that after I gave birth I came back to a room where there were ten other women who had all given birth a few days earlier. They all wanted to play cards and eat pizza and I was exhausted and just wanted to sleep." When it came to coping with classes and motherhood, she recalls only adversity: "There was no childcare anywhere. The only thing Harvard provided was married students' housing." Harvard punished women students who, in my friend's words, "had the nerve" to be mothers: "There was a prejudice against women in academia to begin with. The idea at Harvard was, if you're going to be a woman the least you can do is to have the decency not to have a child. And if you do have a child you'd better take care of it all by yourself because no one here's going to help you."

My understanding of Harvard's gynophobia lay behind another explanation appended to our MLA resolutions: "Women faculty who do have children must go through the embarrassing procedure of asking their chairman's permission to take leave. . . . The fact that individual women are forced to make such private arrangements leaves institutionalized discrimination intact. Were maternity, paternity, and parenthood leave—leave for both parents to care for very young children—to exist as usual and routine institutional practice, there would be little fear that women would be punished for the fact of their reproductive cycles."

The early seventies found me writing my dissertation and job hunting in a market just beginning its descent into the mid-sixties' recession. I'd already begun to publish, and my dissertation advisers had written warm letters of recommendation. But I'd been my department's lone curriculum-reform activist (the comp lit and English departments were among Harvard's most conservative in the late sixties). To boot, I'd challenged my department chairman in a full meeting with graduate students. After the meeting, he summoned me to his office, drew out a file on me, and threatened me about my career future. Ever the rebel, I wrote a letter to the *Harvard Crimson* exposing the incident, which I interpreted as an example of academic professionalism in all its nastiness. Unsurprisingly, I had a very hard time finding an academic job. When two Boston-area colleges offered me full-time positions and then retracted, I drew the obvious conclusion.

The struggles to find an academic job, assert myself in marriage to a much-respected professor, and keep both personal and professional lives afloat were hard enough without bringing an innocent into the picture. As for my husband, he was avoiding parenthood for reasons of his own. Instead of becoming parents ourselves, we moved in 1970 into a house with two academic couples who had infants. In the intimacy of communal living we saw firsthand the toll child rearing, despite everyone's best intentions, took on the mothers.

Still, one summer I burst out, "Oh, why *don't* we have a kid?"

"Wait 'til the winter," rejoined my husband, "when you're studying full-time. If you still want to do it, we can talk." Now, notice the hermetic nature of this conversation: it was him versus me versus the future baby. Nothing else entered as it might have had we been, say, Danish. In which case he might have said, "Your college's daycare center or mine? And, by the way, are we ready for this?" No, in sink-or-swim-by-yourself America, it was "an individual decision"—one from which he exempted himself.

To do him justice, my then-husband, known for both his loyalty and his sense of responsibility, would have become a full-time father if he'd had to. I was self-preoccupied in studies and political pursuits as men were supposed to be but women weren't. I showed only a patchy interest in other people's children. Soon after the birth of their child, the downstairs couple divorced. He moved out; she stayed. Sometimes she'd take an overnight holiday, on which occasion she'd ask us to stay in her apartment. When the baby woke up crying, it was my husband who lurched out of bed to hold and feed her. This, you may say, was evidence that we'd be splendidly equipped to share parenting fifty-fifty. And, you might add, what would have been so bad about a role-reversed, untraditional sixty-forty or seventy-thirty? After all, women have been at worse odds forever. The bottom line was that I—as I put it to myself—"just didn't want them enough to insist." Nor did I feel it right, given that I myself didn't want to run the multiple-lives marathon, to suppose anyone else should have to, either.

While I was making (or not making) up my mind, a friend of Susan's and mine, Rosalie, who was living alone in Paris after getting a graduate degree from MIT, had a baby. She was in her mid-thirties and writing her second dissertation for a doctorate at the Sorbonne. There were major differences between Rosalie and me. She was hell-bent on having a child; I wasn't. She was far braver than I, as I would never have had a child as a single woman. But she also lived in France, whose national health care system included options that, for U.S. mothers, were as far out of reach as if they existed on Mars. I believe she got three months off before the birth and between six and nine months after. She received her full salary. No one penalized her for her absence when she returned to work. Her health care and that of her child were and still are guaranteed by the state. I don't know about daycare in France twenty years ago, but the very fact that there was universally guaranteed, paid maternity leave tempered the atmosphere in which Rosalie decided to become a mother. She probably would have gone the same route in the United States, where increasing numbers of women professionals in my circles were single parents, but the climate where she lived certainly helped her in her decision. In France, the law took account of the whole human lives of women. The state did not view pregnancy, childbirth, and child rearing as irresponsible self-indulgences for women professionals.

Had there been a similar atmosphere in the United States and its universities in the sixties and early seventies, I might have felt more at ease to have a child than I did. Had Harvard had what we recommended in one of our resolutions—"day-care centers . . . institutionally-funded, parent-controlled, staffed by both men and women, and open to children from the age of six weeks on"—the world of study would have been quite different. There are, of course, other *ifs*. Had I been a dutiful daughter rather than an isolated rebel in my department—had I, that is, not been myself but another young woman—I'd have undoubtedly gotten a full-time job in the region, if not in the city; gotten my career "in place"; and felt more at leisure to have a baby. Again, had I been born eight to fifteen years later than I was, with the benefit of at least some older role models and a curriculum friendlier to women than that of the sixties, I'd have been part of a generation where women of my background felt a surer right to both children and career. I might have been surer in my desire when I made my impulsive suggestion to my husband that summer. And in his turn, he might have said, "Yes, let's!" But then, as the saying goes, if pigs had wings, they'd fly.

CHERYL DENISE

God (According to Pastor Smucker)

likes pretty women
in floral skirts
and a glory of long blonde curls.

On a Sunday afternoon
the smell of a roast in the oven
reassures God and man
that everything is in order.

God shines his face upon women
with soft pink Bibles
who go to women's groups
talk marriage and children
play piano,
sew bandages
to send overseas.

He likes Maybelline women
who make Jell-O salads
for carry-ins.

God is happiest when we're pregnant
as long as we remember
the seed is our husbands',
and there's no correlation
between creation and birthing.

God sends men when we weep,
to stroke our foreheads

and kiss our hair.
He needs men to feel strong.

God prefers us skinny
in fancy dresses
with matching accessories—
we are his temple.

God wants us silent
in business meetings
offering lemon squares
and soothing herbal teas.

God likes our breasts
pointing heavenwards,
as we pray
and do the dishes.

GINA VALDÉS

Acts of Protest

She didn't turn in the womb,
come out head first in accordance with
biological laws: her first non-conformist act.

Instead she exposed to the world
her buttocks: her second act of protest.

And refused to cry: her third defiant act.

The doctor acted quickly with slaps
until she let out a loud wail

rattling the walls
of the segregated hospital
in the race-rioting city,

wails merging with black-out sirens
of a world at war,

clashing with her father
expecting a son.

At birth, poised for a life of resistance,
testing the power of clamor,

primed to traverse walls.

ANN PANCAKE

Ice Fight

If they call me anything behind my back, they call me tomboy. For my brother, they have many names. Where we live, there are several ways to be a girl. To be a boy, there's only one.

I'm thirteen, and it's the coldest winter I've ever known. The river behind our house freezes twenty-four inches down and stays that way for two months. There is a wildcat strike in the southern part of the state, our county can't get coal for the school furnaces, and we're out for weeks. I escape the house to walk the ice.

I wear a pair of my dead grandfather's boots that my father dug out of a closet for me when I outgrew my others. Lucky for me, my grandfather was a small-footed man. The boot tread is worn nearly as glassy as the ice, so after I climb onto the river, I move with a deliberateness that makes me feel bigger than I am. I know the safest ice is a beautiful and transparent bright brown, and I lie on it facedown to marvel at paralyzed bubbles, wonder how it holds given all the vertical cracks. The risky ice is opaque or white, and sometimes I play with it, creep out on it until the thrill capsizes into panic. If I'm really worried, I throw rocks ahead of myself and listen. My father has taught me thickness by ear, and not once do I crash through without knowing that it's coming. Never have I walked an openness as long, as wide, as this frozen river, so few passages in my Appalachian world untreed, unhilled, like this one is. Solitary, unwatched, boldened by the boots, on the ice I fill myself clear to my skin.

I know what my brother is doing while I'm out on the river. He's holed up under his covers in his frigid bedroom rereading his books about Hollywood stars. There are fifteen months between him and me, so neither of us can remember a time the other wasn't, and neither can remember a time we didn't fight. Sometimes we go at it body to body, shoving, punching, hurling each other to the ground. More often we tease and goad and name-call—"pick" our mother calls it, but we both know the word *pick* isn't brutal enough. Occasionally I enlist our four younger siblings to gang up on him. We lie in the bushes and pelt him with crab apples when he rides by on his bike. He tries to do the same, make a "let's get Ann" club, but he's usually less successful than I am because I'm the oldest.

As I leave the river and head home, everything is hard. My boots shatter dirt clods in the front field. Grass hummocks crunch under my weight. Puddles that should have evaporated weeks ago hold solid as wood right to the ground. It is a dry winter with little snow, and the snow that has come cannot melt and doesn't lay, coasts around until it catches on fencerows, tree trunks, steep banks, and crusts over. Even without touching it, I feel the parchedness of that snow in my mouth. Back at the house, Sam closes his Hollywood book and puts a piece of paper on top. Begins another in the tornado series he's been drawing for the past couple of years. *Wizard of Oz* inspired, he rides his pencil in urgent black loops until he's coiled a funnel cloud, then adds, spinning out of it, bathtubs, houses, children, pets. All that it's sucked into itself on its rage across the land.

I don't know how much people say to his face, but I do know he is never beaten up, never even touched, at least not outside the family. Decades later, he will tell me that back home in West Virginia no one ever called him "fag," that didn't happen until he went to college where Pennsylvania and New Jersey boys did. But when we are kids, people occasionally do say things to me. "What's with your brother? Is he gay?" Or "Why's your brother such a woman?" Some of the questions are sneering, jeering. Some are innocent, uncharged; the asker genuinely wants to know. In grade school, the questions are confusing. By junior high, they mortify.

When we play cowboy as preschoolers, our sister Catherine and I are Little Cal and Big Cal, thrusting on our rocking horses—there are only two—in hats and holsters. Sam always volunteers to be Mary Jane, the cook, happy to trail along on foot with a tea towel around his waist for his dress and a diaper over his head for long hair. His pretend friend is a little girl named Judy. Mine is Boogle of indeterminate gender. I like *Daktari* and *Lassie*. He favors *Bewitched* and *The Julie Andrews Show*. I want to be Newton, the centaur in the Hercules cartoon. He wants to be Mary Poppins.

As we get older, Sam stages plays featuring himself, the four younger kids, and me when I deign to join in. He cobbles together ingenious costumes pulled from beds, closets, curtain rods, all to fabulous effect until one of our two audience members recognizes them. "Look at how much stuff you all dragged out!" our mother yells. "This better all get put away!" Before we are teenagers, we have just two "rock" records at our house, *Jesus Christ Superstar* and *Hair*, purchased by our parents in a futile effort to keep up with popular culture. *Superstar* is okay, if a little close to Sunday school, but on *Hair* you can fly clear out of the county.

We spend hours doing just that, all six of us flinging our bodies round and round the dining room table, barely conscious of each other, spellbound by our own spectacular dance moves. We've memorized almost every word whether we understand it or not and wail, "So-do-MEEEEEE. Fuh-lay-shee-OOOOOHH. Cunni-LIN-gus. Peder'ASTY" while in the next room our mother, in her perpetual state of seething duty, cooks the dried-out deer meat and canned vegetables for eight. Sam and Laura—the only feminine female in the family—don tablecloths and stand on chairs so they can watch themselves in the mirror. One arm wrapped around the waist of the other, torsos swaying, Laura's head not reaching Sam's shoulder, they croon "Frank Mills" into Ping-Pong paddle microphones.

Our parents don't divide chores by gender with one exception: it's Sam's job to dispose of dead animals the dogs drag in. Otherwise, we both load the hopper for the coal furnace, we both run the vacuum cleaner, we both cut grass, we both clear the table, and we both work the garden. So outside the family, I'm always surprised, then embarrassed, and finally mad when people separate us into boy work and girl work. Because our father is a part-time minister, all eight of us are regularly invited to oven-fried chicken dinners at the homes of old ladies with reverend crushes. After we arrive, the old lady will press us three girls into kitchen service, and while we fold napkins, fill water glasses, and haul platters to the dining room, I shoot dirty looks at Sam, who gloats from the couch. Before we are old enough to work legally, he and I earn under minimum at a packing shed, me on the line with the other women and the one old man with a bad leg, weighing, bagging, and binding apples, then placing the plastic bags on a long table behind us where Sam piles them into partitioned boxes and stacks them. It's the most boring work I'll ever do. Once, after a morning and half an afternoon, I ask Sam if he wants to trade, and bored as I am, he says yes. We work that way for another hour, me relishing the heft of the boxes, the good pushback in the muscles in my arms, the understanding that at least I'm using my body if not my mind. Until the boss walks in and immediately orders me back to the bagging line.

Although work at home is androgynous, fun is a different matter. In small-town West Virginia, the three most valued activities are church, hunting, and sports, in that order. As a girl, I'm barred from two. Sam is obligated to all three. For years I watch our father march him off with his .22, then his 30-30, Sam's ears scarlet with revulsion, while I pine behind, livid with injustice because I love the woods ten times more than Sam does, and disgusted that women's rituals—canning, sewing, quilting, cooking—are all work and all indoors. Our county doesn't have a girl's sport until Girls Athletic Association basketball in seventh grade, and by then, I'm too self-conscious to put myself on a court. Before that, when I'm still yearning, I sit tensed in the bleachers while Sam flounders through Biddy Buddy Basketball, his flailing arms, his dark cloud of hair. Watch him stumble bespectacled around a Little League right field, the only kid with a blue glove. At home, I borrow the glove to play searing games of catch with Catherine, and when she and I tire of that, we face off in impassioned one-on-ones, dribbling, guarding, swatting, stealing, all without a hoop. I run as fast as I can through the pasture, the cold burn livening my lungs, then veer up onto the deer paths strung along the mountainside. I forget myself in balance and speed and leaps over logs.

Our father hears it on WELD. The strike is still on. Another week of no school. The only thing worse than going, I know by this time, is staying home. Sam's in his room, spiraling his tornadoes and worshipping at his Hollywood books. I'm in mine penning furtive sketches of the boy I'm in love with and laboring, without success, to draw the stories I hear in my head. We have been banished to our rooms for . . . fighting each other? Picking at the little kids? Teasing Laura, excluding Catherine, flicking Michael in the head, who knows? Despite the circumstances, Sam and I are always guilty because no matter how young we are, we're still the oldest.

I roll off my bed, stand over the trash can, and rip my sketch into a thousand dirty snowflakes. I pace from window to window to window, then I stop in my doorway, lap each foot halfway over the threshold, mentally daring my mother to storm up the stairs and catch me. But whatever happened, whatever it is we've done to each other, I know that even if we acted out of rage, out of what I have no other word for but hate, I know this, too: Sam and I stay away from faces. We never bloody lips. We rarely pull hair. We don't physically fight the three youngest kids at all, and our fighting each other and Catherine is mostly a ferocious and infuriate wrestling with punches to biceps and struggles to throw each other down. Only the little kids bite, and we pinch with fingers, never with nails, this rule we even say out loud. I know what happens when you kick a boy between the legs, I've resorted to it several times at school. It never occurs to me to use it on Sam.

So, when I, and I assume, Sam, fight family, we fight always from a restraint below thinking. We fight in the frustration of the always-hold-back. We get only the short-lived release of fist meeting undamageable muscles, the half-catharsis of pinning the other one down, and what is it? Responsibility? A preservation instinct toward shared genes? Fear? Love? Regardless, we have no unfettered outlet except tears and self-hurt, me punching one palm with my other fist, banging my head against the wall.

I press my body against my bedroom window, savor the cold from my belly button up. One dog jogs along the edge of the yard, her mouth flopped open in happiness. I grind my forehead into the condensation on the pane and listen to my younger siblings downstairs chasing each other, laughing. I've already asked three times if I can come out, and I hear Sam call the same from across the upstairs and my mother yap, "No!" And I feel my mind lift out of my head, I feel it rising. I feel it grating against my stained ceiling, I feel it force and squeeze and press. I feel it bust into the attic where my father says blacksnakes live, I watch it thread those snakes, I hear it butt the underside of the roof. Soft thuds. Good hurt. The fourth time I call, "Can I come out?" my mother groans, "Yeess."

I make a face at her she cannot see, grab my hat, gloves, and boots, and hammer down the steps.

On the ice, the dogs range out ahead of me, vanish into duckweed, corn stubble, multiflora rose, check back in. At my heels pads a yellow cat named Mr. Paul who, having lived only with dogs since kittenhood, doesn't know he's a cat, much less that cats don't trail humans for hours. The ice opens to Mr. Paul and me secret places, places I can never reach during a regular winter when the river, if it freezes at all, doesn't freeze this solid and never this long, places I've never explored despite their being less than a half mile from my backyard. Frozen lagoons carry us into bough-arched coves on the river's far side, and I can prowl the banks where summer would never let me with its thickness of brush, the itchweed and snakes. We're given passage to islands I've seen all my life and my father has names for, but that I have never been able to reach, and on one of these islands, I discover the abutments of a century-old bridge, softened in grapevine and leafless poison ivy. Elsewhere, crumbles of smaller buildings, skeletons of rodents and deer, a washed-up johnboat half eaten by a mound of silt. Mr. Paul patient beside me. The good give of my grandfather's boots.

I'm exquisitely warm except where my face meets air, and that sear-your-cheeks cold is exquisite too. I move in the counterpoint between the sound of my breath and the sound of my soles, on solid ice, on honeycombed ice, on the stray patch of old snow. In the middle of that river, me moving in that open treeless flat, I'm not thirteen. I'm not the mean older sister, the shy junior high student, the weird smart girl. Time softens, and in this place and this moving, I am exactly who I was playing in the creek at age four, exactly who I will be thirty years from now along some Northwest alpine lake. I am in step with everything else, I feel it, the rhythm of what beats behind. Even though to the ear nothing sounds except breath and ice, to the eye nothing moves but clouds and dogs, cat and me.

One dog skitters back, scramble-pawing the surface. I pull off my glove, take the hot nose in my hand. I lift my face and see the moon in the day sky like a boot heel track on waterlogged ice.

In fifth grade, a new kid appears in our class. At first, no one can tell if it's a boy or a girl. His soft, neat brown hair curls just over his collar, and he wears plaid pants. Both his half-smile and his huge eyes quiver like match flames, delicate and incapable of shielding themselves. I like Kevin Stephens very much. One Monday morning, Kevin shows up with all that soft hair shaved to the scalp.

Some kids tease him about it, but when I ask him at recess what happened, I am honestly confused and a little concerned. His dark eyes glisten under the stripped skull. "My dad did it so I'll look like a boy."

Our father never pulls anything like that. I never see him punish Sam for his effeminacy or deride him. Not for the preschooler drag, the athletic fiascos, the jumping out of trees with umbrellas in Mary Poppins impressions. Not when the Women's Club dresses him as Minnie Pearl for their *Hee Haw* fund-raiser—and Sam doesn't mind it—not when he and Laura roller-skate to Donna Summer albums on the concrete slab out back. Our father deals with the aberration that is Sam by removing himself from it.

Our father deals with all of us this way to some extent, and it's a method I much prefer over our mother's relentless surveillance and hotheaded "discipline." In truth, she's the only parent who directly comments on Sam's difference: "Stop that prissing around!" But our father stays more remote from Sam than he does from any of us others. And this aloofness sinks a barb into each of Sam's cells.

When I am young, I don't understand. Sam rails nonstop about how much he hates our father. Then why does he still crave his attention, want intimacy? I also don't understand why he can't just see how our father is. Because although this is not something I know in a way I can say, not even in my head, I recognized at a very early age our father's fragility. His self-absorption and remoteness and passivity are in part, I understand, the fallout of a dark sensitivity that nearly disables him. I hear this when he tries to yell at us and can't manage anything louder than a desperate whine, watch it in his defenselessness when our mother yells at him, in how the only thing he ever asks for for Christmas is "a little peace and quiet." Most nakedly I see it in the way his eyes look without his glasses. I witness this rarely, usually only when I wake him from one of his naps, but when I do see it—the short reddish lashes, the small wet blue eyes, his face completely unprotected—his vulnerability is so exposed I have to turn away.

I know he is simply unable to behave like a "regular" father, and for the most part I accept this, like I accept his bad back, which means he can't play running games or pull us in a wagon. But there is this, too: it is through my father that I have learned the refuge of the woods. Have learned it by watching him disappear into them alone, but have learned it also through the many times he has taken me with him. Yes, while my father disappoints me and often also angers me, he also gave me the outdoors, and because I expect so little else, I have little to forgive.

But I am not a son.

When Sam is six and then eight, our youngest brothers are born, and with their arrival, our father's detachment from him is finalized. Because "the little boys," as we call them well into their twenties, are real boys at last, who love football and guns and Tonka trucks and chopping down trees, much like Laura, born right before them, likes dolls and dresses and arranging hair. The three youngest fit their boy-ness and girl-ness exactly as they should, as though my parents bumbled along procreating for six years before they finally made gender right. And the love and attention the younger children seem to receive, which we do not, always feels, rightly or not, tied to the way they match up with what they're supposed to be.

By the winter I'm thirteen, even I understand that the charge I feel around Sam's difference, my aversion to it, my shame when it's mentioned, is out of proportion to the usual embarrassment one feels for a sibling's oddities. Even that early, I sense murkily that something else is at stake. If I shovel deep enough and am then brave enough to look for more than a second at what I turn up, I know this: Sam's being more girl than me also means I'm more boy than him. My brother's woman-ness puts into sharper relief the lack in me.

I've recognized I'm not your usual girl since at least kindergarten, and it becomes more distressing as the fork between "boys" and "girls" widens with each successive year, climaxing in the eighth grade. Right now. Makeup confuses me, nail painting I find absurd, and I'm only drawn to jewelry like the leather bracelets we engrave with names during 4-H camp craft time. I never feel totally safe in a dress. In grade school, my mother and I compromise and I wear one just three days a week, but on tights I will not yield and instead yank on mismatched white knee socks even in temperatures in the twenties and teens. By junior high, clothes bewilder me and hair I regard as something you comb in the morning then hope for the best. All this worries my feminine friends, who tamper with my sweaters and shirts and belt at lunch and experiment with my hair at slumber parties.

I do camouflage in ways that don't make me a complete traitor to myself, like reminding myself not to sit with my ankle on my knee. I carry my books against my chest when I think of it instead of dangling them naturally at my side, and I know never to wear my grandfather's boots to school. It's not that I feel like a boy. I don't. But I don't feel like a girl, either. I just feel like myself.

For the most part, I accept my deficiencies with a muted what-can-you-do-about-it regret, not unlike the way I accept my father's inability to be a normal dad. Besides, even in my state of diminished girl-ness, there is no shortage of boys interested in me, even if they are almost never the ones I'm interested in. The culture in which we grow up grants far more leeway for expressing oneself as a woman than it does for expressing oneself as a man, and while at first thought this seems strange given the sexism of the place, on second, it makes sense: if everything male is superior, why wouldn't a masculine woman be more acceptable than a feminine man? Catherine is a bigger tomboy than I am, but no one ever asks me questions about her. We grow up with loads of kick-your-ass women stomping around, I-can-run-a-chainsaw-*and*-nurse-a-baby types, almost all of them married, or once married, to men.

Not until junior high do I really grasp what "gay" is. I learn about "queers" through rumors about Mr. Simon, the mysterious tight-panted eighth-grade math teacher, condescending and fox-faced, who came from someplace else. None of our female teachers appear to be gay, and "lezzies" are discussed less frequently. And because I'm obsessed with boys in general and madly in love with one in particular, that I might be a lezzy is not one of my myriad anxieties.

My mother's not much of a coach on young womanhood, which, as far as I'm concerned, makes her more of a blessing than a curse for a change. Other girls' mothers teach them how to apply eyeshadow, and some even seem to siphon a thrill off their daughters' adolescent romances. To my mother, my gender is only pregnancy potential, and she lectures me about this incessantly in brusque, veiled language. The only other measure she takes is to order me to wear a bra.

Since fifth grade I have observed with cold dread bra straps appearing under other girls' shirts. My mother doesn't mention "bra" to me until seventh grade, and by that time, my breasts are peculiarly sore, but no bigger than an unspayed beagle's. No one can tell if I'm wearing a bra, I decide, unless I'm in a nearly transparent T-shirt. So, I don't wear one whenever I think I can get away with it.

I'm in one of my favorite shirts, flannel, with just a few girl flairs—a billowiness, buttons only halfway down—to rescue it from full-fledged boy clothing, on the day the vice principal surprise announces the scoliosis check. I march off with the other eighth- and ninth-grade girls, happy to get out of class. Until we're ordered to remove our shirts and stand in a long line in our bras and jeans.

For a second, I think I'll throw up. I immediately invent a lie, beckoning the vice principal and confiding in her that my mother doesn't want me to have this examination. I've already had one. My mother said I don't need another. Mrs. Kelley smiles, tells me it won't hurt, and ushers me back into line.

Most of the girls hunch over, shielding their bras and giggling. A few of the breast-brazen stand erect and defiant. I huddle humiliated, my arms crossed over my almost-flat chest, the only braless girl in the eighth and ninth grade.

This does not go unnoticed. Later that afternoon, while we're changing classes, the boy I'm in love with corners me on the blacktop.

"Are you wearing a bra?" The tone is punitive. Not sexual. Not even curious.

"Usually I do," I say.

"Well, you better," he says. He turns and jogs away.

One frozen interminable Sunday that winter, our father rises from his afternoon nap and announces he's taking us kids on a walk up the river. Often on Sunday afternoons, he'll do something like this, climb out of his detachment and usher us on outings. Our mother, seizing the time alone, never comes along. On these outings, which began as soon as I could walk well, my father has taught us the names of trees and tracks, of hollows, ridges, and river eddies. More important, but without speaking of this other, he's showed me how to be with those things he names. How to look at them and behind them. How to hear the silent vibration that drums through and between them, as palpable as my own heart pushing blood.

Today, this is muddied by my mortification at being seen with my family whom I know, in their dishevelment, eccentricity, and sheer numbers, are even worse than the families of most teenagers. I decide I'll accompany them until we get to the river, then I'll take off on my own in the opposite direction. But when we reach the ice, I find myself turning upstream with them because, I tell myself, there won't be a soul on the river to witness my presence in this pathetic entourage. And, I don't tell myself directly, because I can only think it under words: time with my father, even diluted by five other beings, is precious.

I keep to the outskirts, range twenty to thirty yards off the perimeter of the group. Sam orbits the outside, too, but closer in—him like Mr. Paul, me like a dog. Ahead of us, the four little kids bubble around the pole of my father, them in their motley hand-me-downs, their hoods and tied-on hats with tails, the brown cotton gloves with cowboys on the backs worn by all the little kids in town because Santa hands them out at the bank party. Sam and I are dressed almost exactly alike, each of us in a wool CPO coat we got for Christmas, identical in cut, different only in the pattern and color of plaid. Our boots are nearly the same, too, only Sam, because he's a boy, gets a new pair at Western Auto each year. Sam is in a forest-green toboggan with a maroon stripe around the brim. I wear a Miami Dolphins toboggan not because I'm a fan but because it's the only team our town's clothing store had on the rack.

We move in our disjointed troop over the ice, under a sun dampened by rumpled clouds, between the skeleton-work of naked trees on the banks. Once in a while, little kids will kneel, drop their faces to the surface, and try to see through. When we reach the giant sycamore where we usually turn around, we take a break. The younger ones run and slide in their rubber boots on the rumpled, pitted ice, ice-skate-pretending. I turn my back on them and climb the steep bank to the cornfield above us.

Up here, on the side of the river opposite our house, the fields hold the mountains back a little. I can squint across more than a mile of broad bottom, spot the dogs in the stubble snorting groundhogs and rabbits. This valley is the biggest open I ever enter, and I can reach it alone only by swimming or by way of the ice. It's even colder up here, with more wind than the river, and I pull my chin into the collar of my coat. In this wide open, there spreads out of me a yearning, without shape and with nothing touchable at its end. Up here, there is no place for it to stop against, like there is in closer-in mountains, like there is on the frozen river, a narrower open than this up here. I stand with this widening feeling until it's just about to frighten me. Then, quick, I turn away and scrabble down the bank to a ledge not far above the ice.

And jump.

My boots slip when I hit the ice. I pitch forward, and one hundred and ten pounds crash onto one knee. At first the knee doesn't understand, then the pain missiles in, ricochets through my whole right side, and missiles back to the knee. I'm collapsed on my hands and the unhurt knee, and before I can stop her, the child in me swim-kicks straight to my surface, open-mouthed desperate for sympathy. And hears Sam burst into laughter.

I jerk my head and through my dangling hair I spy Sam pointing at me so the others can see how funny it is too. I surge to my feet to go after him. The knee shrieks, the treadless boot slips, and I fall back on my hands on the ice. Then I remember our father's here. And he hasn't laughed. But he also hasn't said a word of comfort or of reprimand.

"Why don't you do something?" I scream. "I hurt myself, and he's laughing at me."

My father doesn't look at me. As I sprawl on the ice gasping with rage and injustice and hurt, he herds the younger children together. I tug at my pants leg to show the damaged knee, but the denim's too tight, and now the others are floating away. Anger tears—the only ones I ever make because they're the only ones I can't control—heat my lashes and cheeks, and my anger at those tears makes even more. I finally hoist myself to my feet, still clamping the knee, my hair wild in my face. Watch the ice expanding between my family's bedraggled backs and me. As usual, Sam follows a little ways off and behind. He turns for a moment and smirks at me.

The truth is, when we were in grade school, I spent almost every Friday night in Sam's room. On his top bunk until the bunkbeds were given to the little boys, then on a pallet of blankets I'd heap on his floor. The truth is, even though I was fearless outdoors, I was terrified of indoors dark. When I slept alone, it was always with covers over my head, and more times than I wanted to admit I was reduced to bleating for my mother, who would shuffle, exhausted, into my room, murmur that I was all right, then shuffle away. She wouldn't let me sleep in Sam's room on a school night because we talked too much. On Friday nights, if I'd been good, I could.

And we did talk—about school, about movies and TV. He listened patiently while I rambled on about my classmates. We turned the way our parents injured us into jokes, we invented codes, intoned "Sweets for the sweet, macaroon" as our secret phrase for our mother's ability to don a saccharine public face seconds after verbally flaying us. As Sam and I lay there, invisible to each other, the fights never were, would never be. With our bodies vanished, our spirits touched. Twin outsiders, conjoined scapegoats. Solitary together.

By grade school, Sam sleeps silent and still, even through mysterious nosebleeds that wash his pillow red. But when he was a toddler, he was a head-banger, and right after that, a bed-rocker. I can't remember why I slept in his top bunk then, I didn't ask to, but I was often put there. In those times, when we were three, four, five years old, I'd lie in that top bunk, swaying, and let Sam rock us both to sleep.

I constellate at a distance. The pain-pulse in my knee is the perfect background beat for my righteous indignation. My lips are parted, my teeth bared, the ache of intense cold against them both provocation and perverse comfort. I feel the hackle of my shoulders, my arms forked off my sides. I am cocked. I move in that aural paradox of frozen dry air, the way it mutes background hum yet amplifies each individual sound, me stealthing along in the *hah* of my breath, the snuff of my running nose, the shatter of my grandfather's boots on brittle surface ice. No one in the family group looks back at me after that one Sam smirk, my father like a stake with the four younger ones tethered off it.

As I draw nearer, I step carefully around the crusty places. I let my nose drip. Sam is about forty feet off to the side of the others.

I rush him from behind.

He yelps as I knock him down, his voice immediately muffled by his scarf and then my body, and I'm on his back punching him through his CPO coat, kneeing him in the butt. He twists out from under me. My toboggan-padded head thumps the river. We grapple on our sides to keep each other down, our bodies spinning together across ice, no purchase for feet, for elbows or hips. My bad knee slams the ice and I suck air at the shock. Until the year before this one, I was always a little bigger, a little more powerful. Now at twelve and thirteen, we're exactly matched. I snake one hand up his sleeve, surprised by the warmth even through my glove. Clutching him by that bare arm, I make a fist with my other hand and pound his coat-covered ribs while he grabs my face with his spread palm, but I shake free. Then, Sam rips loose, screams some insult, and darts away, slipping and catching himself, adjusting his glasses as he goes. I'm left slumped on the ice, heaving for breath, hot enough to melt a hole.

He trots after the family, all of them currenting slowly down the river under the dimming sky. I see one of the little boys point off to the side at something, and they all look. No one looks at me. I roll to a squat, and then I hunch there, a human bonfire of hatred. The kind of hatred one only feels for family, that very hottest hatred because of how much else is in it: the history, the allegiance, the jealousy, the way they look and smell like you, the play and work and make-believe, the love. How all of that, instead of diluting the hatred, concentrates and magnifies it, as though the complicatedness opens up crevices and shafts and craters inside, giving the hate more places to penetrate. Yet despite that, and because of that, I still fight him with maddening restraint, with half-powered punches, under frenzied self-control not to really hurt, fury screaming against responsibility. I stagger to my feet, not even feeling the knee anymore. Nothing in me any longer thinks. I am animal and I am ancient, hypnotized by the heartbeat in my ears. This time, I don't even walk. I hover over ice. The last stretch, I sprint without touching down.

I slip right as I reach him but pull him down with me anyway, then we're thrashing on ice, and I taste, familiar, his bare fingers in my mouth. I hear his glasses skitter away. He seizes the ends of my scarf to choke. I recognize a great idea and do the same. The cotton burns my neck like carpet on a bare knee, Sam gnashing a steady stream of hate words while I can manage, as always, only hisses and grunts, and he finally pins me under him, still sawing the scarf, the spit from his names spattering my eyes, and then he pivots into a position from where he can both hold me down and kick, his boot hammering my shoulder, me so adrenalized I feel only dull thuds. Then I seize his kicking leg, and he topples so hard I hear a crack way down in the ice. And behind all this, a vague awareness that our father knows, may even be watching. But does not intervene.

The next time it is Sam who attacks me. I see him coming, I brace, I meet him chest to chest. From then on, we ambush each other by turns, ripping off toboggans and sailing them away, grabbing arms to reel the other down, at least once me riding his back, him knocking me loose by dropping and rolling. Then we retreat, panting like boxers, him scurrying to the edge of the others, me taking refuge in the aloneness of the ice. The other kids glance our way occasionally, but they've seen us fight a hundred times, so lose interest fast. If our father were asked why he doesn't step in, I know in the dark of my brain what he'd say: *I'm just sick of your all's fighting. And I don't have the energy to fool with it today.* In a thin, pinched voice while his eyes roam away.

By the time we reach the old grape arbor that runs the length of our backyard, I am so wrung out I can barely stand straight. We must all pass the arbor to get to the house, its grapes long dead from blight, the wooden trellis still supported by cement posts the girth of my thigh. I'm of course in the rear, Sam a bit in front of me, one wary eye over his shoulder, my father and the little boys just ahead of Sam. I see Laura and Catherine racing ahead, I hear the screen, I know the fight will be over the second my mother finds out. I inhale, and in that swell of lung, I gather every particle of power I have left. I harden my face, my teeth, my hands. I barrel across the yard and fling myself at Sam.

We have each other by wads of coat sleeves, each of us bent-kneed and panting, desperately trying to swing the other down. My eyes blur with exhaustion. It's only colors and textures I see—the over-bright green of the frost-sharp grass, the gray-blue quilting of sky, the already dark mountains leaning all around—and I cannot think at all. We are too tired even to punch. He tears off my toboggan and I rip away his. We stagger there, deadlocked in our embrace, until I hear our father say, in a voice unloud and without emotion, as though he's offering mundane advice:

"Hit her head against the post."

At these words, some last reserve volcanoes into Sam. I feel it before he moves. Then he shoves me, hard. My body finally fails. He slings me across the short span of yard between us and the arbor. He slams my head into the cement post.

I feel first just raw scrape of scalp, then a ring—more light and sound than hurt—until it ripples out, the agony hits in the echo of it. I drop on my side, blinded as, inside my skull, a hard black wave batters side to side. I don't pass out, and I feel nothing—no anger, no self-pity, no righteous indignation, no vengeance, not even hate—except my struck head.

Then I'm on my hands and knees, crawling away from the arbor across hard grass to retrieve my hat. I half-see, half-sense Sam and my father—I register the anomaly of the two of them together—almost to the door. I hear my father say, "She won't be fighting you again."

Even now, thirty-five years later, I feel more surprise about his telling Sam to do it than I register injustice or brutality. Simple surprise because our father—passive, self-contained—had never before so explicitly stepped in. I'm not surprised once he got involved, he took the boy's side—even if that boy was one he held at a distance all his life—because convention deemed it "natural" that he would. "Natural," too, the roles he assigned us: conquering male, victimized female. I am not surprised he broke the subtle rules of our fights, our code of restraint, of responsibility for each other, because his all-or-nothing perspective seemed to me the way grown-ups "naturally" thought.

But perhaps the unfairness and brutality don't faze me because the "natural" order of things was exactly what Sam and I had already learned to give the slip. I don't remember in detail what happened after I went down, but obviously I picked myself up, no doubt sought comfort from the dogs, and after some time, feeling sorry for myself, returned to being me. In the end, the boy slot and girl slot our father slammed each of us into held not much longer than the ringing in my head. Even if we weren't aware of it at the time, Sam and I had started the process of making ourselves our own kind of boy, our own kind of girl.

Two weeks after, the temperature spikes. The river breaks. I hear it in the night. Table-big slabs of ice wreck up along the banks, and the secret places on the islands and the far side are once again shut away.

I climb over the stranded ice chunks with my coat hanging open, no gloves, no hat. My boots are mud to their laces. Thaw smell richens my head, the softening soil, the rotted plants, the fecund dead. In the ice, I discover barrels that used to be docks, a hellgrammite seine, a woman's plastic raincoat, the corpse of a great blue heron, all of these surprises, along with the aroma of spring, the river's compensation for binding me again to one bank. I range over and under the puzzle of sycamore root, balance on exposed rocks, relish the hold of boot leather below my calves. The dogs are intoxicated, too, but the ice is too sharp, the ground too mucky, for Mr. Paul. He labors behind me for a little while, and then he vanishes home.

Back at the house, the little boys ride their Big Wheels. Our father takes a nap, our mother stirs the chili, Catherine pounds a basketball, and Laura comforts a doll. The blacksnakes prowl the attic. Sam pores through his movie-star books. Creates a fresh tornado.

I don't yet know that in just ten years, Sam will move to Los Angeles, step into his books and eventually onto the screen, a place and a profession where he can be any kind of man he chooses. I don't yet know that I'll be less certain, live in ten different places in my twenties and thirties, love both men and women. I don't know yet that many women in other regions are more choked than women in Appalachia are, but if I skirt the prevailing current, there are ways to be a woman never imagined back home.

What I know now, along this thawing river on top of muddy ice, is how to stand still enough long enough that the front of my chest falls completely away. How to feel dogs, water, sky, trees, beating in time with what moves behind. How it's only when I find that rhythm in myself that I reach my realest me.

NICOLE HOSPITAL-MEDINA

A Poem for the Waitress on First Street: April 18, 2011

The bartender is not the United States.
—Jack Spicer

i.

The head waitress,
not a college freshman,
has nails like downtown buildings.
The longest shifts nightlight
her child's little bed.
The belly-button ring flickers
electronically
under dinner trays,
above dancing scars.

Honey shots.
We are bees.
She buys—
"Let's track down the boy you said was cute."

ii.

It's compulsive—
to have cigarettes and *cuentos* by the dumpster.
The regular seagulls take swigs
abruptly out there.
We get in trouble for moving
our fingers around in the apron,

texting men to bring us beach sand.
Steve, the only bouncer, keeps vigil.
He's our only father
(from him, I learned that shitty trucks
are shitty men).

"Who wants table nine? It's two kids and a dad."
Fuck.

iii.

There's also that girl that only serves
the most deprived shifts,
but the stamp on her thigh reads: WORK.
The manager laughs at her.
Still, he lets her survive
on morsels
and out-of-sight tables.
She trembles a lot.

So she can't do any side work.

One seagull eats a cigarette butt.

iv.

My apron, short and black, is a skirt.

We all have soft arms.
Pen caps, camo and flushing.

Later we'll float and get blurry—
we chew our fingers rare in the kitchen waiting for an order.

BOUTHEINA LAARIF

Fe-Male

You are encased in me.
Fenced into the female.

Without me
You are a dishonored sword
Imperfect without its scabbard—
An autumn leaf gone afield,
Fiddled with by the wind's
Flirting hands.

With me
You shall be nested
In moon's cradle of light,
In the dark womb of the night.

MARIANNE WORTHINGTON

Failed Meal

Here is the kettle and here is the spoon
A full moon in daylight splinters the sky
My mother is dead, my father, too
Their plots are quadrangles crooked and slumped

Here is the skillet, a halo of iron
A hundred years' worth of hands have heaved
It from the sizzling fires, cornbread and grease
And tedious days of crossing the floors

To cook and feed and wipe the board dry
Here is the basin and here is the rag
Here is the sorrow of hot soapy water
Chafing the wrists and blistering the heart

GINA VALDÉS

Butterfly Woman

My laughter is a black night
full of green birds

My sighs are a flock of crows
diving in a smoky sky
from the heights of pines

I am a woman who writes
under the spell of two tongues
to a whispering flute
and the music of light rain

A woman who seeks
A woman who finds

A butterfly woman
history of migration
in my multi-patterned wings

TERRY ANN THAXTON

Stains

i. white walls

Not really a prison, but a halfway house—a work-release program. It's all white walls, but only after I go through the control room at the edge of the long building, which looks like a house that's not been lived in for many years. One woman sits behind the desk. I sign in on a sheet of paper, curled from age and humidity. Not many outsiders drive here. Twenty felons and me. The men, and few women, the "residents," are allowed to drive (if they have a car) or ride the bus on weekend passes. They wear ankle bracelets. On my first visit, they're suspicious. Some of them have already taken creative writing classes at Fed. Why would anyone come to this place, anyway? White walls with twenty-five-year-old stains. Long white plastic tables with rough tops, like Styrofoam. "You gettin' paid for it? Yeah, that be it." Tables, heavy with dirty hands. "No, I'm not getting paid to be here." The chairs are metal. For a moment, I wonder if I'll see my first husband sitting around the table. I've not seen or heard from him in twenty-five years. What if he's continued his criminal activity and, still violent, wound up in prison? Some of the men are big—three hundred pounds—some small. Some have gold teeth. Three men are in their sixties. Six or seven are in their twenties. Most of them range from thirty to fifty. All arms are crossed. Three of the long tables are arranged in a U, and I pull a chair and sit at the open space of the U, so they'll see I'm not threatening them with anything except paper and pen.

"We had writing classes in prison."

"Don't need you."

"Shut up y'all. This gets us our life skills points for the boss man."

I ask them to tell me their experiences with writing. Most of them hate writing, but they'll suffer through my class instead of having to attend talk therapy or drug class, where someone repeats what we all heard in high school: "Drugs are bad for you." So, we're here. We're going to write some stuff. I try to make it fun, but they think I'm just being silly. How could a college teacher call this kind of writing serious? When class is over, Mike tells me he's won a stereo system at his job so when he gets out we (he means him and me) can have an empty apartment with music.

❧

The next week I bring in a video of a scene from a soap opera and mute the volume. I hand out a blank script: a sheet of paper with the characters listed in the order of speaking. Instead of names, the characters are listed by what they're wearing: man in black suit, woman in white dress, man in leather jacket, woman in red pants. I put the men in groups—something they haven't been asked to do in a long time, maybe since ninth grade. They seem like ninth graders. Sweet. Energetic. Wanting to leave class, though there's nowhere else to go. In their groups, I ask them to write out what the characters might be saying based on body gestures.

"Don't focus on reading lips," I tell them, but many of them think that is what they are supposed to do, as if I will give them a better grade, or any grade, if they get the scene correct. I just want them to write. "Yes, you can use profanity, if it's necessary. Yes, yes, yes. Whatever you want the scene to be." Their questions remind me of when I taught in public school: each time I gave a test, I included a free question such as "What is your favorite food?" The kids were certain it was a trick question, like they might answer incorrectly. One by one, they came up to my desk to ask, "What this question mean, Ms. Thaxton?" or "Ain't nothing like this in our book."

❧

Each week I have handouts for the men, usually a poem or an excerpt from a story or essay, and each week I bring folders—yes, they can *have* them, take them to their rooms—and each week I bring back, typed on a clean sheet of white paper, what they wrote the week before, with folders so they can keep their writing. They tell me their rooms are really cells, even though there are no bars, but even smaller than their cells, so that's something to complain about. I toured the place a month ago and saw the rooms. Yes, I agree they are small—about the size of a dorm room at a state college. But, I try to tell them, *If you finish here, you're out; if you screw up in here, back to Fed.*

"Will these get confiscated?" one of the new guys asks.

"No."

"Can I take any color I want?"

"Yes."

This, choosing which color folders to take back to their rooms to hold all their writing, is one of many reintroductions to the real world. And some college teacher has come to teach them how to write for fun and get points from the system for showing up. A couple of my college students have volunteered to come with me and sit among the felons. My students walk behind them, help them with commas and spelling. The men worry about pleasing me, now that they know I'm not getting paid to be here and not turning in their writing to the boss. They all assure me they've *never done nothing wrong*. They all assure me they *was just smoking a little weed*. I'm not fresh ink.

Fourth week, they greet me at my car when I pull up, shake my hand when I leave. There's Mike, of course, who wants me to go away with him, but I don't worry about him because he's a grumpy sixty-year-old white man who just wants to get back to his life. He was no way a drug dealer, more like a car salesman who got caught with coke on vacation. But there's Dan who brings me a book, a thesaurus, and wants to know if I've seen one of these before. He's always telling Mike to leave me alone. "Shut up," he says, "I'm trying to write." Dan's my age. Reminds me a little of my first husband. Smooth-talking. Charming. Dark hair, nice looking. He's been in prison since he was thirty. Now he's forty-five. Four years ago, he was playing cards in the big room at Fed, and the warden calls him over the speaker—Dan has a phone call. Sister-in-law. That's when he knows something's up. Something's wrong. Sister-in-law tells Dan his wife just died. Warden wants to know if Dan wants to talk to him, get some counseling. "From you?" Dan gets out of the chair and opens the door. "Fuck you." Goes back to his cell. That's when he decides just to read. Nothing else to do in prison. Now he wants to know if I've read the last issue of the *New Yorker*, did I see the story in there, did I think it was good. The first night I'd come to the halfway house, Dan wanted to know if I knew about Allen Ginsberg. It was a test to see if I was trying to fool the residents. He stays after class to talk to me, tells me how crazy the prison system is, how crazy his fellow inmates are, how all he can do in prison is read. "Maybe you should go to college when you get out," I tell him. "No way," he says, "too old." I tell him I didn't start college until I was thirty, and after that spent ten years going to school. It's not until I'm driving home that I realize Dan started prison when I started college.

ii. home(less) shelter

I'm coming back, again, to teach the writing class for teens, and Dana is holding her rhymes for only me. Then Maria pulls out of her bag, like magic, a—*ta da!*—T-shirt bikini (or is it a bikini T-shirt? she can't decide). And then Dana says, "Let me ask you something. Yeah, you know. Yeah right, go on home my boy, I sorry, yeah." (Her own private joke that no one understands, even Maria, who says, "Wha— you crazy girl.") Dana hugged me after class last time on her way out. Why? The darkened hallway? Sixty children? Sixty mothers? All scrambling for the same meal. This place is a Neverland of never-ending neverness.

The children at the shelter grab my legs when I walk in the door—they don't give a shit if I've shaved or not. Nor do they seem to care if I've brought them a bowl of cherries or a picture of myself or a potion to cure their sadness. Tonight, Marco wiggles next to me at the OPS (short for "operations") desk while I wait for the worker in a green T-shirt to finish doling out aspirins—white help—for the key to open the classroom door, and Marco smiles, says, "My class is tomorrow night."

I say, "No, your class is on Wednesday night."

And he says, "Yeah, tomorrow."

I say, "No, tonight is Monday."

He says, "Yeah, my class is tomorrow."

He smiles. I nod. And that's all Marco needs from me tonight, I think. So here they are, standing in the hallway, and there I am, my legs on the blue carpet that's—what? laid down in squares?—filled with dirt from many years of children roaming. They want to hold on to something so they hold on to my legs. The cafeteria I walk past to get to the classroom is white, and people in there are holding Bible study or testing for AIDS. The bathroom I can use (same one *employees only* use) has a plastic table (twelve inches high) on top of which are extra rolls of toilet paper, Lysol spray, and a dusty yellow plastic flower.

❧

Time for class. I finally get the OPS woman to open the door and let the teenagers in the room, and already I'm thinking about the table where I'm sitting and the chair where my hands slide on the arms that feel like oil. I try not to worry. In my car, I have baby wipes to clean my hands. Then, a little boy, three or four years old, runs into the room behind one of the teens. I ask, and he tells me his name, but all I can hear is "Ikeestalka" (ick-ee-stock-uh), and I'm sure I hear him wrong, so I ask him again, and then he won't leave the room. He grabs a toy, so I reach out my hand, because by now I'm smarter than your average middle-class white woman who comes down here to teach people how to write, and I figure that Ikeestalka will take my hand, and he *does*. I'm always hoping that my son doesn't remember living on sidewalks, or in shelters, abandoned cars, and trailers. He'd just been born. Two weeks old, and his father, my husband, decided he didn't want his/our son to be near my parents, so he sold all of our stuff—baby food, clothes, everything—and drove us, with forty dollars to our name, out of state.

❧

I tell the teens not to wait for me, to go ahead and start writing something. Ikeestalka leaves the room with me, and each of my hands is holding one of his, which is when I ask where his mom is. He doesn't hear me, and now Ikeestalka is leaning back in a stretched backbend while he holds both of my hands. Now he's seeing his world upside down, but he won't point out his mom, and no one answers, even though it seems obvious to me that I'm trying to unload this kid. I keep asking, "Where's your mom?" until the older woman who's still sitting against the mustard-gone-bad-color walls says, "She's right there," and she's pointing at a woman who does not look at me or at her son, Ikeestalka, who's still seeing the shelter upside down from the end of my hands. People are asking the woman in the green T-shirt for their aspirin, and she's saying to wait a minute, she has to finish the chore list, and by then his mother has left the area because I ask the old woman against the wall where the mother is and she points down the long hallway. Finally, the old woman stands up and takes Ikeestalka from my hands and tells him to wait for his mother.

❦

Tonight in class, I ask the four teenagers to write a dialogue between themselves now and themselves when they were five. Shawna, who hates to use her hand to write—she gets really tired—begs me to write for her, so I leave my chair, go down to the other end of the table, and transcribe as Shawna talks to herself at five. The other volunteer from the phone company is here to help, but really all she does is do the writing prompts herself. She ignores the kids and writes her stories. Shawna calls herself "Angel" at five years old, and halfway through the piece, she starts yelling at Angel, but then she tells Angel that she (Shawna) would rather be back there at five, and not know about any of what comes between five and twelve (the age Shawna is now). Shawna tells Angel, "Stay put, don't come over here to this side of the room. Even though that teacher, Mrs. Carlton, is a mean and ugly witch, she ain't nothin' like this place here, where one day we will leave, I'm sure of it." Someday we'll get out of here, "and we won't be livin' in no hotel neither. We'll have a house, a real place to live."

I left my husband for good when my son was six months old. By then, we'd lived everywhere except a real home. I've always wondered how much of those six months he remembers, how many of the experiences affected him, made him feel "less than," unworthy of living a good life.

❦

Last week, I gave them an assignment to write a letter to an imaginary friend about what it's like living at a homeless shelter while you're a teenager, and Dana writes to "Julia," tells her to come get her, that she's trapped in a cage. She stops writing for a minute and I sit down next to her and she stares into the wall and says, "I think sometimes it would be better to sleep on the sidewalk than live in here where there are used sanitary pads on the bathroom floor."

I try to explain how it's not better on the street. "I've been there," I tell her. But I don't have time to think about when I was twenty, living in the backwoods where people dumped their garbage, or when I slept in open-air car washes, or on sidewalks in strange cities. But I can't think about this now because Dana is telling me about the bus driver announcing to the entire busload of kids every day on the way home from school, "Next stop, homeless shelter," and how the other kids make fun of her because of where she "lives," and she can't believe she's been here for so long. All I can do is remind her that here she is surrounded by other people who know what it's like.

And then, later after class, I'm leaving, walking back down the blue and mustard hallway, past the signs that say, "Sorry for the Inconvenience/Repainting walls/ Thank you," as if the wall, mustard-gone-bad or white putty or green wallpaper from years ago, matters when Mary is just trying to make it to dinner on time before they close the doors or for the role-playing job interview, and then Marco spots me again, from behind the door of his dorm—peeks out, smiles, waves.

And then I'm in my car, and then I'm home.

iii. staples

Twenty-five years ago, I was a woman who was kicked and punched and slapped and thrown out of her house for not having dinner ready on time. Who gives a shit if it was two in the morning? The man was home from fishing and he wanted me to cook the dinner. No, honey, I wish I'd said, don't ask me to dance again, don't ask me to wait for you to bring home the fish. Don't ask me to hold the knife between the flesh and skin while you sit in your animal weariness, your rifle whipped across your knees. Ask some other broad to dance this jig. All morning, I picked lint from your jacket pocket, found your hair between stones along the front walk, hid dollar bills behind the paneled walls, waiting. Find someone else to pull to your chest, show her your big gun, that forgotten canoe. Take her with you into the tired Gulf of Mexico. Etch your ownership into her arm, sling your hand across her moon-baked cheek. I have spent oh too many nights on my back, ideas rising from my gown of darkness. Will I miss you? I have an idea: sleep with your mouth against that wall tonight, dream of the world's flatness and the crumbling corners of this house.

But I never said that, and it took three years for me to figure out how to sneak away. That was twenty-five years ago, and now I am pulling up my chair to the workshop table at a domestic violence shelter, which I wouldn't have had the guts to go to back then, when I was twenty. Did they exist in the eighties? I don't think so. Even if they did exist, I wasn't brave enough to leave my house. I was afraid. Afraid of getting shot myself, or him shooting someone in my family. Tonight, at the writing workshop, is Linda, an African American woman who has just arrived at the shelter. She heard about the class from her new friend-roommate Emma, a white woman. She puts her hand on Emma's shoulder. Most people, when I tell them I volunteer at the domestic violence shelter, think it's all African American women, as if white men don't hit, push, shove, slap, burn, or shoot their white wives. More white women are here, always, than African American, but the community education director tells me that the numbers in all ethnic/racial groups are about equal, though some statistics show white men tend to be more likely to be abusers. So many arguments about who, what, why. Who cares? Linda has staples in her head. Emma's arm is in a cast. Sarah, at the other end of the table, is too afraid to speak aloud. Still. She's been at the shelter for three weeks, and still won't talk to anyone. That's why she comes to write: she writes, and we read aloud (for her) what she writes.

I couldn't face another abused woman for twenty years. I'm here in the safety of five of my college students for the eighth time this semester, to teach wonderful, fun, exciting ways for these women to express themselves in writing. No one talks about the staples in Linda's head that run from just above her left eyebrow to just above her ear. The room is small, and the tables, four of them, are made into a square, so it's like a real college workshop. Marcia, the college student in charge tonight, gives the participants a writing prompt, and they begin to write. That's when Linda touches her own head, and Emma looks up from her writing and asks if her head hurts, and Linda says, *Yes it does,* but she whispers *thank you* to Emma. Now my students and I and the other women are looking at them both, and Linda tells us that when she was taking a shower today after she arrived, the water pressure from the shower was hurting her head and Emma brought a cup from the kitchen and filled it with water from the shower, and then Emma let the water fall over Linda's staples. "It felt so good," Linda says. With her left hand, Linda touches Emma's shoulder, while her right hand moves along her scalp. She touches each one of her staples.

When I first started volunteering at the shelter, I couldn't talk to any of the women. I cleaned the kitchens, swept the hallways, dusted the tables and bookshelves. I swept the sidewalks. They'd see my weakness I was certain; I'd stayed with my abuser too long. I hadn't been able to leave and come to the safety of other women as they had done. I couldn't believe they let me wash their plates and forks and cups. Couldn't believe they'd figured out how to walk out the front doors of their own homes. Here they are with each other. They pour water on each other's cuts, they spread aloe on each other's burn marks, they clothe each other's children, they whisper strength into the meadows of each other's lives. They are learning to speak again. So soon after leaving.

Me? It took me three long years to leave him. Ten years to tell anyone. Twenty before I said, "He punched me while I was five months pregnant, and I lost the baby." Still I cannot say it any other way. Should I even tell people that he put the fetus inside a clear plastic bag, sealed it up, and took a picture of it to remind me that I was not a good woman? There are other things I will never say. It was twenty-five years before I offered to soothe someone else's scars. Twenty-five years to say, "Yes, it happened to me, too, and here, I want to write it out with you."

On the Body & Sex

LISA MINNEY

Mental-Pause

I sat down today and cried.

I cried because our baby ducks were all killed by a raccoon yesterday. I cried because it was Memorial Day and I desperately miss my father even still.

I cried because my husband and I just celebrated our thirteenth wedding anniversary, and he is still in love with me despite my multitude of faults.

I cried because I verbally abused him last week, because I was mean to my aging mother, because I have just come to realize how often I have made myself and others miserable.

I cried because I am premenopausal, and in the midst of the heaviest period I've dealt with since I was fifteen years old.

No one wants to talk about menopause. Only those who suffer from it care to discuss it, or will dare bring up the topic in public. Chin hairs, memory loss, pimples again on my cheeks (both sets). Restless legs, general anxiety, mid-day exhaustion. My body is freaking out. I think I am losing my mind (my husband knows it's so), and the cause is an illicit subject.

I picked up a book on menopause last year at the local library book sale after I'd had a few hot flashes. The book, *Menopause: Managing the Transition,* gives an overview of traditional and holistic options for dealing with such joys as hot flashes, night sweats, headaches, memory changes, cognitive changes, bladder changes, vaginal dryness, low libido, breast changes, hair rebellion, increased chance of heart disease, increased chance of cancer, increased stress levels, and no-doubt-about-it weight gain.

While I quickly felt relief that I did not suffer *all* the tortuous symptoms listed, I came across one sentence that twisted a cramp of terror in my very soul: "Menopause is like puberty backwards."

Oh dear God, no. Please, no.

Immediately, images flash in my mind. Two-inch-thick maxi pads plain as day in the crotches of required cotton gym suits. Red running down my leg after less than an hour with a super-plus tampon. Blood on my boyfriend's classic car seat. Cramps so constricting I spent hours curled up in a ball.

I also grew up in a house where, unfortunately, my mother hit menopause when I hit puberty and my older sister moved home pregnant.

I grew up in hormone hell.

It is not exactly a period in our lives any of us want to talk about or remember.

❧

The women in our house were screamers and throwers. We threw things for punctuation in our ranting: "I hate you!" (*Crash!*) "It's not fair!" (*Crash!*)

Dishes were a common loss, as a majority of arguments sparked after dinner over whose turn it was to wash and whose turn it was to clear. Whenever we were forced to all be around each other and interact for more than a few minutes, there was a fight.

I had forgotten about being a thrower, until last fall when I barely missed my husband's head with a pewter jewelry box. The look of surprise on his face was classic, not only at this behavior he had not witnessed before in our twenty years but also at my accuracy.

If he hadn't ducked, I would have hit him. The wound would have certainly been bloody.

I retreated to another room to get ahold of myself, hands shaking. Who was this person? I haven't seen her since I was . . . a teen.

I remembered another smashed jewelry box, a red-enameled wooden one my sister threw past my head through a bedroom door, where it exploded against the wall in the hallway. I don't remember what I picked up to throw back, but I do remember there was debris everywhere by the time we finished.

Puberty, backward.

❧

Puberty, for me, brought an overflow of unmanageable emotions. Hormonal, I am drawn past the rugged to the raw. I feel emotions from my very core, where they gurgle like hot magma and erupt. Pure, primal, dangerous emotions.

Anger becomes fury. Fear becomes desperation. Passion becomes obsession. Strummed heart strings become heart-wrenched. Love threatens to overwhelm. And in the middle of a seemingly innocent sentence, there will be a sudden, overflowing urge to break down and cry.

So, I cried today. I cried for dead ducks, for sharp memories resurfaced, for lost loved ones and for loved ones hurt afresh by this menstrual malady called menopause—including myself.

I let the tears flow, even gave out a low moan, for once the dam was broken I cried for stained car seats and broken dishes and every harsh word spoken I can never take back. I cried for successes and failures, for my losses and disappointments, and all the losses and disappointments of the world. I cried for reasons I could only feel and not remember, for terrible pains unrecognized and unnamed.

When the tears were exhausted and I was purged, I wiped my eyes with my fingers and my nose on my sleeve. I felt flushed, relieved, and lighter. I straightened my back and set my shoulders, knowing what I did not know as a teen. Angst passes. Tears dry. Life is generally good. But sometimes, you just have to sit down and have yourself a good cry.

SARAH SADIE

Stretch Marks

Once, when we were in a hard stretch,
my husband wrote me a note that said
I can't imagine thinking your body
is sexy, in twenty years.

It wasn't what he meant.
What was implied—he told me later—
was that although he couldn't
imagine it, he knew he would,
because now, twenty years already in,
he did, and at age nineteen
he couldn't have imagined that.

Love is what's between the lines.
We stopped writing notes.

What could be less sexy than
a woman writing down plain truth
about her body and her marriage?
This body is stretch-marked
from my shoulders to my knees,
as though a thousand pearl-eyed fish
shivered kisses as I surfaced
through time's suck and hinge.

Rucks and pockets and sprouted hair,
brought on by pregnancies and arguments
and weird hormonal shifts, now my skin
looks like the skin of a lake
when a chilly breeze ripples across.
Or skin of ocean.

(I have come to believe
life and love are questions of dilation.)
Against the shiny, minor goddesses
I set moles, gray hair,
and crow's-feet, signs of good humor,
of pain endured and pain's release.
Odysseus returns, and realizes it doesn't

matter so much, what Penelope was doing
in the meantime. True minds again met,
their bed still a tree, and hadn't he
had his adventures too?

KATHARYN HOWD MACHAN

Journey through the Door into Always-Always Land: 1966

Between my father's death
and my first kiss
it came,
the blood suddenly there
maroon on my cotton underpants
in that chill Long Island
Howard Johnson's ladies' room.
That was the first time
I bit the wings off fried butterfly
shrimp, too;
I have always suspected a correlation.

We'd gone to visit my brother's godfather
with the giant hobby train set
racing through his cellar.
When we got back from lunch
with the brown-bagged box
discreetly tucked under my mother's arm
his wife showed us upstairs
and my mother closed the bathroom door
proud with the Mystery
and said *You know from the books*
I gave you what is happening.
Did I ever tell you (she had told me)
how when I was 11 (I was 13)
I fell from a tree (I had eaten the shrimp)
and later the bleeding began and I thought
I was hurt but your grandmother said

suspiciously sniffing my underclothes
No It's something all women get
The Curse Accept it
You'll be all right You'll have to put up
with it from now on Here use these rags *and*
she showed me how to pin them on
and later how to wash them out
over and over and over.
At least things are more comfortable now.

I listened to the words suddenly real
watching her take out the tiny mattress and
show me how to hook it on
the pink elastic belly belt.
We went down the flights of stairs
(my thighs burning aware and clumsy)
into the godfather's wife's welcoming smile
down to the big room
full of the stench of electricity
where the long sleek train
rushed round and around so powerful.
  Where've you been? my big brother crowed.
Tell us where, oh where you have been.

MARY IMO-STIKE

The Stain

I worried about blood on my clothes,
on the back of my skirt
from sitting in stale classrooms
on dim and stuffy winter afternoons;
like the stain of genocide
but never hidden, it grew and spread
coming to full light on the East Main Street bus,
beneath the boundary of my coat's coverage.
Unmistakable, unforgivable, the worst stain,
it defied all my pretense, the hiding, covering,
being pure, being good and a girl
from Mercy High School
whose parents paid tuition
so she could attend with the suburban girls,
the daughters of dentists and lawyers.
I rode two city buses a day in the slush to get there
and they saw me bleeding like a slut.

My shame spread like the stain.
I'd laughed and pretended it didn't matter,
hoped for the day I'd be thirty years old
and living in the suburbs, too,
with a professor husband
who wears hunter green sweaters
and sons who need me.
I dreamed of driving a car with leather seats
so I'd never worry
about the blood.

My life has given me struggle
and the wisdom that there is no cause for blood shame,
an insidious tool of the patriarchy,
that kept me unconfident, doubtful of my worth,
unbeautiful and repressed,
stuck in the place they picked for me.

Now I whisper across time
to the girl on the bus.
"Claim your life, your blood.
Love your bright and dark
oddly shaped, conspicuous,
magnificent
Stain!"

BONNIE J. MORRIS

Puberty's Enchiladas

It's December 1973, and in Chapel Hill there's a new restaurant called Tijuana Fats. That's where we're going tonight for my father's birthday, the sort of place my hippie parents can afford. The very name evokes our California past, the Baja trips and taco stands we came from. A dinner out for four ex-Angelenos, tired of southern barbecue and grits. My father in long sideburns, biker boots; my mother in a peasant dress and beads; me with my retainer, twelve years old.

It's a moment of profound sophistication, for by now I understand my school friends are rich kids who eat out all the time, and we're just here for a special birthday treat. But my friends' parents fight, their meals are silent strain—and my family's dinner table rocks and rolls with laughter and good talk. I'm thinking of these blessings as I eat my enchiladas, eating my past years in California, my present ones transplanted here and now. The hippie music swings. The low lamps over the table and the recessed nooks of Mexican ceramic wall art add their glow. The folded napkin hides my orthodontic retainer while I eat (*don't throw out the expensive retainer now that you have the beautiful smile*), and something strange is happening to me. I can feel it. Best not to say anything. Check it out later. Lean forward, the blue plate enhancing the enchiladas, three of them, burnt-orange in their tuck-and-rolled loveliness. Eat. But not too much; there will be birthday cake later—my grandmother's recipe, the one decadence from her German farmhouse heritage. *What is happening to me?* My father is happy; he is thirty-nine today. He has a gorgeous wife, two smart kids, two cats and a big red dog, two big green yards to mow. He is drinking a frosty margarita. This is his night. Look down and concentrate on Spanish rice, Spanish rice, Spanish rice.

When we arrive home later, in the coat-shrugging key-jangling lull between walking in and getting the cake out of its hiding site, I head to my bathroom. I now have my own bedroom with a tiny built-in bath—only the week before, my parents completed renovation on our attic loft and moved upstairs, allowing me, the growing twelve-year-old, to inherit their downstairs room with bath. So now I can throw my car coat across the room and dive into green-tiled toilet privacy to confirm that yes, during my father's thirty-ninth birthday party, my first period began. I walked into that restaurant a girl and walked out a woman. There's no bat mitzvah planned in my un-kosher family; *today I am a woman. Bless these enchiladas.* That will have to do.

And I yell out the sentence so many girls have called: "Mom, could you come in here for a minute?" And it will *never be this intimate again,* this ritual of calling out, *Hey, Mom.* At every life landmark after this, Mom will be far away, not beckoned, or not told much. Losing my virginity, five years from now? Not shared with Mom! It's just this once, this growing up, and Mom has the cake knife in her hand, called to my side in the midst of smoothing chocolate frosting on my father's cake. She looks in, where I'm exposed to her, and verifies the red stain: yep, that's it. But I don't get a smack across the face, the smack that her own mother, born in Poland, had to suffer at menarche. I get a plate of chocolate cake, after I'm trussed up with *the Belt.*

My dad stands there, forgotten. It's supposed to be *his day.* Next year he'll be forty, and already he's got worries: now his daughter can get pregnant. No one says much more to me, my parents stand there looking hip, but also frozen, and I head to the phone: the critical thing is to call my best friend, Jacky, who's already been through this and will squeal and gasp and gloat. This is the call she is waiting for. Fortunately, it's one of the rare nights when she's not grounded, punished, with her phone privileges suspended. "Guess what?" I crow down the phone. A momentary pause, and then—"No!" she shrieks back knowingly. "You didn't!" And that's the whole exchange. Really, what more is there to say? For at least a year or longer, we've been reading passages from the Judy Blume book *Are You There God? It's Me, Margaret* over the phone to one another. My own first period is almost anticlimactic by this time. My parents keep the light off, trying to be quiet, inconspicuous.

I go back to my desk and write two words on the calendar square, December 20, 1973: *IT HAPPENED.* What did I think, that night, falling asleep, a woman full of cake and enchiladas? What did they murmur to one another, my parents in their loft?

Five months later when May came and I turned thirteen, I announced I was too old for a birthday party with a bunch of kids. I was hanging out with new friends who were older, hipper, cooler, including long-haired guys. There was a guy I liked, and a girl I liked, and a guy the girl liked. So, could I have dinner out at Tijuana Fats and invite along these two guys and this girl? And celebrate my teens with enchiladas? And afterward, have cake? A dinner party—out. Sophistication.

This was the night we broke away; because after playing soccer all over the front yard, and dining out on enchiladas we didn't have to pay for, and coming home with plenty of evening left to kill, one of the guys said, "The party is dead," and I retorted, "Then let's go outside," onto the far lawn, where my parents couldn't see us. Over into a corner of the vast, dark yard, heady with Carolina pine and spring blossom, we made a cross below the birdbath, girl across from boy, boy across from girl, in clear configuration of a date night, holding hands. Anyone could have held anyone's hand and it would have served to say how young we were; that I loved her the most, my new friend Jennifer; or that Mike and John were soccer buds, who liked goals more than girls at that point, much to our dismay; the four-way cross that led to easy talk, and nothing more, no thought of sex, which we craved far less than birthday cake; that we were trusted out alone, but within calling distance of a house; that two of us had parents whose marriages outlasted everybody's; that all of us were popular, strong-bodied, and alive. There weren't any dangers, any pressures, any college plans yet, any fears. Able to eat cake and gain no weight; enchiladas troubling no one's dreams.

That was the night before I knew that three of us would move within three months and one of us would die within three years. Everything would splinter like a plank, and I would be the carpenter/historian who tried to nail the former memories down. No one aware that anything might change, just lying on our bellies, talking. Not boasting, telling lies, but talking real, so sheltered, so grown up.

My mother drew us in with final bowls of ice cream to finish off the night: adolescent reduction finished with ice cream. Choices: there was peppermint, crushed with tiny red pieces, or Neapolitan, and you could watch the three stripes dissolve in the ceramic bowl or eat each color separately and neatly, or stir it up as stiff mush, as I liked. None of these friends had brought me a birthday present. The whole night was their gift. And, spoons cooling in chilled bowls, we sat and smiled and waited for their folks to pick them up. None of us could drive. It was all of us, alive.

KALI LIGHTFOOT

Puberty, 1956

I was 12 and I wanted to learn to play Schumann's *Träumerei*
on piano. We didn't have a piano, and I couldn't even
play "Chopsticks," but like Robert, I was in love with Clara
Schumann.
Well, actually I was in love with Katharine Hepburn, who played
Clara,
and the piano, in *Song of Love.*

That year I also fell in love with Deborah Kerr in *The King and I,*
Ingrid Bergman in *Anastasia,* and June Allyson's voice
in everything. I wept, dreamt, and did not swoon
over Elvis on *Ed Sullivan.*

Watching July 4th fireworks with my best friend Madeline,
I offered to stand close to keep her warm. I knew it wasn't innocent,
but didn't know just what it was—except new and terrifying.
I stayed away from her for all the next day, and as it turned out,
for the rest of our lives.

BEATRIZ F. FERNANDEZ

Reunion

She's well-preserved, they will say,
I know they mean it as a compliment.
Neat, well-kept, like rows of cans in a pantry:
meat, tomatoes, peaches in heavy syrup.

In the ladies' room,
I unroll a tube of lipstick,
apply berry red to my mouth—
the color my lips used to be—
and think of the dark suspension of time
inside cool corrugated metal.

Nascent bacteria and mold spores
held in suspended animation.
The pristine surface lurking beneath
like the face of an unexplored planet
under turbulent nitrogen clouds.
Waiting for the curling back of sky,
for the bright violation of air.

JESSICA SPRUILL

After Years of Being Told I Have the Body of a 12-Year-Old Boy

I prayed for them.
God, I know this probably
doesn't seem very important, but—
I anointed them with fenugreek oil
and smelled like Indian food for a week.

God, please. Just a little bigger, maybe
let them bounce ever so slightly when I jump
on a trampoline?
But, no.

Bee stings. Mosquito bites.
Sup, Olive Oyl?
Fuck you, Miranda. Your barely B breasts
lifted and smashed against each other
inside your Mary-Kate and Ashley bra.
You handing me a tube of hydrocortisone cream.
Do you get a AAA discount?
Ha.
Let's be honest.
        My tits are pretty
        goddamn magical.
I mean, they don't do much exactly
but I have kept men mesmerized
for years with mostly these
handful (mouthful) smallish

meringue-peaked perky tits
and the occasional home-cooked meal,

et cetera.

I spent a decade covering them up. The first
time I had sex, I didn't take my shirt off
because I was afraid they would ruin the moment.

Since then, they've felt the night wind
out a car window, been on wild display
for the open road to see. Reveled in
summer daylight. Delicate, pink
nipples burned red by sun and baby oil,
hardened by river water and aloe vera.

It's taken me thirteen years
to stand naked, shameless
in front of men and women
and mirrors and it's time

I stopped praying
over my body. Stopped
making sacrifices in
hopes of a bigger, better
temple for men to worship,
to kneel before and suckle,
to feel their lips around my nipple
as they whisper, *Baby,*
I'm gonna buy you
new tits for your birthday.

I spread cake-icing across my chest instead,
stick candles in it, burn them down
'til wax and sugar roll in hot rivers
across my skin. I am celebrating
these sweet-honey bee stings, these
warm-blood mosquito bites that swell,
ache. These are my breasts and my God,
I love, love, love them.

RENÉE OLANDER

Dear Torso, Stone-Carved

Dear Torso, Stone-Carved:

Are you still there on his porch, smooth-bellied and gleaming in the corner?

He remarked often that you were my torso, your lilting breasts my breasts—but how could that be? You're too heavy to lift, legless and armless as a quadriplegic, headless as a corpse. No voice can emerge from your truncated stub of a neck.

Your curvaceous stone reaches down past the contours of your taut belly and elegant navel, down to your sensual tufting, suggesting indentation, labial lines, though your vulva's unseen. Of course, you see nothing, eyeless as you are, can't tell that only these pleasing parts, your breasts and sex, are whole, everything else truncated.

It always caused me drag that he didn't honor you with a solid stand, a table or even a cinder block underneath—the least one might do for one so amputated, whose undeniable beauty sunk just below dick level, a veritable bonsai next to his strapping six foot six.

But I never said—didn't speak up on your faceless behalf—why was that? Or am I misremembering now after the centuries since you first appeared? In fact, perhaps I asked early on, repeatedly, about his plans to place something beneath you, something simple and stable, not a pedestal for Pete's sake, and he said I just complained—called me a nag. He could be so insulting and angry, sometimes scary.

If you had a tongue you might ask, how did the porn creep in? It started with a Valentine or two, then videos. Previous girlfriends loved it, he said. Was I to be a prude? I didn't say early on that I could see chafing on the actors' skin, my eyesight better than his, or that I'd read disturbing reports about the industry filled with runaways.

Turned out he had a closet full of DVDs, some he proudly declared "female-friendly." He queued up his favorite scenes so they exploded onto the screen as soon as I entered his apartment, and then he expected me to perform. So awkward! Then I felt as if I'd be a hypocrite to speak up and change course. I worried he'd dump me. Good grief.

Sure, we had chemistry, but in hindsight I see how his rock stardom and smooth tongue made me dumb. Mom used to say, "You can't be a rug if you don't lie down."

Regrets abound, dear Torso.

I wonder now, given climate change, sea level rise, and such a bitter winter: are you still out there so vulnerable, as if struggling for a little dignity?

If I had it to do over, I'd figure some way to smuggle you away when he wasn't paying attention, which of course was most of the time. I'd give you shelter, do my best at love and respect. But it's too late—I'll just have to do better by other sisters in the future.

Sincerely,
His Ancient, Recent Romance

ANNE HARDING WOODWORTH

Sex at Six

Pretty soon I could ride a two-wheeler.
Most tries, I fell off.
It was a boy's bike with that bar
my crotch got stuck on crosswise.
I got bruised in a blue-and-black
yellow-red-green-and-purple kind of way
that made me prouder than a kid with a cast.

I showed it to Roger, who came over to play.
He marveled at the sight (first time
he'd ever seen a girl), must've gone for years
thinking we were a much deeper richer hue
than could ever be imagined
of tantalizing places.

RACHEL A. HICKS

The Biopsy

When nurses whisper and tell you to wait, some young blonde girl that won't look you in the eye, but will only tell you questions must be directed to the doctor—that's when conversations happen in a long hallway, muted syllables with a few words poking out and making their way under the door—*well, it's her age . . . not sure . . . mumble, mumble.* The door slightly ajar as I sit on white paper that wrinkles and squeaks with every small movement, echoing loudly off the white walls. Naked from the waist down and wondering if I should have shaved to avoid embarrassment, my pale chicken legs shake but my gray eyes tremble more—a shooting range in front of me, large utensils to pry me open, four different bottles that will soon hold four bloody pieces of me—me, me, me. I make it all about me but when it's my insides and my legs that will soon be propped up in shame, I can't help but think about being seven, about loving unicorns and long blonde ladies I drew on construction paper. If these white walls could talk, then they could morph and manifest into that one white unicorn I have always thought about. One that will stand and wait for my weak body to get up from this long table and ride away into a white sky full of plump pink ether clouds.

LINDA FLAHERTY HALTMAIER

Cloaking Magic

I cover it up even when I'm alone,
drape it in scarves Scheherazade
might deem excessive,
cloak it in layers of black-on-black,
tugging at the fabric

to be sure the illusion holds—
this belly of gurgling shame,
cauldron of twitchy judgment
and failings made flesh—
streaked with the taint of bird-women

in spandex and neon trainers,
this belly that housed a
human genome project—
conjuring earlobes and eyelashes
from bagels and cream cheese,

coding instructions for pinky fingers
perfect as spiny starfish.
This belly that connected me
to my mother,
a portal to the sacred site

where one became two—
in an alchemy that
has terrified men, held them in awe.
This belly,
full of magic and mossy wisdom,

deserves the light of day,
a parade with streamers—
but a gentle pat beneath a
waterfall of scarves
might be a good place to start.

ELIZABETH JOHNSTON

Tackle Box

I find more bitter than death the woman who is a snare, whose heart is a trap and whose hands are chains. The man who pleases God will escape her, but the sinner she will ensnare.

—Ecclesiastes 7:26

Some interstate in the south. I'm around seven. We've been in the car for hours—en route to Irmo, a suburb outside Columbia, South Carolina, so Dad can take classes at USC to become an officer in the Marines. We're in his sporty black Nissan. My mom and younger sisters, Jenna and Katie, are in the brown and yellow station wagon behind us. Bart is barely a kidney bean in Mom's belly. I press my forehead to the cool window and watch my reflection superimposed over the trees rushing by. It gets dark, and Dad asks me if I want to talk to the truckers on the CB radio. He picks up the mouthpiece and rotates the channel dial. Voices crackle over the speaker. They sound like aliens speaking a garbled foreign language. "Watch this," he winks at me, then presses the receiver and starts to lisp in falsetto, *I feel pretty, oh so pretty, oh so pretty, and witty, and gaaaaaaaayyyyy. . . .* This usually gets a response from one or two truckers. "What's your twenty?" a voice wavers across the radio. They want to know where we are, what highway, what car. Sometimes we talk to them until their signal gets too fuzzy. Sometimes they yell at my dad, and he laughs so hard tears roll down his cheeks and he has to turn the channel before I hear too many profanities. "You do it," he nudges me with the speaker. I don't know what to say, and whisper a timid, questioning, "Hi?" into the crackling space. Sometimes the truckers will talk to me, tell me about their kids back home. Other times they tell my dad to get me the hell off the radio. In those moments I'm aware, as young as I am, that we're intruders in their world. Then one calls me "Honey" and "Pretty thing" and says he likes the softness in my voice. My insides rustle and it's like I've dipped my toes into warm water. My dad snaps off the CB. "That's enough of that."

We listen in silence to the radio, stare forward as the yellow lines of the road roll like a conveyor belt beneath our car. When Hall & Oates comes across, Dad turns up the radio, drums his fingers on the steering wheel, sings along wistfully. I watch his face flashing in the darkness, lit up by the headlights of passing cars like someone's opening and closing shutters. He's not laughing anymore. He's serious about this song, I can tell, these lyrics about a hungry woman who eats men.

"What's a man-eater?" I ask him. It sounds dangerous. My eyes try to penetrate the woods outside the window—so much darkness pressing in. I imagine some she-monster with yellow eyes stalking our car from the bushes. Dad replies solemnly, eyes straight ahead, "A woman every man wants." I am still riding the high of the power I felt with that last trucker—his desire to know more about me, a need so dangerous my dad had to silence him.

Every time I looked in the mirror, though, I knew I was decidedly not a man-eater—not yet, anyway. Man-eaters, the kind I came to see on the big screen and on magazine covers, did not have stringy red hair or freckles or glasses. And the teeth they used to chew up and spit out men were straight and blindingly white. My teeth looked more like those belonging to a Venus flytrap. The bottom row turned every which way but straight, and my left and right incisors had grown in at an angle, overlapping the front two teeth like fangs. Sometimes the kids at school pretended I was a vampire, raced away from me as if I might suck blood from their necks.

It only added injury to insult that my mother was a real-life beauty queen. At eighteen, she had been crowned Miss Ligonier, the trophy of which was displayed prominently on the bookshelf of every living room in every house into which we moved. It was a gold figurine about the same size as a Barbie, on its head a crown and in its hands a scepter. The scepter was about the size of a sewing needle and slid into a hole in the trophy's fist. It wasn't supposed to be removable. Jenna and I used to take the trophy down from its bookcase and stroke its hard, gold dress. Eventually, we loosened the scepter and found we could take it from her hands. We gave it to our Barbies until Mom found out and yelled at us. Tears brimmed in her eyes as she cradled the trophy, trying to fix it. After that, she kept the trophy out of our reach.

My father was convinced that every man wanted her, so he watched over her jealously. His fears were not unfounded. Once at a Kmart, when she was pushing my baby brother in the cart and we sisters were trailing behind her like ducks on a string, a young Marine, probably no older than eighteen or nineteen, touched her on the shoulder. "I'm sorry," he said, "I just had to tell you that I think you're the most beautiful woman I've ever seen." I was probably around nine, and this was impressive. "Look at your mother, girls," Dad would say to us, gazing up at her with hungry eyes while she'd fill our plates at dinner. "Isn't she beautiful?"

And she was. But she didn't wake up that way. We knew her secret: the orange tackle box. For the better part of the day that she spent vacuuming floors, dusting cabinets, and folding laundry, she was downright plain—thick, red hair gathered into a tight bun like a knob on the top of her head, small eyes fading into a pale and freckled face. But an hour before Dad came home, Mom would stop whatever household chore she was attending to and head up to her bathroom where, under the cabinet, she stored a fisherman's tackle box. The contents were magic, invoking into being the beauty queen hiding inside my mother. Where men might separate lures, lines, and hooks into each compartment, Mom had neatly arranged row after row of eye shadows, mascaras, and lipsticks. I'd lean against the doorframe of her bathroom and watch as she "put on her face." First there was the pale, almost white concealer she'd dab under her eyes, then the liquid foundation she'd swirl across her cheeks, forehead, and chin. Next, powder and a sweep of pink blush. She'd lean into the mirror, carefully swipe blue eye shadow across each eyelid, step back, examine her work, lean in again to fill in any creases. Next, the eyelash curler, a stroke of eyeliner, a flourish of mascara. She'd brush out her eyebrows and pencil them in so her dark, almond-shaped eyes slowly emerged as if coaxed.

But the most magical part of the tackle box was the assortment of lipstick tubes piled in two or three of the compartments and organized by shade. All shades of red, they touted names like "Cherry Lush," "Ruby Dream," "Scarlett Empress," "Femme Fatale." I loved running my fingers over the smooth tubes, removing their caps, rolling up colors so deep and rich my mouth watered. First, she'd line her lips, drawing in a fuller pout on bottom, a cupid's bow on top. Then she'd choose a lipstick and drag it slowly across, back and forth, press her lips together, and repeat. Again, she'd step back from the mirror, survey her reflection, dissatisfied, rummage through the tackle box for something to right it. Lean in again, fix the mistakes. With each sweep, stroke, and blot, ho-hum servant girl slowly transformed into Cinderella. What I wanted more than anything was to look like her when I grew up.

Indeed, it was this beauty regimen alone that kept me from climbing onto a chair and tying a rope around my neck. That she could transform herself so completely gave me hope every time I looked in the mirror at my own plain-Jane face and straight-as-a-board body. ("You're a pirate's dream," my dad joked. "A buried chest.") Still, I assured my friends that the story of the Ugly Duckling was my own. My mother was proof—*of course* I'd inherited her genes. Plus, all five of my dad's sisters were beautiful and his own mom was so gorgeous she'd been married six times. How could it turn out otherwise for me? Friends of my parents concurred when they'd come over for dinner and I'd skip downstairs on break from playing dress-up, my adolescent face inexpertly plastered with lipstick and eye shadow. "You're in trouble," the men would elbow my dad and wink. "Get your gun ready." I'd blush, pleased.

And, eventually, it happened, with the assistance of puberty and its helpful sidekick, CoverGirl. Each morning, I woke up early to put on my own face, jostling with my sister, Jenna, for real estate in front of the bathroom mirror. By then, I didn't need a tackle box as some marketing genius had created Caboodles, essentially a tackle box but in appropriately girly pink and purple. Because it was too big to carry to school, I dumped its essentials into a plastic pencil pouch that I stuffed into my backpack. As soon as I got to school, I dashed to the bathroom to check that my makeup had remained in place during the harrowing thirty-minute bus ride. I repeated this process in each of the ten-minute breaks between classes, joining the line of teenage girls who were also reapplying their lipstick and eyeliner, brushing their hair, and otherwise checking for any break in the surface that might betray us to the boys.

The boys were the thing. The thrill of knowing we were desired was like static electricity coursing through our veins. Every moment of our teenage years became a pageant. Friday nights, my dad would drop a group of neighborhood girls at the mall and we'd treat it like a catwalk until it closed at nine: strut around the top floor, then take the escalator and sashay around the bottom, then ride the escalator back up and start over. We never actually *talked* to these boys. It seemed to us they spoke an entirely different language, one composed of guttural grunts and groans. It was enough to glide past them in their huddled masses and feel the hush our presence caused. Sometimes one would break the silence, whistle or moan, or another would lick his lips, a lascivious "niiiice" unrolling from his tongue like a carpet at our feet. Without speaking a word to them, we possessed the power to interrupt their compact and gated world, to make their heads swivel in our directions, to command their bodies to straighten and stiffen, to invoke the gazes that caressed the length of our emerging curves. Sometimes as we swept by, they'd collapse into each other like sailors thrown about by the force of a wave. We imagined them set adrift, desperate, clinging to the hope that we might turn and save them. We thought the most romantic thing in the world was to be desired from afar, a belief confirmed and encouraged by any number of love songs our boom boxes crooned: "Lady in Red," "Jesse's Girl," "Private Eyes," "Every Step You Take."

It wasn't just teenage boys wanting us, though. On nights we couldn't pester a parent to drive us to the mall, we made do with the gravel catwalk alongside the main road beyond our houses. We were allowed to walk only as far as a stop sign at the corner. Still, we'd saunter down and back, down and back, practicing our swagger. The point was simply the thrill of the horns beeping as cars slowed down, adult men hanging their heads out the window like dogs, calling to us "baby" or "honey" or "sugar lips." Sometimes they'd slow down too much, as if intending to pull over. We didn't know what to do, had no plan for desire that materialized itself into an actual encounter, especially not with a mustached man, so we'd giggle and run into the grass, feeling safe behind the wood fence posts that separated our backyards from the street. And we mostly were.

The truth is, we didn't really understand this power we had inherited with our bodies, with being born female. We, too, felt set adrift—without anchor or direction, our bodies like rafts floating on some vast sea in which we were told lurked all species of danger. Somewhere on this sea there was safety, an island paradise called marriage. All we knew was we had to get there, and in one piece. Not broken. Not damaged. But we were provided no oars, no compass. Sure, we were given "direction," of a sort, but it was like being handed a map to use on an ocean with no landmarks. Our school counselors and health teachers talked to us all the time about how to "just say no," and our fathers guarded our virtue like border police. Then, too, there were the sermons. Church elders constantly lectured us about what to do with male desire should it ever present itself in a tangible way: run. Our bodies did not belong to us, but to our fathers on earth and our father in heaven. One day, if we were lucky, they'd belong to our husbands. Our bodies were temples, they told us. But temples need worshippers, or else they're just empty buildings.

There were plenty of worshippers at church. The churches to which we belonged were of the evangelical brand, notable for their populations of zealous converts who'd led sad and seamy lives before being lit on fire by Jesus. In one church, our youth group leaders were two handsome young men both of whom had been male strippers. In fact, our pastor had been a pimp, his wife a prostitute about whom he told stories of beating before he found his way to the Lord. Their wives were dour-faced women, saddled by arms full of infants and diaper bags and clung to by toddlers with sticky fingers—they scowled at us when we ran up to hug their husbands after service. We ignored them. Those hugs were soft and warm, their husbands' beards scratching our cheeks, musky cologne pressing into our noses and lungs. Every Sunday I looked forward to the five minutes the pastor would take from the sermon so we might greet and hug those in adjacent pews. Jenna and I positioned ourselves strategically so we'd be sitting directly beside, in front of, or behind the boys or men we most liked to hug. "You give such nice hugs," I remember one growling in my ear as he pulled me into an embrace—something inside me clenched with pleasure. All of this, of course, under and approved by my father's watchful eyes.

In another church, our youth ministers were recovering alcoholics who would talk to us about why we should wait for marriage to have sex and tell us how hard it would be since many men would, of course, want us so badly. They'd refer vaguely but wistfully to the girls they had "ruined" before their conversion. After group prayer, we teens would play capture the flag in the parking lot, while our illustrious leaders would guard the bases, keeping us warm when we arrived there by hugging us to them or rubbing our hands between their palms. One of them was enraptured with a fourteen-year-old friend of mine whom he nicknamed "Face" because, he said, she was so pretty. It hurt my feelings that he only called me "Red," tribute to the much-maligned color of my hair and decidedly not my beauty. "Too bad I'm too old for you," he'd tell my friend, hugging her to him, or, he'd wink, lift her chin up to his face, cluck approvingly, "Trouble. Trouble. Trouble." Eventually, he started dating a woman in the choir and shortly thereafter began to ignore us; when he resigned from youth group, we felt betrayed and whispered loudly about his new wife's snaggle-toothed smile and pointy chin when she passed us in the pews. We were certain she had cast some spell on him, forced him to abandon us.

There were also the men who'd show up for the first time on a Sunday morning, sit behind us in the pews, and afterward ask if they could call. We'd give them our numbers, knowing they'd never get past our dads, who would ask them how old they were. Once, but only once, Jenna called one of them up herself, and he showed up at our house on a Saturday while my parents were out shopping. She was thirteen, he was twenty-eight. I wouldn't let him into the house, so Jenna met him on the porch instead. I watched them through the blinds as they kissed. It was the kind of kissing inexperienced kissers do, tongues battling in the hollow of wide and motionless mouths. Jenna came back inside, flushed. "He said I was jailbait," she confided. "What does that mean?" I didn't know.

I was fifteen when I French-kissed for the first time. It happened while watching *Road House* in a movie theater with a nineteen-year-old named Eric. My friend Sandy, who my mother complained was "fast," had set me up with him. I'd met Sandy at church, and Eric was her ex. They'd already had sex. I was supposed to be at a sleepover at Sandy's, but instead I'd let Eric pick me up from her house and take me on a date. He kissed me as soon as the lights went out in the theater, pressing me against the hard-backed seat and spilling my popcorn onto the sticky floor. He tasted like cigarettes and beer, though I didn't know it at the time. The second time I snuck out with Eric, we made out in the back of his mother's car during a Fourth of July party. We stretched out on the backseat while Boys to Men played on the radio, but I wouldn't let him slip his hands up my shirt or beneath the waistband of my shorts. It was hot inside the car, and he was frustrated, so after a while, we went back to the party and he disappeared into the crowd, leaving me alone to wander the yard among strangers. Everyone was drunk—his mother offered me a Budweiser, and I carried it around, not drinking it, letting it sweat in my palm. I retreated inside, where dirty dishes were piled on the counter and the carpet smelled of dogs. Upstairs, the toilet was stained brown with rust. In the bathroom mirror, I practiced my smile. It felt quivery and loose like it might slide off. I called Sandy from the phone in the kitchen, and her mom picked me up. I told her my stomach hurt.

Eric didn't call me after that, although I did see him one more time. It was in a McDonald's after I'd been canoeing with the youth group. I had fallen in the water. My clothes were dirty, my hair scraggly, and my makeup melted in rivulets down my cheeks. I had just paid for my milkshake when I turned around to see Eric. He nodded at me, and I rushed past him, embarrassed by my Alice Cooper appearance. Later, referring to my appearance, he told Sandy that he had dodged a bullet. Eric was a high school dropout and an alcoholic. His tongue had felt thick and dry in my mouth, his fingers calloused. I was an honors student and, except for my brief flirtation with lying to my parents about my whereabouts, morally irreproachable. But his assessment of my worth was all that mattered.

If I had been careful before about making sure to put my face on before I went out in public, I now became a zealot. With boyfriends in college, I woke up early to sneak into the bathroom to reapply whatever makeup had worn off overnight. I bought only waterproof makeup in the summer and didn't go under the water lest what wasn't waterproof washed off. If a man didn't desire me, I read it as a sign that I needed to procure whatever lure would bait him. Perhaps my hair needed to be less red. Or more. Perhaps my green eyes should be blue. Or purple. Or turquoise. (A smitten eye doctor supplied me with six months' supply of colored lenses for free.) For many years I was convinced it was my pale skin and freckles—a suspicion initiated by a fellow student's remark in high school that I would be "even more hot" with a tan. When I suffered one too many sunburns trying to tan my tender Scotch-Irish skin, I switched to lotions and sprays that left me orange—but that was better than pale. For a time, I wore pantyhose under shorts because I was so embarrassed by my pasty legs. One night, I looked in the mirror and realized that everything about me was fake—bleached hair, colored contacts, painted lips, acrylic nails, spray-tanned skin, adhesive eyelashes, waist-cinching corset, padded bra, platform heels. I was a fraud. False advertising.

But by then I was taking classes in poststructuralist theory. What was "real" anyway, I reasoned. What was identity? Isn't identity unstable? Always shifting? Isn't that how we decenter power? I used my courses in feminism and philosophy to rationalize the fact that there wasn't really any "me" to begin with. "I" was a series of constructs, an assemblage of parts I could compartmentalize, rearrange, brush on and, just as easily, strip away. I was a Colorforms doll. Mrs. Potato Head. An Etch A Sketch—shake and start over. This man liked a woman who wore baseball caps and big hoop earrings—I went shopping. This one wanted a woman to take home to Mom—I went to church. Another had a thing for Claudia Schiffer—I bleached my hair and bought big rollers. This one was into athletes—I joined a gym. Sometimes when my girlfriends and I went to bars in El Paso where we met college boys from UTEP or GIs stationed at the nearby military base, I'd even make up a new persona. I was Savannah. Or Callie. Or Elena. I was a medical student. Or a dancer. Or a runaway. I had no scruples about lying. After all, I knew they weren't really interested in me. An Elena was as good as a Savannah or an Elizabeth. I was all surface. Smoke and mirrors, I'd joke.

How tenuous a hold women have on the power they believe they possess. When I was seventeen and still living at home, I pulled a book from my parents' bookshelf. It was about marriage and was written by a Christian woman. My parents were evangelicals then, and most of our reading material involved how to be better servants of God. This book had a foreword written by the woman's husband. I remember reading something to this effect: "My wife is a beautiful woman. Still, how hard it must be on her to know that every ten years, a new decade's worth of young men no longer find her desirable." What hooked my seventeen-year-old brain was the instability of power—that at some point, no orange tackle box could save her. I hadn't considered this before. It was like suddenly realizing there was fine print in a contract I had already signed. I remember looking into the mirror and thinking about what my mother's friends would say to me when they'd come to coffee—things like, "Oh, to have that body again!" Or, "Oh, how time flies. Enjoy that face of yours now!" What were they talking about? Would men *really* stop desiring me? Up to this point, getting older had meant only that I would get prettier. I'd grow boobs. I'd be able to wear makeup. I had never before thought of getting older as being *bad*. Suddenly I realized that I was sailing toward a horizon on a world that was not round but flat. And there wasn't a damn thing I could do but brace for the fall.

This knowledge made the performance I was giving all the more important. I began to really feel the pressure as I was finishing college. Although an honors student with plans for graduate school, I was convinced that I was running out of time to accomplish the most important goal: marriage. My mother had been engaged three times before her senior year of school. My cousins and many of my friends from high school were already planning their weddings. "Some women never get married," an older cousin consoled me when I showed up, dateless, to Thanksgiving dinner. "It's okay," she patted my arm, unconvincingly. At the time, I was dating a med student, but tradition instructed me that the *man,* not the woman, gets to propose. After three years together, he still wasn't proposing and was making plans to move elsewhere for his residency. "Of course he hasn't proposed. Why buy the cow if he's getting the milk for free?" my father intoned. "But I'm not a cow!" I protested.

One night I went to dinner with my roommate and her parents. Over drinks her mother laughingly told us about how she got her husband to propose: "I spray-painted the window of his car with the words, 'Shit or get off the pot!'" I cringed at the metaphor. But I got it. Soon after, I told my boyfriend, blankly, "I'm twenty-three. I'm not going to look like this forever. Either you ask me to marry you, or I need to go out and use what I've got now to find someone who will."

No surprise that we broke up soon after. So, I went to grad school. I finished graduate school ten years ago and have been teaching gender studies classes at a community college for almost as long. The conversation hasn't evolved much. My students read and discuss poems by feminist poets like Anne Sexton and Adrienne Rich and Kim Addonizio. I lead them in discussions about the traps of a media-driven society obsessed with an unrealistic feminine ideal. We mourn for young girls growing up under the guidance of shows like *Toddlers and Tiaras* and *Extreme Makeover*. We reminisce about our mothers' beauty routines and the suitcases of Barbie dolls we kept under our beds. We admit to each other our obsession with the mirror, our dieting woes. We shake our heads and cluck our tongues at sexism masquerading as girl power in popular songs like "Single Ladies (Put a Ring on It)" and "All about That Bass." They are comforted to know that their professor, long-steeped in feminist theory, still battles with her own vexed position in regard to beauty and desire. I, in turn, feel guilty for allowing them that comfort, which I worry confirms for them that there is no way out of the [tackle] box and therefore no reason to seek, much less attempt, escape.

Last year I turned forty. In our culture, this means I have officially entered the point of no return, crossed over into the no-woman's-land of middle age and its menagerie of cougars and crones, am preparing to fall off the edge of the world. Woman overboard, my body parts sagging, shrinking, sinking. Here, then, is the whirling sea of my life: my ex-husband dating a woman seventeen years his junior, my father engaged to a woman who just turned fifty, my mother choosing an aquarium of brightly colored fish instead of a husband. I myself am remarried, this time not foolish enough to imagine marriage as a destination. If I'm on a raft, my husband's on it too, both our hands in the water paddling. I take my face off before I get in bed. I trust him to love me—faceless and bare, hooked and gutted.

Still, there are nights when my husband falls asleep before me, and I close the door to our bathroom, stare into the mirror, push my disloyal skin back and up, beseech it to stay and not sag. When it refuses, I reach for the vials that line my shelves, for their promises of youth and beauty and perpetual power. As if from over a hill, I hear Botox and Juvéderm and their minions calling, like Christina Rossetti's nineteenth-century goblin men, "Come buy, come buy."

They sound so kind and full of love.

BOUTHEINA LAARIF

A Woman's Body

Deep into the guts
Of an oil-green sea
An oyster is thrust into
A nest of weeds.

So is my body.
Bolted, warm, silent
Wrapped in a plumy, jade cover,
Waiting to rise with the sun.
Pierce the encroaching smog
Fumed by the elders' pipe.
I feel my body, ready, ripe
To bloom as a fruit out of season
But grown right.
To blossom as a bud, crimson
Red of the fight.

I raise my head and fix the gilded sky.

Gasp before I grasp

Hope's nacreous crests.

MICHELE K. JOHNSON HUFFMAN

Natalie Land-Locked

Sometimes when I'm online and I don't want to tell them
everything I am, I pretend my name is Natalie.

Natalie does not fear the ocean,
its dark and deep swirling of mouths,
its calamitous urges. No, Natalie
wants to sink down, feel ancient
muck on the pads of her feet, see
the roaming, indistinct figures.
Natalie does not want a light
in the depths. Natalie does not
want to wave a beam backed by
the artifice of *we can belong here*
too. If she is faced with light
in such a place, let it be uncertain,
let it be plasmic. See, Natalie does
not want to damage or even move
plants with her body. Natalie believes
the sea is the best place to avoid
being a body in the first place.

Natalie in the Dirt

Natalie has had her fair share of dirt
on her hands. On her arms, on her
whole nascent form as it brought itself
up from the scrum. Natalie has crafted
a careful autonomy, a solid structure
that, without her there pulling the strings,
would go on, willing itself to be and be
and be. Rather than relying on the soft
brain and salacious heart, Natalie has
traded them for stock footage
of local sporting events and clip art
scavenged from common use sites.
Natalie has said sayonara to loose
tendons, the slackening nervous
system, the pliant skin. Now, Natalie
raises one baked-clay hand, run
through with steel wires and bungee
cords and waves aloofly at all those
who pass organically below. Natalie
will wave, flash her white pearls and
nod her ceramic, freeze-framing head
until we all pass from her sight.

Natalie on Men

Natalie has two kinds of body:
one fibrous and tender, one steely,
intent. Natalie doesn't let anyone
finger her fibers. Natalie only clicks
I agree after she's read all the terms
and conditions. Natalie is unafraid
to bear witness; she is always
bearing it. Natalie refuses to use
her sexuality to get ahead. Natalie
desires true love. She can't help it
if her ass shakes every time
she walks out of a place. Natalie
is always walking out of places.
Natalie enjoys watching *Antiques
Roadshow* in the evenings.
Like I said, Natalie wants true
love. Natalie has had sex;
her body afterward reminded her
of a silver brooch pinned
to that glossy velvet backing,
post-appraisal. Pointed, shaped
ore wrapped around are-they-real
gems is not one of her two bodies.
Natalie has heard of longing
and has decided it is worth the wait.
Natalie will wait like the lungs
for a sigh, like jam in a jar.

JANE CHANCE

Spit

What I always wanted was to spit out,
blind to the mandate of the stiff penis.

Once, I hitched south away from snow,
the man in the truck saying, "No, don't!"

So, hold your breath and swallow,
I think, my mind turned swamp.

I whittled myself small, joy scant
pleasing him, thin coat to weather

desire. My own, a chipped cup
left behind on the shelf.

Now, *Oh* and *No*
are different routes to the same town,
and I drive my own car everywhere.

TUESDAY TAYLOR

Lipstick and Earrings

Long hair, red, never wore any wigs.
Bold, brassy, sassy, and a little trashy.
He was a *she* with an attitude,
taught him by old movies,
calendar pictures of pinup girls. Him
wearing pink lipstick, pinup curls,
painted nails, satin panties and lace bras.

He'd teach me:
men will try to get your cookies if you let them.
Sit like a lady, watch me.
Cross at the ankle, not the knee.
Sit with your knees together.

Dresses that hung to the floor.
Drag-shopping with my uncle.
Only my brother and I can call him Uncle.
Uncle Jimmy, she,
Prudence Dianna Lovejoy,
a queen.

Pumps in every color.
He would let me line them up in his closet,
pretending they were my shoes.

Pantyhose with baby powder.
That's how you get them on, he said.
Foundation, cake it on.
The lights are bright when I'm on stage.
Blush you'll never need, pretty pink cheeks.

A man taught me how to be a woman.
Eyeshadow, liner, mascara, and lipstick.
Tuesday, you'll never need lipliner.
Yes, men, most will cheat,
It's not you, it's them.
Never kiss on the first date.
A girl has to have standards.

Don't sell it on the first date,
imagination is all men want.

Lipstick and earrings that dangled.
Falsies I would put under my shirt,
pretending they were my own breasts.

You're going to grow into a beautiful woman,
said to me by Ms. Gay West Virginia.
I'd watch him transform.
Paralyzed by the masterpiece
of cross-dress.

Be who you are and be proud, he said.
God and I we have talked.
He made me a queen.
Men will adore you
just like I do,
said to me by
a man who lives his life as a woman.

As a little girl, I'd run downstairs, introducing him
Now presenting the Queen of all
Queens, Prudence
Dianna Lovejoy.
My uncle Jimmy. She!

On Love & Leaving

MERIDIAN JOHNSON

Somewhere with Cows

But the dark embraces everything.

—Rainer Maria Rilke

At night, the cows crowd my two-mile-long driveway in rural northern New Mexico. Black Angus so dark that I often only catch sight of the green-yellow glow of their eyes in the headlights. And sometimes, also, the yellow Department of Agriculture tag found on their ears.

If it weren't for the gravel road and the slow speed required to drive here, we might meet with a much different form of contact. Possible collision with cows. Go slowly. Watch for the shimmer of their eyes, the tapetum lucidum, that light-reflecting surface that helps many animals see better in the dark.

Things in the dark that are also the color of night can sneak up on you. And that is how it felt to receive news from my husband that he is complete in his intimate relationship with me. Am I just being polite?

Or I could say: Dumped. Broken up. Separated. Cheated on? Though none of these qualifiers feels quite right. There is a night-ness to the feeling. A dark quiet stillness, a handlessness, as though I cannot properly grasp a thing. As though the spoon is not stirring the soup. As though water is not pouring into the glass. As though a bowl dropped to the floor doesn't make a sound.

I am clearly not alone in this separation predicament, as something like just under half of American marriages end in divorce. So now I feel welcomed into the club of women and men who have gone before me. Initiated into a new experience of being human. Having one image of relationship shattered.

I remember recently thinking how strange it would be that I would never again have to experience the brokenhearted sensations of my youth, as though marriages like mine were supposed to last forever. As though, despite difficulty and deep discontent, people like my husband and me just don't give up.

To be sure, I feel the new place I am in, the "somewhere" that I cannot quite name or define. It feels like an aftershock from an earthquake. It feels like the wet ceiling of moisture left over in the sky after a blast of storm has just branded the land.

But this earth-shattering sensation isn't a "place" per se, except in the sense of cycle that it signifies. A new cycle in life. As mother. As poet. As teacher. As woman. I flinch at the thought of being a "single woman" again.

Was I ever that?

But shuddering and shock aside, I am woman, and as Joseph Campbell once said, "Woman is where it's at."

This feels like ground I can stand on. I know that my role as woman, as human, is still essentially a creative vocation, a fiesta of creative energies coalescing, calling to be played with, contained and expressed. Celebrated. There is more birth to be the instrument of.

And so, I have work to do.

We humans have the great capacity to reinvent ourselves. To shed layers of real or imagined perceptual understanding of selfhood. We are the stars. And if we are the stars, or the light that's emanated from them, then what great bounding cycles might leap forth from the darkness of unknowns that lie before me?

I sit in my simplicity tonight—a smile I wear alone in my room, a knowing that moments like these make the story of one's life. We remember that we can see in the dark. We can see during the hard turns around curves, the speeding up and slowing down of understanding, the rigidity of logic that always gives way to organic flow of meaning making. On this road. Somewhere. A new place. A new way of seeing. The dark gives rise to somewhere-ness. Black. Sleek, unforeseeable fissures in the present that reach out for us, jump into our awareness like the shimmer of animal eyes in the night. Something within knows the darkness of all this.

This is an invitation to embrace pain, discomfort, adjustment, transition, tenderness. A bigger love. A longing to grow. Expansion balanced with contraction. These words. Just trying to name the place. My heart. The man I have loved for many years. The love still there that won't stop growing even if. Even if. When. If. At the time when. When some other form stirs and invites me forward.

Calls.

But.

It's not about finding someone else to love or call husband. It's about what is available in darkness. The lover who is in all things. Who comes forward to hold and comfort and inspire. Dwelling somewhere. Everywhere. Here, now.

Picture a woman walking in the desert at night, speaking or even singing to cows. Oh, cows. Your great presence stirring beside me. Oh, night. I believe in you.

RUTH SABATH ROSENTHAL

A Box, Full

of photos—a glaring paper trail of my failed marriage—
the snapshots (first) locked away (intact) during
the legal separation when I'd learned that my husband,

a shrink, had a love life outside our bedroom, in
an adjacent room (soundproofed, but alas, not
fool-proofed!). A room he had the gall to call *office,*

on a couch on which I'd heard tell he had many women
going nuts for him, including, it appears, in retrospect,
a patient or two. One such paramour, who became

wife #2, would surely have needed more patience
married to him, had she not divorced him, too,
one would think. During that legal separation,

perhaps she, also, had reconfigured her family photos
as I had: With a cuticle scissor, taking great pains
not to nip the children, she'd cut out the soon-to-be

ex's heads and flushed them down the toilet, leaving
the children smiling up at hole-after-hole-for-a-face.
After the divorce, she'd cut his bodies out and

tossed them in a trash bin (along with an envelope
full of negatives)—the children left leaning on
a slew of missing father figures.

And, like me, it's likely wife #2 suspects there is
a poop-load of similarly doctored photos buried
deep in a score of women's drawers—evidence

the psycho-shrink has been, one way or another,
fully eliminated.

For Want of Red

I see men ogling red-clad women: see-through-
cheap red—backless and sleeveless, breast-tight,
cheek-taut. What ecstasy, peeling layer after layer

of red, the glistening ruby-ripe cores revealed. Oh!
to see those bodies slink past "All You Can Eat"
to "The Pink Pussy Cat" down the street,

to nosedive into hardcore fantasy, rock and roll
in it! Hey, in the thick of it all, the stud-wannabes
appear masterfully cool—slick cucumbers

escaping getting caught red-handed eyeballing
each eye-catcher. In the dogged pursuit of red
the cocksure voyeurs invariably return home,

likely without the slightest shred of red showing.
My old man, a looker from way back, comes
home, more often than not, looking quite in the pink.

Home to me, his postmenopausal wife whose red
faded dress grows more threadbare daily, eyes
bloodshot, bawling over the tear in our state of union.

Forbearance worn thin, I look to my spouse to
redress despair—at the very least, notice me.
The louse looks my way, turns away.

CATHY CULTICE LENTES

After All These Years of Marriage

every room in the house shouts for attention,
secrets cower in corners, all those signs
of trouble I tried to ignore.
Under the bed—
last year's anniversary card,
one black sock,
a dusty Polaroid taken
of the two of us
when the kids were young.

In a kitchen drawer, I find your old pipe,
stem broken, but stashed away as if it could
be repaired. Did you try?
Some things are beyond fixing.
I stand now, finally ready,
trash bags and boxes
open to what comes next,
heart-halved, but two hands
able and steady.

RACHEL SQUIRES BLOOM

Problem Solving

If I only had the email addresses of all those boys
who were so sure I'd spurned them in high school,

I'd write to tell them that they'd read things all wrong.
I'd ask them to send photos of themselves running Microsoft,

piloting planes, turning ideas into gold, inventing
cures for common colds and broken hearts.

Their reserve seemed to hold knowledge the rest
of us lacked. I longed to shake them from silence,

beg them to look beyond my long lashes and soft hair
to the poet inside pleading, *read me, know me.*

But their faces turned only toward scrawled-on notebooks
or stared out of windows, looking anywhere but at me

as though they possessed no protection from my gaze.
I wish I'd dared to bridge the hush to convey

that shyness is not limited to those whose eye contact falls
short, that aloofness signifies diffidence as often

as snobbishness. I'd inform them that their reticence
doomed me to date after wasted date with boys

who cradled footballs closer than I'd ever be held,
consigned me to jovial fools whose visions of women

were limited to two-dimensional garter-belt glossies.
If only I had the email addresses of those boys who shot

furtive glances from behind thick glasses,
ducked their heads in my presence with soft snickers

that through the lens of years may have been sighs . . .
Had I known how to interpret the language of longing

perhaps things would be different, perhaps I could revive
a crushed hope, solve one problem

that they'd scrawled on all those papers
that they failed to look up from as I passed.

MARGED DUDEK

The Anniversary Cake

It is February 2003. Magically, in Seattle, it has been sunny for two or three days and unseasonably warm. It feels almost spring-y, though admittedly, the sunny parts of the day are punctuated with flat gray puddles and the sound of buses splashing through them.

About a week and a half ago I left my husband. I had been distancing myself from him for a short time. I took cheap tennis lessons from a funny old pro. I started going to movies alone.

One night in December, I go to a bar and eat a tiny piece of a psychedelic mushroom stem that is offered me, and I walk home from 45th and University to 42nd and Whitman very mildly tripping. I tell him when I get home, and that I'm a little scared, because at this time, drugs just aren't something I do, and I have never eaten "shrooms" before, even a half a stem, so I don't know just what to expect (it's odd but passes forty minutes after I get home).

While I'm in the tub, he says, "I have felt dark forces gathering all around you for a while." I know I have to leave, and soon. I am not a shaman but I know there are no dark forces, other than him, who would not trust me to go to poetry readings, or drive. Or take the bus after 7 P.M.

I'd wanted to leave before, but when his father died in November, I couldn't. Now, it's February, and the last straw was drawn two weeks ago. I have left the apartment. I have nowhere to live and very little money. The line has been crossed, and from now on, I am going to be decisive about what happens to me, even if it means leaving the cats. There is nothing that can tempt me back now, buddy.

But, I've become accustomed to caretaking. There is a great void under the decisiveness, a strong desire to run back and not abandon everything we've done, the little "wiggle, wiggle—squish, squish!" we said to one another when we used to snuggle in bed, the turning down of his collars when I hung his shirts. So on. Wedded bliss. It has its perks.

❧

So, I have a strong drive to reclaim my soul, but I am still a newlywed. This is only our second anniversary of marriage. You're not even supposed to start counting the years until the third year.

I left four days before the anniversary.

❧

I've been working at this nice, low-key restaurant for about a year. I do okay. But, it's too close to where we lived. I have to get a new job. But I can't just *give up* the old one. I need bus fare and I need to pay the friends who are letting me crash on their couch—to say nothing of needing a few thousand so that I can get my own place. With a determination dusty from long disuse, I don a turtleneck and make myself look not terrified. I lie on my résumé, I lie in the interviews. I get a job three days after leaving William, at a fancy, hip bar on the main street of a hip, fancy part of town that has the advantage of being William's least favorite neighborhood. I'm a bartender now. I'd better learn fast or I will get fired. But, if I can fake it, and have a natural talent for muddling limes (turns out I did), then I can be relatively rolling in the dough soon enough. It's a young part of town. Lots of money in the booze biz.

❧

So, I have both jobs. At one I'm terrified I won't survive, and at the other, I'm sad because I have to leave. I like it there. I like the Wallingford Marged. The Capitol Hill Marged has just wriggled screaming from the earth, and who knows how she'll fuck me up.

It's soon enough after getting the new job that I haven't given notice at the other one, in case the new job falls through.

So, my life has gone from

> up at 5 A.M., at the restaurant at 6 A.M., work to 1 P.M. or 4 P.M., depending, and then back to my husband, where there will be pasta to make and *The Simpsons* to watch and cats to pet and laundry to fold,

to

> waking up at 4 A.M. to catch the bus to the first job, making up reasons that I can't stay until 4 P.M. (because they love my husband there and I can't bear to tell them I've left him), so that I can leave by 3 P.M., catch the bus to the other neighborhood, where I work from 5 P.M. to 10 P.M. or midnight (because I'm training they don't keep me late, thank GOD). Then, I take two buses to get to the apartment where I'm staying. I eat when I can—cheese omelets and cocktail olives while I'm on shift. I sleep when I'm able. Even though I have only a few hours to catch sleep, sleep won't be caught. I can't net the fucker. I'm too stressed. I do, usually, get a few hours. There were stretches of work/no sleep, so bad that I now know the virtue of trying. Turn out the lights. Listen to the cars. Close your eyes. If it's not sleep, it's a close enough approximation to sort of fool the body.

It's a few days, then, after our wedding anniversary, and a regular at the Wallingford Marged Restaurant comes in on my shift with a cake box. He is a single old man with a lot of laugh lines and diabetes and a son who doesn't talk to him. He and I get along. He likes that I am young and have married. He likes that I like simple life. He has no idea that I have just become Urban Warrior Marged, and am no longer Appalachian Transplant Marged. He has baked us a cake. It is white, and lined in blue, with yellow birds on it. And, in the banner the birds hold, it says, "William and Marged." He says, "Have a great third year, you two."

I have to smile, to pretend that my heart is not in his soup. I have to say, "William is going to *love* this. You know how he feels about cake." I have to say this, and finish my shift, and I have to not cry, and I have no time to figure out what to do. That cake is proof—that incredible gesture from a man who sees what I have with my husband from the outside—proof that we still look good, that the dysfunction does not shine through.

I sneak outside and I put the cake in a dumpster.

He sits happy in the knowledge that we will celebrate our love over the half-eaten body of his generosity.

I tell him I called William to come get it, and that I just took it to him. I assure him William was very excited, was off to the grocery to get a split of champagne for us to toast, that we had been unsure how to celebrate our anniversary, and he had provided us a focal point.

That moment ranks in the top five lowest points of my life.

LAUREN BRIMMER

Recurring Dreams

I have this dream where I collapse and melt into the sidewalk. I have this dream where my friends pick shards of glass off of my body in the moonlight and it is cathartic. I have this dream where we run into each other in a bathroom in a city that is neither of ours. I have this dream where I electrocute myself with a blow-dryer and become all light. I have this dream where you are touching me outside of a bed. I have this dream where we are drinking red wine on a raft and we don't wonder where it's going. I have this dream where you turn and look at me like I am not bad for you. I have this dream where you are with someone who is a compilation of all of my flaws made opposite. I have this dream where we are all in that living room again and the light is dripping in again and we are all laughing at the familiarity
again

I Have This Dream

I have this dream where we don't only have bad things to talk about. I have this dream where I don't sweat alcohol. I have this dream where I never wake up in your bed, face wet with sadness, unsure of what happened in between the space of now and last night. I have this dream where you don't sleep on the couch when I cry. Where the next day you don't say to me, "You just looked comfortable how you were." I have this dream where your empathy is not faked—where empathy cannot be faked. Where you don't say, "I am feeling empathetic right now," as if empathy is not something that lies aching in the guts of those who possess it. I have this dream where I never slept with any of your friends. I have this dream where I don't sleep with your friends when you don't text me back. I have this dream where your fingers do not poke at my bruises. I have this dream where I don't bruise easily. I have this dream where you don't blame my cuts on yourself, just because she did. I have this dream where you realize that what women do to their bodies usually has nothing to do with you. Where you don't say, "I just have that effect on women," when referring to circumstances too grim to associate with such a phrase. I have this dream where you do not feel like a drug. I have this dream where I do not lie in your bed out of convenience, out of proximity—out of there being less than ten blocks between us. I have this dream where you do not feel the need to remind me that I am not the only one who gets to touch you. I have this dream where you touch me with an ache, as if there is something other than what's outside of me that you want.

MARIANNE S. JOHNSON

Today at the Gynecologist

Naked, wrapped in a paper gown paper towel at the OB/GYN because it is that time of year again, and likely my last time for all practical purposes, and I brought a collection of poems to read while I wait, written by someone you love, and poetry always makes me think of you anyway, and the bulletin board in the exam room is bursting with baby pictures, all kinds and colors, whole broods of them, pairs and newly minted cherubs, and one dark-haired one looking terribly ugly in terror, and I wonder how you manage your yearly peek-and-poke with these cheesy reminders that none of the hundred faces on any of the boards anywhere belong to you and never will, and I remember one lost, returned upon the water, and you are the only person who knows the weight of those stones in my chest, and maybe it was that episode on HBO last night that triggered this, that girl show that you love, the scene in the bathtub where a distraught, near-sobbing Jessa bursts in on Hannah singing in the tub, and Jessa slips off her dress, a skin-to-skin, and climbs in with her, like climbing back into a watery womb with her, without questions or permission or judgments, or maybe it is my mail that you still have not answered, my letters naked without reply, that makes me want to crawl into a warm bath with you, a face-to-face, then lace your fingers in mine and soak until our hands are conjoined.

RASHIDA MURPHY

Maybe

Maybe somewhere in Marrakesh
A woman shook her hair out of her abaya and sighed into the desert air
Maybe somewhere on Mt. Carmel
Lovers clasped hands and saw olive groves plunge into the sea
Maybe somewhere in Babylon
A child slipped away from his mother and caught his foot on an ancient root
Maybe I held my breath when we met
You reminded me of olive groves and salty seas
Of cinnamon smells that linger in country kitchens at three o'clock
Of mulberry trees forming canopies in an orchard
Of children's laughter and whispered secrets
Of ancient forests and illuminated stories
You listened to me
You looked at the shards of my life and said
I've been here too, you know
When church bells condemned
You nudged me with phone calls and interstate flights and book parcels
You sent flowers tied in blue ribbon and envelopes with crooked writing
I dreamed of cool forests where I could lie down beside you among the honeysuckle
Eat cherries. Wear scarlet. Wait for the ease you promised.
Wait for the unfurling of leaves and the beat of moths' wings
Wait for the future
Wait for our lives
Wait for tinglings, nerve endings, senses, faith, poetry, love

BETSY CORNWELL

The Search for One Thing

"Give it one week of hard frost," my new husband says, "and all the green will be gone."

He has slowed the car to let two adolescent does cross the road, and we watch them vanish neatly into the ditch on the other side. In the four-thirty November gloom, the perfect white of their rumps is nearly all we can see. As they pass through the high brambles of the ditch, Richie admires their fleetness, their nimble feet. I say the deer must only risk the danger of the road because it's winter and they are hungry, but he says they wouldn't be wanting yet. That's when he warns me about the week of frost, and the green.

But here, even in winter, Ireland is so green that to walk through the countryside is almost to think you are underwater. And here a ditch is not a hole, not an absence, but its opposite. An Irish ditch is a raised thicket, a dense living tangle of blackberry and ivy and gorse. Twining through the ditch are innumerable tiny tunnels—through them mice and spiders wind. No snakes here, of course—remember St. Patrick—but the tunnels mimic their absence, their silent, assured sinuousness. I follow their paths with my eyes.

When I first came to this country, I remember thinking that even if I jumped from one of its many cliffs, I wouldn't fall but float, until the cool wet wind of this place carried me back, softly, onto the grass that is so green it is like water, like every kind of life pulled together into one.

I came here to renew—something, although I didn't yet know what. And to escape, well, everything.

❧

Two years ago, at the end of my graduate program, I was broken down and burned out: spent twigs for a spent fire. I did everything quickly, heart in my mouth, because I felt sure that if I took any extra time, I would collapse into ash. I was teaching three times the prescribed student limit, tutoring, writing, finishing my thesis and my classes, and editing my first novel for next year's publication—all jobs that filled me with whiplash joy and panic and soul-crushing insecurity. A person I loved had shown me such grinding ambivalence that I'd had to let him go, and I spent far too much time imagining our never-to-be future together. There was a cushion-laden corner of the floor in my cheap apartment that was alternately a nook for grading papers and a nest to curl up in and cry until I fell asleep. I ate whatever I thought would make me feel better, mostly cheese and Vernors ginger ale. My heart was broken and my belly ached.

I had a particular dream that kept me working: I wanted to go to Ireland. I'd come in second for a Fulbright arts grant to write about selkies in Dublin, and the near miss had left me determined to get there on my own. But when the summer came and I looked at my finances, I realized that even with my book advance I would have to choose between Ireland and more earthly concerns like health care and rent.

That day, my father called and said he wanted to know my schedule for next year because he was taking the family to Africa. We would go on safari and sleep in tents together.

But I have spent much of my life figuring out how to avoid being in the same place as my father, especially at night. And for the first time, that day, I told him so. One advantage of being so very tired, on the threshold of adulthood, is that your childhood nightmares start getting tired, too, and it is harder for them to frighten you.

"I can't go," I said in a voice that shook but was still my own voice, coming out of my own body. "I can't sleep in the same room with you."

The other end of the line was silent. After a few seconds, he said, "All right. That doesn't make me happy, but I understand."

We hung up soon afterward, and one weight was strangely gone from the fears I carried.

A few days later, he called again and offered to buy me a ticket to Ireland instead, since I wasn't going to Africa. It felt like hush money—if I was brave enough to tell him I remembered, whom else might I tell? I said I would have to think about it. I felt sure I would say no, but that dream was a hard one for me to give up.

I went into town to have coffee with Trish, a woman twice my age who feels like someone I grew up with, a friend whom I often call my spiritual guide. The Catholic school we attended, with its Planned Parenthood protests, homophobia, and rape apologism, tempted me to throw up my hands at even a nebulous, agnostic God—but it was Trish's faith that kept me searching for my own. She combined her devout and somewhat radical Catholicism with dashes of Buddhism and a sharp flair for the intersectionally feminist, and I've always loved her for it. I liked to say that she was *tapped into something*, because it was the only way I could find of explaining her radiant wisdom and kindness, the light that shines through her. (When she's not giving spiritual counsel to frightened young women, Trish is a professor of sociology and a brilliant poet.)

As soon as she sat down, I started crying—big, gasping sobs from a shy woman who can rarely even manage to raise her voice in anger. I don't know if I'd ever shown that much emotion in public before.

Trish stroked my arm. I wept into my giant bowl of latte.

When I quieted, she laughed and said, "Honey, I wouldn't go through my twenties again for anything."

Suddenly, I felt much better. I wiped my eyes, and she asked me what was wrong.

Trish is third-generation Irish American—three of her grandparents were born on the island where I now live—and it was she, in the end, who brought me here. I told her what my father had offered, how it felt like a bargain I didn't want to make, and that I never wanted to owe him anything ever again.

She looked at me steadily. "You never will," she said. "He could give you money until the end of the world and you'd owe him nothing." He'd taken more, she said, than he could ever give back. Though some well-trained part of me thought I was being a bad daughter, I admitted she was right.

"But . . . ," said the bad daughter, on the verge of tears again. I found I couldn't finish my sentence, and I took a deep, shaky breath. "God, I'm so tired. I'm sorry about this." I waved at my eyes.

Trish shook her head. "Go to Ireland," she said. "You'll rest there, you'll write your book. It's where the world keeps its magic. And don't go to Dublin. In fact," she pulled out her tablet and did a quick image search, "you need to go here."

She showed me a page thick with pictures of green cliffs, dark waves, and small stone-bound fields. A girl's feet dangled over the edge of one cliff, her legs mid-swing and relaxed.

"The Aran Islands?" I laughed. "It's mostly sweaters there, right?"

"The Aran Islands," she said. "See? You're happier already. Go there," she thought for a moment, "for at least a month. It will heal your soul."

My soul leaped out for healing, and I knew that I would go.

Three months later, I sat in the warmest corner of Tigh Joe Watty's, one of only two pubs on the whole island. I was smiling, and every part of me felt light. Tall, redheaded Uinseon McCarron danced a beautiful Australian girl named Sjonelle across the dark wood floor, and the rest of us at the table watched and admired them, their easy grace and easier smiles. Dave, the handsome, acerbic owner of the hostel where we all worked, came back to the table with pints of cider. I hadn't written anything in weeks.

I did not understand, when I first came to Ireland, why I wasn't writing. It was the first time in my life that I didn't feel overworked, and suddenly I couldn't work at all.

I'd been manically, neurotically productive for years, trying to scratch my way into prep school, college, graduate school, New York agencies, and publishing houses. And now here I was, *not* a student for the first time since I was three years old and my parents enrolled me in university preschool. I had gotten into all the places I'd been told my whole life to strive for, done all the things my growing-up self was supposed to do. I had my master's, and my book wasn't coming out for almost a year. I could support myself until then, meagerly, on my advance and hostel work exchange. I was, odd as it seemed, grown up.

All my life I had wanted "to write full-time," but here I had all the time in the world, and I wasn't writing at all. I woke up early every morning determined to work, and I hovered over the Cinderella retelling on my computer, making small changes that meant nothing. I always ended those sessions at least a little disgusted with myself.

My afternoons, though, I set myself free, wandering through the cobblestoned Latin quarter of Galway City to the rushing gray mouth of the Corrib. I walked the promenade from Galway to Salthill and back, looking out at the quiet bay, cold wind slipping over my face and silvering my hair and skin with salt, breathing air clean as miracles.

I've spent most of my life inside my head. In childhood, my body was the site of fear and confusion at the hands of an adult protector. I became expert at curling up inside myself, where my senses would know and remember nothing. The desires and doubts of adolescence only made me retreat further. My body hardly ever did what I wanted it to—I have never even been good at sports.

As I grew older, this disconnect led me to think that my body had no needs of its own, and certainly not much value. It carried my mind and my heart around, and that was all. When I felt worn out at the end of school, I thought it was only my soul that hurt. I didn't notice the knots in my back.

I struggled over my writing in Ireland, and as Trish had instructed me, I worked to heal my broken heart. It was my lungs and my legs, though, that first grew stronger, walking along the promenade, making beds and mopping floors at the hostel.

Salt and clean air, and enough work to make you need them.

Healing was in my body, was stitching into my very cells, before I could even see it working, before I could see new words on the page. When I came here I thought I was failing, but something was already starting to grow.

In college, I studied literature and fairy tales. Some—*The Selkie Bride, Cinderella, Red Riding Hood, Tam Lin*—I'd read in different translations and retellings since I was a child. I have always loved, more than anything, *stories.* Stories helped me escape those parts of my childhood that I could only talk about years later. I told myself stories, too, even as I progressed into adulthood. I thought I knew what I wanted, whom I would love, how my life would lead. I was a good student, a follower of rules. Whenever I searched for something, I believed I knew what I would find, and when, and how.

I write fairy tales for a living now, and like many feminist writers, I try to give my heroines the agency that they sometimes lack in older versions of the tales. The aims of women of my generation and the one before—and many, many brave and hard-fighting women before us—are all for choice and action. By action, I mean achievement, agency, *doing*. I believe in these ideals—they keep the world moving forward and help to give it some chance of (maybe, someday) being just.

But lately I have been thinking that these older princesses and witches and peasant girls have a kind of wisdom to offer us that has lately been lost: the wisdom of passivity, of stillness.

Those seemingly unfeminist stillnesses are nearly always there, in the most enduring of the old fairy stories. Snow White, Sleeping Beauty, Red Riding Hood curled up in the wolf: what are they thinking, unthinking, as they lie there undoing? Are they glad, unchosen as it is, for the rest?

Whether they are or not, the stillness is part of the narrative and, therefore, is itself part of the moving forward, the *doing* of the story. Even when they are still, their stories go on. And I have found, in the time that I have spent in this place, that stillness has a strength and power of its own. I believe now that I needed not to write for that time. There are many fields here that lie fallow.

Soon after I met my husband on Inis Mor (the largest of the Aran Islands—oh, Trish, how right you were), he told me something that has twined itself through my heart ever since. In Irish, he said, "*Faigheann iarraidh, iarraidh eile.*" In English: "The search for one thing leads to another."

I came to Ireland to write a book. I could not write, but if the soul is a place of quiet and stillness and peace inside oneself, I found mine, and the island and I healed it where it had been starved and broken. I met my partner, and I found my home. And nine months later, in the spring, living in East Galway with Richie, I began to write again.

On Family & Heirlooms

ANDRENA ZAWINSKI

After My Mother's Death

I pulled the sheets awash in fleur-de-lis
straight down in a swift swoop of cloud
off the deathbed onto the planked floor
where they lay lifeless spent blossoms.

Last week, we bundled and carried them
down to the basement Kenmore, she hovering,
breath labored, hands trembling, it gushing,
chuffing, and spinning its way to the end.

Her Ivory Snow made me sneeze as it did
days we worked the Maytag wringer washer,
she cranking its arm, feeding bedclothes
through the roller, coaxing me to pull pull pull,

my small hands cold and aching, six-year-old legs
shaking, as I pulled pulled through the pillow cases
I would later iron into smooth warm squares
to rest my head, doze into a powdery clean sleep.

Today as I stand folding my own shams and sheets,
funeral flowers rise up fragrant with upturned earth
where gravediggers put down rose wreaths and lilies,
scents she liked least with so many friends' burials.

Again on shaky legs, I hear her saying pull, pull, pull—
you can do it. But that day of my mother's death,
I stretched out on her bed imagining the mortician
loading her body into the dark car, cold and alone.

I languished there pressing the small of my back
    flat against the padded tufts of her bare mattress,
        lay the way I saw her there nursing her weak heart
            after a hospital stay she said would be her last and was.

Then as suddenly as I imagined that hearse hauling
    her body away, I rose up, a Lady Lazarus, pulled the sheets
        back onto the bed, burying my nose in their heap,
            their final sweet moment, the last scent of her,
                the one I had memorized from birth.

Rosie Times

"How do you know you are going to die?" I begged my mother. With strange confidence she answered, "When you can no longer make a fist."

—Naomi Shihab Nye

My mother, born into the flapper era, never bobbed
her hair, never sported drop waist dresses with a cloche,
nor did she cover her face with pancake and rouge,
lifting her skirt above her knees in speakeasies
or on Gatsby verandas. She came of age in World War II.
Draped in white coveralls, hair wrapped in a red scarf
under a hardhat, clear goggles shielding her amber eyes,
she welded Pressed Steel's boxcars outside Pittsburgh

like women in Toledo hauling Jeep parts to Ford lines,
like those assembling fuselages on bombers in Long Beach
or for Boeing's Flying Fortresses in Seattle,
like women filing bullets for the Army,
or building ships at California's Richmond docks,
like those feeding blast furnaces in steel mills,
sparks flying at the giant cauldrons of molten steel.

Liberty Girls—the women on railroads, in shipyards,
as pipe fitters and riggers, bus drivers and mechanics,
like those shooting riveting guns or ferrying planes,
ratcheting with wrenches or lighting torches,
arms linked across America with the plains women,
with the farm women, the desert and mountain women,
with the city women, even with Marilyn Monroe,
who as Norma Jean, attached propellers to planes.

My mother never jumped drunken in her clothes
into a fountain like F. Scott Fitzgerald's new women,
but she did drop, donning her mail-order rayon sheath,
from a rowboat into the lake, belting out the high notes
of "Indian Love Call" at a USO picnic. She learned
to love the night shift as a blackout air warden
and became the woman who I would later blast
for not pulling free from my father's fierce grip.

I have become the woman who no longer wonders
how I dared knuckle into my own fist, raise it high
for rights in rallies and marches for reason and right
because I had a mother who dared give up a job
as a nursemaid for the rail yard and factory,
relinquish the girdle to the rubber drive, who never
threw off the helmet for the apron, and went on
living as if she could do anything—making a fist.

MAGGIE THACH MORSHED

Land and Water

It's early, and my mom wakes to a blue-gray haze. It fills the house just moments before the sun finds the right place in the sky to start the day. The house is still and quiet, but she is up, which means there are things to be done. If she doesn't do them, no one else will.

We have just spoken, a Skype call erasing the eighteen hours between her in her home in the Central Valley of California and mine in Seoul, South Korea. A weekly phone call used to feel like a cumbersome duty reserved only for firstborns like me. As I've gotten older, though, the phone calls are comforting. I stick to this routine even as we are thousands of miles apart. I last saw my mom three months ago, but we will reunite soon to attend my cousin's wedding.

In twenty-four hours, my mom will get on a plane headed for Vietnam. Her suitcases have been packed for weeks, so she starts this day like she would any other. I know because in the months leading up to my move to Korea, I observed my mom's daily patterns. It was the only way for me to keep my mind off the anxiety and doubt I had surrounding my life's biggest decision.

This tendency was nothing new. Growing up, there was never a time that I did not long for a strong mother–daughter bond. To my dismay, there were times I felt a deep chasm between us, a distance shaped by the fact that thoughts and feelings could not be translated from English to Vietnamese or vice versa. We were bound by what we could not say. To be close to her, I observed her. I noticed the things she did, the responsibilities she had to take on. So even though I am not there with her on this morning, I know what she is probably doing.

I imagine that while my brother and dad sleep, she makes her way to the den that has been transformed into her sanctuary. My college diploma hangs next to my sister's, and a different altar takes up each corner of the room. The peaceful-looking Buddha statues gaze out, wanting nothing. Photos of each of her deceased parents sit on a bureau directly across from the diplomas. Subtle smiles spread across my grandparents' faces, as if they are happy with what they're seeing. This is how my mom wants it—what she left behind and what she left for on opposite walls, bringing balance to the room. She lights the incense and the smoke wafts around her. Morning and incense smoke rise at the same time. When illuminated by the soft morning glow, the smoke drifts through the room like a ghost.

She goes to the kitchen and starts packing lunch for Ghandy, my brother. He is the child she almost lost: once in the womb and once in a bathtub filled too high. My mom never thinks about what could have been. Maybe another college diploma to hang on the wall? Perhaps. But she never asks questions because he has escaped death twice and she will love him for that.

While my sister Goldy and I were in college, my brother was in a classroom for developmentally disabled adults. He has been there since he aged out of the public school system at eighteen. He goes to the day program for interaction with other people like him, other people who can't walk or talk. Other people who can't keep the drool from seeping out of the corners of their mouths.

Inside the house, my dad is most likely still asleep and will be until my mom leaves for work. After Ghandy is taken to the adult day program, she has only an hour before going to the nail salon to rub people's feet and pumice their calluses. My mom removes dead skin and paints the toenails of high-maintenance college coeds and bored housewives. They talk down to her and speak slowly when she asks, "What col-uh you want?" They roll their eyes and sigh loudly if she pinches them with her cuticle nippers. They tip her a few dollars.

My mom is no different from the Vietnamese immigrants who flocked to the nail salon business in the late 1970s. She has been giving manicures and pedicures for fifteen years now. She will retire soon because she can't stand the continuous bending over. And even though she wears a mask, the nail polish fumes have started to give her headaches and make her forgetful. The salon takes so much out of her.

After long days at work, she sinks into her queen mattress and eats fruits that have already been offered to the gods and our ancestors. Her house is her haven, a piece of land she can finally call her own after almost thirty years of living in rented houses. Filling up white spaces on the walls, lacquer artworks embedded with mother-of-pearl inlay and framed embroidered pieces fight for attention. Flower arrangements and potted plants take up corners in every room. Pictures of us three kids—the images of an American life seen through Vietnamese eyes—settle where there's space.

My mom is happy we were born here. But throughout my childhood, it was clear there was a distinction between my mom and her kids. We were home. She was not. There was always a sense of longing for Vietnam with my mom. Once, when my dad picked me up from school, he tortured me with his twisted sense of humor. "Your mom decided to go back to Vietnam for good. She left this morning." I cried so hard that even upon seeing her the moment I walked through the door, I stormed to my room in order to let my worst fear heave throughout my chest in private. Now, my sister and I are gone. I wonder how many times she thinks about going back and satisfying that longing that hung over her all those years.

I see my cousin, the one getting married, at Tan Son Nhat Airport in Saigon. My mom arrived yesterday, and I have just arrived from South Korea, where I am teaching English. I climb onto the back of my cousin's motorbike. My olfactory memories erase the ten years since I've last been here. Smells of meat grilling over charcoals and green onions and garlic popping in oil trick me into believing I am seventeen again. The same food carts occupy the same cement real estate. The fashion here is dictated by the humid weather, not time. Motorbikes fight over pieces of asphalt as if they were unclaimed plots of California land during the Gold Rush.

My cousin takes me back to 76 A/7 P. 10 Phu Nhung, the L-shaped house in the heart of the marketplace where my mom grew up. Since my grandparents passed away ten years ago, the house has been divided. New walls have been built, separating the inheritance of every surviving family member.

No portion of land was too small to pass down. My cousin received what used to be the front entryway, a ten by fifteen foot area where the family used to park the motorbikes. It has been retiled and is now a small kitchen and narrow living room. My cousin built the house up—he and his sister live on the second floor while his father is on the third. Saigon is filled with houses that look like precarious Jenga towers.

The motorbike whimpers before coming to a complete stop. Thin red sticks poke up from a dusty urn on a corner of the doorstep. These are the remnants of incense burned to guide spirits to the house. I wonder if my grandparents' spirits knew I was coming today. My mom comes down the steep stairs with a plate of hot egg rolls. I remember the stairs that used to be there, when this was my grandparents' house. My memories are transposed over what is actually in front of me. I see my grandfather's wooden bed—transparent like incense smoke—over my cousin's couch, my grandmother's hammock in the kitchen.

"Are you hungry?" my mom says. I'm so happy to see her, but the matter-of-fact demeanor in the way she mothered me growing up has not waned in the time that we have been apart. She doesn't ask me how my job is or how I've been. She doesn't hug me or kiss me. I know not to take this as an insult. She asks if she can feed me because for my mom, food is love.

"Yeah, I'm starving," I say, knowing how to speak her language. "I've missed your egg rolls, Mom."

Cooking in the house that she has always called home, my mom appears different. She is not just my mom. She is a daughter. She's the young girl who was too naive to realize leaving for something better also meant leaving something behind, something she would never be able to get back.

My mom came to the United States in 1983 after almost three years in four different refugee camps. For most of that time, she survived on a bowl of rice twice a day. She saved up her salt and oil rations for the days she couldn't stand the monotony. Her prized possession was a fully intact plastic bag she could use to catch rainwater. The four liters of water she received every day was never enough. Drink, cook, or bathe—she could never do all three.

Still, the hardest thing about being in a refugee camp wasn't the agony of waiting day after day with nothing to do. Or trying to stay clear of the malaria, scabies, or any other infections that flourished in the camp conditions. It wasn't the uncertainty of going to a new country or the worrying about the parents she left behind. It was shitting. The hardest part about being in the NW 82 refugee camp on the Thai–Cambodian border was shitting.

To do so, she had to go to a bamboo hut on the outskirts of camp. Her biggest fear was having to go in the middle of the night. The refugee camp was filled with anguished spirits, both dead and alive. She didn't know what could be lurking out there in the dark. The hut housed a big hole that led to a pile of human excrement. Roughly two thousand people were squeezed onto a mudflat about the size of a football field. When the waste of all those people piled up too high, a new outhouse was made. The stench simmered in the tropic humidity.

She met my dad, a ranger from the 81st Airborne Vietnamese Special Forces, in the camp. When their names finally reached the top of the resettlement list, they went to the Philippines to learn some English phrases and American customs. They were headed to Utah, where a sponsor awaited them. My mom was relieved that their sponsor was, like my dad, Khmer Krom (ethnically Cambodian people who live in the southern region of Vietnam). She was told the sponsor would help them settle in America, provide food and shelter until they could do so on their own. But it was a different story once they got to Utah. My mom felt they were more like a burden than welcomed houseguests. The sponsor made them sleep in the basement and split their earnings with him when they got their paychecks. When she told him she wanted to go to a vocation and language school instead, he showed his disapproval by refusing to give her a house key. Often, the worst part of her day was ringing the doorbell to be let back into the house.

She worked at a glass window company, and my dad worked at a gun manufacturing factory in Provo. They found new friends and finally got out of their sponsor's basement. They even moved out on their own for a little while, until they didn't have enough to pay rent every month. A fellow Vietnamese refugee heard they needed a place to stay and told them they could stay with him, but it wasn't long before he asked them to move out. His sister was coming, and he needed the space. Once again, my mom and dad had nowhere to live. On the brink of homelessness, my dad reached for his wallet to retrieve the number of an old Cambodian man, Ông Già.

My dad met Ông Già at a holiday gathering in Salt Lake City. Ông Già had a trailer that my dad hoped was empty. He left my mom momentarily to find a phone. Surely, my mom thought, Ông Già would take in a fellow Cambodian and his newly pregnant wife. My mom wondered how she could still feel like this in America. All she wanted was a new beginning on solid footing.

❧

Don't look back. Keep going. Don't think about what could have been. Keep moving. Never look back. Those are the words my mom's American life was built on. My mom came to America newly baptized. In the water that separated her old home from her new, she held her breath and let it wash over her. But how could she ever forget it all? Was this her path? Was she meant to leave her home forever? She took those doubts and regrets and pressed them together. Made them indistinguishable. Wrapped her hands around them until they made a tight ball, until they made a pebble. She pushed that pebble deep into her brain to a spot that was hard to reach. It remained undisturbed until I said something to knock it loose.

Before I moved to Korea, I told my mom I had just left the man I thought I would marry. Before that, I quit a job and moved to another state for him. After languishing for almost a year with no work and no purpose, I realized we were not the right fit. "Where will I be without him? How did I get here?" I sobbed to her over the phone. I imagined my mom's disappointed face as she clicked her tongue and shook her head over the last five wasted years of my life. I expected her to tell me "I told you so" since she was against the relationship and our twelve-year age difference from the beginning. But no dismissive word ever left her mouth. Instead, she told me she understood.

"Before I left for America, the man I was supposed to marry married someone else," she said. "I couldn't stay. I cried so much. I told your grandmother." My grandmother told my mom the same thing my mom would say to me. "Go. Go as far as you need to." It's funny how despite time and place and circumstance, mothers and daughters can live the same life.

❧

It's been thirty-two years since my mom left for good. This trip back to Vietnam is her sixth, but only her second since her parents passed away. Coming back to Vietnam is like pressing play on a video that has been paused—my mom instinctually picks up where she left off.

My mom is on the back of my aunt's motorbike, and I am riding with my uncle. We're getting sodas and ice for the wedding tomorrow. From this familiar vantage point, the streets of Saigon are what they've always been: the lifelines of the city.

They pulsate with continuous traffic. The heart of the city still beats the same. But we see some things that are unrecognizable. Small shops have been torn down to make room for Louis Vuitton and Chanel boutiques. The Windsor Plaza and Park Hyatt appear and disappear like pictures in a slideshow. The hotels' shadows swallow up motorbikes and pedestrians only to spit them back out.

Later that day, my mom supervises as my cousin gets his house ready for his wedding. My cousin cleans the altar and makes sure it's presentable for when he brings back his bride to burn incense for our grandparents. My mom inspects the job he's done and gives her approval. The pictures he cleans are the same ones my mom has in her altar back in California. My grandparents are with my mom wherever she goes.

My cousin wakes up early on his wedding day, and we wake up along with him. My mom sends me with my cousin to get fresh flowers from the market while she stays behind to get ready. By the time we get back, my mom is in a black and fuchsia *áo dài,* a traditional Vietnamese dress. She must have tried on ten before she decided on this one. She has already put on the earrings that she's been saving just for this day, but she asks me to help her fasten the matching necklace around her neck.

When the wedding starts, my mom and I are separated. Behind my cousin, my mom stands by the rest of her siblings as representatives of our family who ask for permission to enter the bride's house. I stand with the bride's sister and the rest of the young people. Only parents and elders are allowed in the altar room, where my cousin and his new bride burn incense for her ancestors. Gifts of boiled chicken, areca nuts, and tea are in silver tins covered in red and gold handkerchiefs. Incense smoke circles the room.

My mom beams with a childlike happiness. My mom has been to places and seen things nobody else in her family has. Despite it all, she has landed right back at this moment, perhaps right where she's supposed to be. As she stands next to her brothers and sisters, I remember the black-and-white pictures she used to show me when I was a kid. I look hard at my aunts and uncles, searching for the features that helped me distinguish them before. They stand in a straight line, as if my grandmother had lined them up herself. They are kids, and they are adults. I am seventeen, and I am twenty-seven. Ten years have passed, and time has stood still. This is a place where time is no marker of any kind. Time here is like water. The wave that pushes you farther out can be the same one that brings you back to shore.

❦

My mom and I share the bed in my cousin's room while he sleeps on the floor with his new bride. I wake occasionally because my mom won't stop rustling. She doesn't drift into her dreams as easily as she used to. The reason she can't sleep could be the six-inch-thick piece of foam that passes for a mattress here. Or the hum of the air conditioner. Or the fact that there are no windows in the room, making it seem more suffocating at night. But all those things aren't really the problem. I know the real reason is because she misses my brother.

In pictures of Ghandy as a child, nothing seems to be out of place. As a toddler, his cheeks were so supple and his dark brown eyes so deep that people hardly even noticed that he didn't walk or talk. He was just a baby, people thought, even though other kids born around the same time were developing much faster. He was a beautiful baby. What a shame, people would tell her as he got older. He would have been so handsome. But my mom does not think about what could have been. She won't allow herself to. When it comes to Ghandy, she only lives in the present because the past and the future are where the regrets and what-if questions live. No matter how many coarse hairs might grow above his upper lip or pimples might sprout on his face, he is her baby.

When my sister and I were young, we used to argue about who was my mom's favorite.

"Who do you love more? Me or her?"

"Neither of you. I love your brother the most."

That answer is still true today. My mom says my sister and I will be fine. She never worries about us. I wonder if she realizes her other children might need her as much as Ghandy does. But for the rest of Ghandy's life, my mom believes her sole purpose is to make sure he is taken care of. She never hesitated in taking on this role. That's what it took to handle the doctors, the neurologists, the social workers, the therapists, and the special education teachers. Despite never becoming fully fluent in English, my mom made sure they all knew what Ghandy needed.

She did a good job of holding it all together when he was growing up. She treated every appointment and evaluation as a mundane task, like grocery shopping or eating rice. But there were times when it all became too much, when one small crack led to a spider web of crevices. The cracks would spread out and crumble the wall she had built around herself.

Like the time when Ghandy was eleven and went to the dentist to get some cavities filled. The whole family had to come because there was no babysitter to call on. Ghandy was not a typical patient because he couldn't sit still in the dentist's chair. He didn't know what was going on, only that strange people were holding his arms and legs down. He squirmed and bucked his head. They gave him a sedative. Putting him to sleep was the only way he would stay still long enough for the dentist to treat the cavities.

An hour passed. Ghandy was still not asleep, and the dentist wouldn't return until he was. My mom had the dental assistant turn off the lights so Ghandy could drift off. My dad paced in the waiting room when he wasn't smoking in the parking lot. I wanted to stay in the room. My mom had no energy to object.

She scooted Ghandy over in the chair to make room for herself, slipping her arm underneath his head. She shushed him and patted his chest gently. He didn't want to be comforted and he snapped at her, finding a piece of flesh under her bicep between his rows of little, sharp teeth.

My mom jumped as he clamped down. She ignored the pain in her arm. She shushed louder. He became angrier. His groans became more desperate. She continued to pat his chest, just as gentle but faster. Faster and faster she patted. She tried to focus on the staccato rhythm to keep from giving in to the sobs sitting right behind that big wall she had built. But she felt the first piece of the wall fracturing, and it was only there in the darkness that she let herself cry in front of her children for the first time.

My grandparents are buried in twin aboveground graves just outside of Saigon. The wedding is over and the most important thing to do now is to visit them. My mom rides with my uncle, and I am with my aunt. My aunt and I lean left and right on her motorbike to negotiate the potholes filling the streets. We have brought gifts for my grandparents: *bánh bao* (steamed pork buns) and *bánh bò* (rice cakes) for my grandmother, and *càfê sữa đá* (coffee with condensed milk), and *trà* (tea) for my grandfather.

We park the motorbikes and walk toward the graves, which are at the end of a small field. The altar is shrouded by thick overgrown blades of grass. Possessive vines weave through the bars of the metal fence that protect the two tile caskets. A year's worth of dust has collected over the portrait of each grandparent. My mom wipes down the caskets. My aunt sweeps the debris into the corners. In this moment, everything will be clean and food will be plentiful for my grandparents. My mom sets out the offerings. My uncle lights the incense and hands two sticks to her. She lifts the incense up to her forehead. Her prayer is long and slow. Her lips move as if she is in conversation. Maybe she is. A slight glimmer of neon orange moves reluctantly down the incense, emitting a smoke that swallows her up. She is lost in that smoke.

When I was young, my mom told me she would return to Vietnam because she wanted to be buried where she was born. This always seemed like a threat to me. As the neon orange glimmer leaves a trail of ash in its wake, I think, *Would the incense that Goldy and I burn in my mom's memory reach her wandering spirit if she were buried here?*

My mom and I follow the other Westerners to where the coconut candies are being made. We are on a tour in Bến Tre Province. We watch young women wrangle rice paper wrappers around cubes of coconut globs. This candy factory is a makeshift operation. There are no walls, just an intricate frame of wooden posts topped by a roof covered in dried coconut tree leaves. There are oversized metal mixers churning a milky-colored substance that looks like thick saltwater taffy. Some of the women pour the taffy into molds that make long ropes of candy, and when the taffy hardens, it is cut into cubes.

"I love the smell," my mom says. "You can't get this back in America."

The tour group forms a line on a shaky dock and people are placed in long traditional wooden work boats. A young local girl guides our boat through narrow ravines under a canopy of vibrant green coconut leaves. It feels like I am gliding through a hidden passage. The water is not what you would see in a brochure for an island getaway. It does not glow with an aquamarine hue. It is not so clear that you can see to the bottom. It is the color of dirt, a brown that matches the earth from which the coconut trees sprout. It moves you along swiftly and quietly.

There are all kinds of people on this tour. Half are English-speaking Westerners. But there are also groups of Koreans and a handful of older men from various Asian countries paired with young local girls. I notice one girl in particular who can't be more than nineteen. She's shy and reserved. A matchmaker, a middle-aged Vietnamese man, acts as a liaison between her and her new suitor. He encourages the suitor to put his arm around the girl. Even though my mom and I are Vietnamese, we somehow fit in with this group of outsiders.

Once our purses are filled with packages of coconut candies and our bellies are filled with fried fish and rice, we board a boat back to Saigon. This boat goes much faster than the wooden one. We don't glide through coconut tree groves as if we're sneaking up on some rare bird. We zip across the waters of the Mekong River. The velocity creates a wind strong enough to break the gripping humidity.

"What are you thinking about, Mom?" I ask in Vietnamese, noticing she is more reserved than usual.

"I'm thinking about your grandmother and how I brought you and your sister and brother back to Vietnam right before she passed. I don't know what I would have done if we'd lost her before you guys got to see her."

"I'm really glad I got to see her too," I say. "It was really weird to see her grave after only seeing it in pictures. I remember seeing pictures of you, Mom. Of you going to visit the graves on your last visit, and you were crying. Your face was red. Everybody else seemed fine, but you looked so upset. I've never seen you like that. I thought that's how you were going to be yesterday."

"I cried because that was the first time I visited their graves." And just then, I realize that was the first time my mom came home and was no longer a daughter. An umbilical cord had been severed—the bond that had tied her to the land was gone. "I didn't need to cry this time. I just wanted to visit them. It was a happy visit. There was no reason to be sad."

"Do you think you'll be back there again?"

"I don't know."

I am surprised by her change of heart.

"There's no other reason for me to come back. I used to worry about everyone. But everyone is okay. They have their own families. Everyone has a home."

I take my mom's hand but say nothing. I feel the peace in her answer. Between the two of us, so much is said with no words. The buzz of the boat's motor whirs around our ears like mosquitoes. We look at the never-ending horizon that stretches beyond the Mekong River. We are bound by a silence and contentment for wherever the water will take us.

LIZ DOLAN

For Once I Am Able to Save Her

I thought my mother blessed to be born
and raised in a country without dentists
until the year they yanked out all her teeth.
Pearl headstones fell each week.
Now her false teeth swim in a blue Aegean
atop the porcelain sink. I remember
her mouth stuffed with bloodied cotton,
and wonder how she survived the rumbling
subway home. For her torture, I blamed dwarfish
Mrs. Hegel, the clinic's Mengele,
who cowed both dentists and patients,
shooting orders at her gap-toothed son,
her raven-haired go-fer,
his shriveled arm dangling like a light-pull.
Twice a year I huddled inside those
whitewashed walls, eating ether, falling backwards,
blinded by rays of a florescent sun.
Now in my dream the light shines in Kilcoo
where Mama falls backwards into the waters
of the mountain rill streaming by her cottage.
I dive, my arms cradled, breaking her fall
the skin of her back opaline as a baby moon.

ELLEN BASS

The Orange-and-White High-Heeled Shoes

Today I'm thinking about those shoes—white
with a tangerine stripe across the toe and forceful orange heels—

that fit both my mother and me. We used to shop like that—
trying them on side by side. That was when there still

was a man who would cradle your heel in his palm
and guide your foot. Sometimes he would think he'd made a sale,

only to have one of us turn to the other—
and he would have to kneel again, hoping to ease another naked sole

into the bed of suede or leather. I thought those shoes
were just the peak of chic. And—my God—

you bought me a pair of orange cotton gloves to complete the ensemble.
Why is there such keen pleasure in remembering?

You are dead ten years. And these showy slippers—
we wore them more than half a century ago. The first boy

had not yet misted my breasts with his breath
and you were strong as a muscled goddess, gliding nylons

over your calves, lifting your amplitude into a breastplate.
Who will remember these pumpkin-colored pumps

when I die, too? Who will remember how we slid into them
like girls diving into a cedar-tinged lake, like bees

entering the trumpet of a flower, like birds disappearing
into the green, green leaves of summer?

BARBARA UNGAR

Call Me Medusa

Some years ago, when I had braces
and headgear, I'd pull my hair
through the openings in the cap
contraption so as not to flatten
the curls. Hence my nickname.
I just gave them a sullen stare.

You'll be glad when you're older, they said.
Beauty always a thorn. My two sisters
share my snaky locks and stony looks.

The girls in our family all come in threes:
our cousins the Grays, the Graces, the Norns.
Always an oldest, a youngest, a beauty.

I was none. I was a brain, eyes, and hair.
If not a beauty, are you then a monster?
Some say I was beautiful, raped, punished
for it, then beheaded in a rearview mirror.
Even cut off, my head could still turn men
to stone. Even decapitated, my corpse

could still give birth to a winged horse.
The blood from my severed neck
could turn seaweed to coral and sprinkle
the desert with vipers, amphisbaena,
snakes that swallow their own tails eternally.
Even Eden depends on me.

PAULETTA HANSEL

Pentimento

There are five sets of doors between my mother and me. The first two doors are sliding doors, and automatic, though they are not always triggered to open if it is the weight of a wheelchair, rather than a standing person, moving through first. The third door pulls outward. It is human-powered and unlocked. The fourth I unlock with a key card and enter an atrium. I walk past the elevator doors to my left that lead to the Assisted Living section of Memory Care where my mother began her stay before flunking out a couple of weeks later. Never mind, we didn't like it up there anyway. The staff was unfriendly and the private duty aides sat clicking their freshly polished nails on their cell phones as the glum elders gathered around the nurse's station not talking to each other or even to themselves.

The last door pushes inward after a swipe of my card, and it is here I stop and smile, no matter how I am feeling. I try never to enter with the sadness I carry with me on my face, or to show dismay at whatever I see inside those doors. It is getting easier to smile now that there's less likelihood of finding my mother parked in a wheelchair. Now, often, she is up and staggering about with an aide, or sitting on one of the many couches or at a table, talking near, if not with, others. And sometimes she is smiling even before she sees me.

Going out those doors is more difficult. If I am leaving with my mother in her wheelchair ("I am your motor," I tell her), it is the complicated dance of butt first and a quick turn as not to use my mother's feet as the doorstop (sometimes the turn becomes a swerve and I tell her that her driver is drunk). Then those feet go first through the next door, this time my shoulder holding it open. From there, it depends on where we are heading. Usually we turn right, to the courtyard door, which opens with a push of a button, as long as there's no elder in her own wheelchair blocking the way.

If I am leaving alone, I kiss my mother goodbye and hope it is not her brave face I am seeing, lips pursed so as not to have them tremble before she cries. If I am lucky, it is her don't-bother-me-with-kisses-I'm-fine face.

My husband says it's like sending your children to kindergarten, hoping they'll be happy, learn a lot, not get in fights. But kids in kindergarten get to come home.

❧

I am studying my mother for signs of the woman she was underneath the layers of dementia. They are there. Today at lunch she snapped at me for pushing food on her. "Pauletta!" she said sharply, and my hand with the fork went back down to the table. Quickly! No questions asked. A rare opportunity to be a scolded daughter.

❧

"She was busy, busy, busy today!" the nursing home aide tells me. My mother wants so much to be the busy woman she was. She is always touching things, moving things. Because my mother is considered a fall risk, the staff tried to keep Mom in her wheelchair for most of her first couple of months here. I believe it was her persistence, rather than my advocacy, that has loosened their resolve. She has not given up. It would be easier for everyone around her if she did. But she hasn't, and though I am exhausted after my visits from chasing her as she lurches around the nursing home, I am grateful that her feistiness remains.

❧

I am not sure what I thought it was that would be last to go. Love, I suppose. That she would know us, and want to be with us, her family—and that is all still true. She usually knows me, though the context of where we are and what we are doing here is often lost. Maybe there are some things that her mind chooses not to know.

❧

They have given my mother a baby doll to calm her down. Even two months ago, when she first arrived, I wouldn't have believed that my mother would have had anything to do with such an obvious ploy. Sure, she sees children we don't see, but she wouldn't see a living, breathing child when we see a plastic toy, would she? Apparently, she would. It's the prettiest baby she's ever seen, she'll say, as she coos happily and cuddles him—then holds him by one leg and drops him to the floor. If it works to curb Mom's ratcheting anxiety, it's fine with me. Better baby dolls than tranquilizers. Though some days she has both.

One day I walked into my mother's room and saw a mother I have never seen before. The crying mother was bad enough. This was the scrapping mother, hitting her hands at the aide and telling her she'd never amount to anything, just like her mother. The aide looked at me and said, "Well, she's right about my mother." The further Mom sinks into dementia, the more startling are her moments of psychic clarity.

I said, "Mom, don't talk that way to her. She's my buddy. She'd never do anything to hurt you."

"She grabbed me by the throat and tried to strangle me!"

"Mom, she did not."

I sat beside her on her bed and put my arm around her for a while. "Let's get out of here," I said, getting up to gather the things we needed. "Here's your hat." I put it on her head. "What's your hurry?" A joke funny only to my husband and me.

We did our daily ritual of leaving the locked unit to sit in the shade in the facility's courtyard, her in a wheelchair and me in a wrought iron garden chair. We talked about the day lilies that have sprung up through the creeping phlox that was blooming in the early days of our visits, about the ever-present wall lizards and the robin hopping from one place to the next. "Well, who knew robins really do go bob-bob-bobbing along," I said, and she laughed when I sang the song.

"All right now?" I asked.

"Yes," she said. "But don't tell me something didn't happen when I say so."

"Okay," I said. "It's a deal. Let's shake on it." And we did.

❧

My mother and I talk more than we used to. We have both always had the knack for silence. When I was young and at home she was too busy for much conversation, and my nose was usually in a book. I loved the rare occasions when she would sit with her sisters around a table and tell stories about me as if I was not there to hear.

Much later, after my father died and we lived again in the same town, though not the same house, our weekly dinners centered around her favorite shows: *Jeopardy!* and *Antiques Roadshow*. We would go antiquing and wander the aisles as often apart as together. We chatted in the car and in her living room, or mine, but we could sit quietly for hours. And as mother's dementia progressed, she talked less and less in company—she became the listener at the table as her family told stories about her.

And then there was the phase when I felt I must argue with everything she said, as if by will alone I could force away her delusions:

"No, Mom, there are no children in this room."

"Nobody stole your silver."

"You have plenty of money in the bank."

Now that I'm learning to agree with everything, instead, there is an ease to our conversation:

"Is that right?"

"Well, that must have been something!"

"No, I haven't seen Daddy today."

Mostly, now, my responses are based on tone, rather than content. She speaks very low, and fast, and even when I do hear her, I don't always know what she says. When she speaks clearly, it can feel as if I'm eavesdropping on her half of a conversation and am struggling to keep up.

"What did you put in his pail for dinner?" she asked me the other day.

"Half-runner beans and new potatoes," I said. "But I was too lazy to make the cornbread."

It didn't matter to me who he was, and she defended my cornbread failure as busyness, not laziness.

Sometimes I am mentioned in the stories she tells me, having apparently gotten into all sorts of trouble with money or men. Yesterday, it was my sister on the hot seat. I told Mom, "Renée is coming to see you Thursday."

"Oh, no, she's going to drive me crazy."

One morning she said, apropos of nothing I knew, "She just went to sleep and didn't wake up."

"Who?" I asked.

"Your old teacher."

There is no way she could have known that Mrs. DeHoag had died a week or two before.

"I don't know how you know these things," I told her.

"I don't either," Mom said. "Sometimes it just starts as something small, like I see John on a skateboard."

"That sounds like a good memory to me," I say, and just leave it there. "Should we go have some lunch?"

❧

Today, pulling her pants back up after a trip to the toilet, I notice the folds and folds of skin from her far too rapid weight loss. They will never again be filled, and yet will never rest comfortably against her bones without the flesh that once filled them.

❧

And too, I am learning a new sort of language, that of touch. I never thought to realize how touch-deprived my mother must have been in the eight years since my father's death. She began receiving weekly massages a few years ago, but it was not until the move to the nursing home intensified her already increasing anxiety that touch became part of her daily life. She is never so calm as when someone's hands are on her. We all brush her hair, stroke her back, hold her hand. Sometimes now I climb onto her narrow bed behind her, and she'll pull my hand up to her chest and hold it as she must have held my father's hand, as I hold my husband's as we spoon into sleep. It doesn't last long. She's not much of a napper. But, for a moment or two, she is at peace, and so am I. "Pauletta is spoiling me," she told my aunt. The other residents of this Memory Unit ask me again and again if I am Larnie's mother.

I visit my mother for several hours four or five times a week, and our cousin Gail, her former live-in companion, comes on the days that my siblings or I do not. On Sundays, my husband, Owen, comes with me. He has taken to photographing our visits. I post them on Facebook, and on Monday I read Mom all the comments from her friends and former charges at the daycare center she ran for more than twenty years more than twenty years ago.

"Tell Larnie I love her."

"She looks so pretty."

"I wish we could come see you."

"Make sure she doesn't forget I'm her favorite."

And Mom smiles and laughs. "Thank you," she says to each one. "Thank you."

MELISSA HELTON

The Women's Gown

Creased linen hangs on me,
generations old, under which
Grandmother and Mother swelled
and split and shrank with lineage,
fabric faded as fieldstones holding
me in the body.
Flames crown my head,
lick at the air, a dance
of oxygen, plasma
uncontrollable.
I dream of evaporating,
particles spreading, disconnecting
and saying goodbye
to each other, yielding
to air currents and whatever
may come next.
But the linen keeps my molecules
bonded, a shell in which
I incubate and spin, a holy
robe that keeps the sin
of pride from me.

JAMIE WENDT

Pins, Ropes, and Wooden Stakes

You can tell a lot about a mother by her clothesline.
Dirtied rope splitting like Havdalah candles,
designer shirt appearing each month like a full moon,
the dye shining a midnight river.

You can tell a lot about a mother by counting
the days she lets dry clothing dance,
how many stains cover bibs after scrubbing,
the number of patches on pants and socks,
the way she stands between the rope lines
feeling the slap of wet cotton on her tired body.

Once the children have grown, she will remember
unclipping her son's starched collared shirts
crunching like the opening of his prayer book
for the first time all year.
Her old wedding dress rippling under pins
like an ordinary nightgown, restless
from having also brushed her daughter's virgin ankles,
a rebel in the wind, an heirloom in chains.
Her black lace bras snap against the rope
with more fury than thieving crows.

LIZ DOLAN

Sepia Photo

One-Room Schoolhouse, 1917

In the highest row stands Master Breen
his hands folded like Cuchulain across his chest.
His mustache tips brush up against his checked cravat.
My mother, auburn-haired and girlish, stands to his left
in brogues and a coarse wool dress she sewed herself.
At ten each morn she serves her master tea.
I beg her, stay in Tullaree forever.
You'll miss the warmth of the cows' udders
and the bleating sheep in the upper pasture.
Don't cross the sea, Mama.
You'll scrub until your knuckles bleed
pink tears on our white blouses;
you'll dust and sweep with Yeats
turned to stone in your chest.
Your son's head will be crushed,
three infants will die. Your husband, another master
you will serve, will wax as thorny as pyracantha.
Cushla, at Eastertide, sixteen patriots were shot
in Dublin. I'm a papist scullion in Ulster
which soon will be chopped off like a gangrened arm.
My brother will inherit the land.
You've never been starved by the raw wind
from the banks of the Bann. You choose your masters
in this life. Our whispered faith, sustained as we knelt
on nettles, will gird me like the radiant skin of a snake.

MICHELLE ELVY

Moments in Sand

Fragments between Sea and Sky

1. Departure

Whipping wind, cracking canvas. Anchor up; lay a course for west-southwest. An air horn blasts farewell to us across the bright Mexican sky. We set sail, wave one long goodbye to North America. Our home is a compact thing, all that we own jammed into a space the size of a walk-in closet. Books and Grandma's china neatly packed in cupboards; memories stowed in safe places. Ghosts stalking my heart.

I steer us out of the anchorage. Bernie's on the bow; our two daughters race along the rail to catch one last glimpse of friends shouting *adios*: Shelly and Jim and a dog named Grover.

Over my shoulder, a terra-cotta sun heats the February sky.

Ahead, there's nothing but wide open blue, a world of possibility.

❧

For several weeks, our six-year-old has been telling everyone that we are sailing to the equator. Never mind that we are going farther and that the equator is an imaginary line we traverse along the way. For her, the equator holds exotic connotation. For me, too, really—crossing from one hemisphere into the other is a significant milestone in a sailor's life. But there's more to it than that. We pull out our charts; I hold my two daughters' small hands and trace our way past the equator to French Polynesia, the Cook Islands, Tonga, New Zealand. But beyond that, my hand wavers; I don't know where to go. This departure is different from the others, neither a short jaunt to Hawaii and back nor a circular route through the inland waterways of Alaska that leads eventually back to where we started, to the comfort of Vancouver's False Creek. It's a leave-taking without an end in sight. Stepping off the edge of the map. A world of unknowns.

For all we know, the earth might be flat after all.

This time we have left for good. It is 2008. We are filled with excitement about this ocean crossing, the long offshore passage, the months of exploring new places we've only ever dreamed of. Even our children understand that we are leaving this continent and everything familiar for years to come, possibly forever. And as often as I delineate all the complicated reasons we're out here, I know deep down that there are things that put me on this path long ago. Moments that changed everything. Some don't have dates; some do. Some are dark, murky memories. Some are crisp, clear things I wish I could erase.

March 16, 1994. *There's been a plane crash.* Five words that changed my life.

At forty-one, I am setting out around the world with as few possessions as I have ever owned. I have no career, no house, no pension plan. I've lost any sense of place I used to know. I've got everything I need packed into a small boat. I've got wind in my sails, and the largest ocean on this planet stretching before me.

I've got that date, March 16, 1994. I've got those ghosts.

I've got today. And today it's good to be going.

Moments in Sand 1

Delaware, 1979
My brother leaps
off the end of the jetty
sand flings from his feet
He's airborne a second or two
—feels like forever and I think he'll keep going, fly away
Origami-boy, sudden swan,
limbs tucked then released, gangly and long
He unfolds, stretches, becomes elegant,
blond mane whipping, wings out wide,
jet-fast now, there's no stopping him
—and he's gone

2. Silence

When we were kids, we celebrated birthdays with big cakes and presents. My grandfather cultivated his own hybrid roses along the fence in his small Virginia backyard and decorated the table with them. One year my grandmother made a huge sponge cake with a rose in the center. The rose was called the Pink Michelle. It was beautiful.

I can't recall which birthday that was. Was I seven? Eight? I was young enough to see the pink rose as the most perfect thing on my cake, and old enough to know it was special that this small perfect thing was named after me. But was it 1973 or 1974? I could not tell you that.

And was I seven or eight when hands were laid on me, tugging me from light to darkness, pulling our secure split-level house into quicksand? The house filled with love, and then sank under the weight of it all. I could not tell you the exact date that terror crept into my bed and under my covers. But those hands are as true as the pretty pink flower in the middle of that cake.

⁂

The morning music of small voices and sails, of wind and water, is broken by a sudden assertion of silence. We are hundreds of miles offshore. We are on our own. And my second daughter is beset by an alarming quiet, glassy-eyed, panic registering on her raised eyebrows.

She is not getting air. She is not breathing. She is just standing there, staring. Silent.

She was born silent. No cry, no wail. Torn placenta and an emergency operation. They told me later that they thought they could not save her.

I love my second daughter's boisterous voice. I would not quiet it for anything.

⁂

It's when I grab her and ask if she is okay that the panic—hers and mine—becomes real. She points to her mouth while her eyes search my face. *Fix this, Mom.*

Instinct drives me. I grab her and thump her on the back, bend her over to dislodge whatever is stuck.

The hard candy went down her esophagus whole, squeezing against her windpipe. It comes up in a mucous glob, along with everything she ate last night.

Sobs and more sobs—short intakes of breath as she clutches me. As I clutch her.

She's crying fully now. I am ecstatic with relief.

⁂

Fix this, Mom.

Every mother's desire, and failing. I am lucky. My daughter is safe.

I know my mother will never let go of the one thing she could not fix.

Mother and daughter stand in the kitchen, late night. It's December 1987—home for the holidays. They talk about the father's abrupt departure. The violence, the betrayals, the questions no one can answer. The girl stands in quicksand. History and memory make a slow sucking sound.

The mother tells stories the daughter has never heard. Stories of a boy whose youth was shattered when an uncle touched him behind closed doors. Stories of parents who didn't know. Of a man, forty years later, collapsing in front of his wife, the shame already tearing him apart, the marriage already crumbling, silently, under the weight of it. Stories of counseling, of help that doesn't take. Stories of anger and violence. Stories that at least explain some things.

The daughter is sinking fast.

The mother sighs and looks at the daughter and her voice is crystal, sure—because she's still standing at the edge of the quicksand, does not yet feel its pull. "At least we can be glad this never happened to any of you."

The daughter's reality changes forever. She knows this to be untrue. She knows that she's sinking into murk so fast she may never get out.

"But it did happen. It happened to me."

Saying it is like reliving it. The daughter feels it; the mother sees it. A father turned monster. Large hands moving on a small body. Hands reaching up, in, over, under. Movements that could not be stopped, protests silenced with a cupped hand. Gnarled memories that can't be unwound.

The mother's eyes are glassy. The tears: *How could I have let this happen?* The panic: *And for how long?* And even if the girl will one day tell her mother that it was the mother that kept the daughter from sinking entirely and disappearing into the quicksand—who else could it be?—there is only panic engulfing the mother's heart: *I cannot fix this.*

Moments in Sand 2

Berlin, 1989
A sand painting
fluid, fragile
bird into bridge into moon
east meets west in rivulets of movement
Bird flies—

Berlin morphs
Us and Them pulling down walls
climbing to greet and kiss
on a bridge arcing time
This moment, this moment
matters most
while moon plays with tide—regular as, well, the moon
Sand painting shatters, reality is only
light and shadow
and I live in the in-between

3. Knowing Where You Are

My oldest brother Marc learned to navigate before GPS. The last of the twenty-four satellites making up our current constellation was launched the same year my brothers died, in 1994, and the system became fully operational one year later, in April 1995. Like other navigators before the time that GPS became a household word, Marc used Loran, the radio navigational system that relies on multiple installations of low-frequency terrestrial radio transmitters to determine a position. He would be astounded by the electronic toys he could have today, how precisely we locate ourselves as we sail across oceans. He would like that we have a sextant on board, but he'd also like that we carry two handheld GPS units. He'd like that we always know exactly where we are.

The plane carrying my brothers and two other men crashed in 1994, just minutes after takeoff from a small airstrip near a place called Dulce, in the northern mountains of New Mexico. I know a lot of things about this place. It was originally called Agua Dulce—Sweet Water. The town is a part of Rio Arriba County. With only twenty-five hundred people, Dulce is mostly Native American and is the tribal headquarters of the Jicarilla Apache Reservation. The Jicarilla people speak a southern Athabaskan language. The term *jicarilla* comes from Mexican Spanish, meaning "little basket." Dulce's elevation is 6,778 feet above sea level. The reservation land encompasses 1,364.046 square miles. The community owns and operates an FM radio station, KCIE. The Jicarilla band was the only band that did not cooperate with the U.S. government in its search for Geronimo.

On the NTSB online query page, three crashes come up for the Dulce, New Mexico, airport: a Cessna 172P crashed on April 7, 1999; a Bell OH-58C crashed on March 19, 1998; and a Cessna 172RG crashed on March 16, 1994. The last one is the only listing whose "Event Severity" column is labeled with red lettering: "Fatal." Years later, I still will my eyes to connect the black "Nonfatal" with the date March 16, 1994.

But the truth of it is in the report.

❧

"Fatal"—a certainty I carry with me. I know how my brothers died. I see it all. No matter how many times I try to put aside these images, I end up there anyway, in that sweet water place: I am at the plane crash site, on the mountain, in the police car, at the reservation clinic. I am with Marc when he watches Kirk die. I see Kirk's eyes searching Marc's as the medics intubate him and try to save his collapsing lungs: fear, panic, pain, then nothing. I am with Marc when he dies four days later, no amount of emergency medical care able to save his crashing organs.

These things are not in the NTSB report. But these are things I know better than the facts of the report, the facts of the place.

Dulce lies at 36°56′22″ N, 106°59′23″ W. I bet Marc knew exactly where he was when that plane went down.

"What are you running away from?"

When that question was put to me many years ago, I could not answer. I only knew that sometimes you have to leave. That sometimes knowing exactly where you are is not enough.

Moments in Sand 3

Spa Creek, 1999
More mud than sand
but the silt of this brackish bay
holds her childhood—crabs in
buckets, a foot split on glass,
bandaged in a skiff by a friend
with shaky hands, murky memories
of young love
The Chesapeake, her home once,
now stranger than sand-painting in Berlin
Sister brother mother gather
at the creek's edge,
a quiet Christmas with candles, a moment to remember
Briskly now: back up the street to the warmth
of mother's home, salted ham biscuits and
crescents baked golden, rolled with pecans
Girl looks back to creek, her home her heart
while the tide pulls her away

4. The Beach and the Wind

When we arrive in New Zealand, I quickly acquaint myself with the literature and poetry shelves in the Whangarei Library. For my birthday, my husband gives me *The New Zealand Book of the Beach,* which introduces me to short story writers of Aotearoa and further connects me with the coastline—my entrée to any new place. Maurice Shadbolt has said famously that "New Zealand begins with the sea and ends with the sea," which speaks to my immediate affection for this land. And Graeme Lay notes in his introduction to the book how the beach plays a central role in New Zealand's past, present, and future. The beach—matter ground to shifting bits of time—is where history and memory play. The beach is, more than anywhere else, where sea and land and sky meet in optimistic collusion, shoulders shored in symbolic protection, eyes looking out to the horizon.

The sand on New Zealand's shores slides comfortably between my toes, soft and warm: a place I could come to call *home.* But I don't stay long, not even here.

Not *running away.* Curiosity begets curiosity. One story leads to another. Conversation turns to action. *Wanna? Yes, why not?*

And there I go again, plotting my waypoints one at a time, even if they happen to lead away. The ghosts come with me. And the fragments of a broken past. And everything else I need too.

And the wind—the miraculous wind—carries me forward.

Moments in Sand 4

Urupukapuka, 2009
From one end of the beach I see my children
all the way at the other, silhouettes rushing
at water then retreating up sand
as waves chase and almost catch
their feather-light feet
They stop, lean in, consult, hover
then purposefully work, carrying things
back and forth
bringing items to evaluate, discarding many
keeping only the right ones
I am too far to see the treasures
they choose and assemble with care
but I hear their voices tinkle my way
on the grey air, soft chimes in my ear
Their tiny forms squat over a mound
of feathers seaweed and shells,

larger scallop shapes wedged round the edge,
a barricade
against everything
a stick-and-seagrass cross at the head
they know how to build a proper penguin grave
Up close now, I hear them whisper wishes for
this *wee blue one: forever* and *safe* and *hush*
I wait for them to finish, for some things you
cannot rush

LIZ DOLAN

A Secret of Long Life

In exchange for books of thirsty grids stamped S&H,
a glossy toaster popped up in Momma's kitchen,
a marvel unlike the one whose silver wings flapped
flat singeing fingers and scorching toast.
To Aunt Susannah's brood in Kilcoo,
Momma sent our outgrown clothes.
In exchange for bags and bags of rags, she packed
a carpet weaver, conjured a field of acanthus leaves.
Toasty feet on bloodless Bronx mornings. Anemic
tea leaves nourished pothos and gardenia.
She spun scraped bits of beef into gravy so bronze
it made us weep. She did not take more than she gave
and thus, given long life
and a fur-collared Persian lamb coat
my sister and I bought her with our first paychecks.
Although we thought we had outgrown such thrift,
today my sister stocks up on bargains.
Neither she nor her hair will last long enough
for all those bottles of sale-shampoo.
And I have begun to record purchase dates
on creams and lipsticks to tally how long they last.

JENNIFER L. FREED

You Believed

Never hug and kiss them, never let them sit in your lap. If you must, kiss them once on the forehead when they say good night.

—John B. Watson and Rosalie Rayner Watson, *Psychological Care of the Infant and Child* (1928)

When your new baby cried in the night,
the force of his wail rising, rising, not
subsiding, as Doctor said it would,

when you lay rigid in your bed, fisted hands
against your side, eyes wide
against the dark, waiting
for the wails to end,

and in the day, when your son woke
and screamed again—
silent only when you gathered him up
to feed him,

of course—of
    course!—
you had your doubts.

And yet
    you held fast
to Doctor's advice.
What did you
know, young mother
that you were, compared to the man

who had tended so many?

You believed
in his science, latched on to his
calm, measured words,

tethered your wild need
to nuzzle and lick,
to lift your sweet child
to your lips
and carry him through
your days.

You sat in your chair, left your boy
in his crib, and he cried and he cried and you
cried beside him, rocking and holding
your arms.

O the will,
the will
behind your wide blue eyes—the will
to raise my father
right.

RENÉE OLANDER

The Apparatus of the Dark

Notes to myself on longevity
after a lightning storm on the beach

1.
You can touch, Mama said.
She placed my palm on her stretched skin,
She pulled my head close so I heard
A child

            I squelched my urge to recoil from ripe
Motion there in my mother. I searched for the door
She said doctors would open.

Afterward, after prayers with her,
I lay in the night
Straining
For a sense of origin, a point
Like a faraway star I came from.

2.
Imagine atoms
And clusters of cells
Driven to grow like banks of clouds.

3.
My mother conceived seven lives:
Five survived, one miscarried, one died
A few hours after birth—
Mama buried a life alone
And Dad sailed home from Korea.

Next I slid
Premature,
Twice declared dead,
Packed in ice,
Till I shrieked my lungs alive.

4.
Mama's body burned.
Her ashes went to sea.

Our last touch, my lips
Brushed her forehead,

Cool as shaded clay.

5.
This evening I went out for broken silver
Beyond sailing scuds at dusk
And high tide. Bitter air came from somewhere
Something
Tossed up inadvertent.

Soon I'll burrow in bed and seek
Childhood dreams where palm fronds
Were God's fingers touching down.
I'll study markings: *sacred scared*
How moon rims dip past sight.

MICHELE TRACY BERGER*

The Poison Our Mothers and Grandmothers Drank

2002—Dream: I am surrounded by my grandmother, my mother, and other indistinct female figures. They are dressed in ceremonial blue and white tunics and we are pressed together on the concrete walkway outside the second floor of my Oakland apartment building.

I pay attention to my dreams. They are a night rhythm that feeds my waking life. I record them, honor them with titles, and pore through pages of old dream journals as if meeting cherished friends. While visiting an art gallery in Pittsboro, North Carolina, Sharon Blessum's *Medicine Women* photograph brings back a significant dream to me that has taken years to reflect on and absorb. It is so clear in my memory:

There is a hush and I am given a chalice. My grandmother, whose husky voice is just as commanding in the dream as it was in life, tells me to drink from it. I do not want to drink it. I know it is poison. I am upset in the dream and try to push the chalice away.

I search for the precise description of the dream, knowing it is buried somewhere in my twelve journals, which chronicle my move from the west and much of my eight and a half years in North Carolina. After upending my already disorganized office, I find the journal with my first recollection of the dream. And, luckily, just a few pages after the entry, I see my notes from the therapy session where I first discussed the dream with Ruth, a skilled Jungian psychotherapist. When I read my entry, however, I am crestfallen, because there is a gap between what I initially wrote about the dream and how the dream exists in my memory. I struggle to make sense of the differences.

* ***Author's note.*** During fall 2010, local writers were invited to visit the Joyful Jewel, a gallery in Pittsboro, North Carolina, and see which piece of art inspired them to write. My piece was inspired by Sharon Blessum's photograph *Medicine Women.* In the photograph are four small, iridescent torsos of mannequins with names like Copper Shaman, Shaman of the Heart Chakra, Shaman of the Seventh Chakra, and Water Shaman. Some of the torsos have feathers sprouting from the backs of their necks, and others showcase big, chunky necklaces. In December, the Joyful Jewel hosted "Visions and Voices," where writers were asked to read what they'd written after their visits, and the corresponding artists were asked to display their objects and say a few words about the art-making process.

Journal entry scribbling about the dream:

> Dreams—active. Grandmother + mom-me drinking witch hazel—medicinal? What does that do? Remember this fragment the best.

The detail of witch hazel surprises me. The sharp smell of witch hazel has faded from my memory of the dream. Why didn't I remember that witch hazel was what they offered? I know witch hazel well. In my mind's eye, I see the tall bottle's red and black label. My mother used it for everything, just like other poor urban women did in my neighborhood. She sprinkled it on cotton balls and rubbed us down with it for fever, or to take the sting out of a bruise, or as an astringent to dry up a pimple. I wonder about the symbolism of witch hazel, as I know it is a significant medicinal plant. Nothing comes to me.

Not satisfied with the brevity of the journal entry, I consider if I might have combined this dream with another. No, I assure myself . . . that is not right. This is the written aspect of the dream, a fraternal rather than identical twin to the one that lives in my memory.

My mother, small, nut brown and steadfast says I must do it. I must drink it even though I feel I will die. A sense of obedience and loyalty washes over me. I defer to them. My inherent trust in them sustains me as I drink the poison.

I read on to the entry from the therapy session:

> Ruth said I got a trigger [about] the "witch hazel dream," [and] that I was interpreting things so literally—but it's about the *dark feminine,* the transmutation of the woundedness of these women that can pull you down into something else-by my own "psychic witch"-old knowledge-ritual. And it *is* tough—and it is strong medicine.
>
> I drink the poison and I am dying. I shake and tremble. . . . It is a terrible agony.

I was never fully satisfied with Ruth's interpretation, though I could not come up with a better one at the time. Years pass and my time becomes laser-focused on planting roots after a cross-country move, navigating my partner's lonely road of depression, and establishing myself as a published scholar.

I return to California in 2006 and meet Barbara, a friend from my first job as a professor at the University of Nevada, Las Vegas (UNLV). We visit Kabuki Springs Spa, a Japanese-style spa in Japantown, San Francisco. For all my outward bravado, I am a little nervous and shy about going to a communal spa where nakedness is the norm. We have chosen a day when it is all women, and I am grateful. We beeline it to the sauna and then lay around with cucumber slices on our faces.

I talk about my new life at the University of North Carolina at Chapel Hill (UNC). I talk about how it feels to work with so many first-generation African American college students and the nonstop mentoring that I am doing. I share with her how Black students trust me with their deepest secrets, regrets, and triumphs, how hungry they are to see themselves reflected back to them, and how I was probably one of the few Black female professors they would ever have in their college experience.

I confide that I swallow daily doses of ambivalence about academe, but that I also feel needed at UNC. How could I help others if I wasn't in a position of security? Indeed, when I made a casual remark to a Black female student about maybe not staying for tenure, she held my gaze and said, "Dr. Berger, you have to get tenure. We need you." At that moment, I felt the groping of a collective unseen "we" that reached out past its immediate needs and wanted to engulf me.

I share all this with Barbara—and also my fruitful and very satisfying budding work coaching and lecturing on women and creativity. There is something about being naked, wrapped in a towel, sweating, and surrounded by other women that encourages a recall of the "drinking poison" dream. I talk with Barbara about the dream and am suddenly reminded that my grandmother used to read five to six newspapers a day and loved the written word. She had entertained high aspirations of becoming a journalist (already in full bloom in adolescence, as evidenced by her securing an interview with Harlem Renaissance notable Countee Cullen for the high school newspaper). However, she found it impossible to give her gifts to the world because of her skin color and sex. I think of my mother, a frustrated, half-trained modern dancer, who experienced a lifetime of "no" and the slow grind of poverty, abuse, and alcoholism.

As a biracial woman and historian, Barbara reflects on her choices and challenges at UNLV. In our conversation, I feel as if I am on to something about the dream—that there is a lot of poison out there that women of color wind up swallowing. In another journal, I spy some notes taken right after my visit with Barbara. They point to a way of understanding the dream that I had overlooked:

> The act of offering and drinking the poison that my grandmother and mother initiated me into was an alchemical process. It was not meant literally to kill me, but to help me to become conscious of the nature of challenges that others and I face. Such recognition unleashes the power of authentic awakening.

As I see how my life has unfolded in North Carolina, I now believe that the dream gives me insight into how to help other women—especially women of color—recognize the "poisons" they face in their lives. Racism. Sexism. Dispossession of spirit. Erasure. Poisons that are so eagerly offered to them in society. I can support other women to transmute society's poisons into a greater transformation of the self.

The dream also points to healing the unfulfilled karmic desires of female ancestors who came before us—who swallowed the poison and died. They swallowed the poison because they found themselves alone often, afraid constantly, and shamed routinely. They swallowed the poison because anger basted their vital organs, rotting them from the inside out. They swallowed the poison because they had lost touch with their own night rhythms, wisewomen guides, and nocturnal magic. I draw on this knowledge as guide, midwife, soul treasure hunter, mentor, and witness for my students and clients.

The poison does not kill me. I stand shakily and meet the women's eyes. My vessel is stronger than any poison. My luminous body lives.

MARIANNE WORTHINGTON

Porcelain

I wash Grandmother's Japanese china,
a pattern with such an old-fashioned name:
Arlene. A gentle sudsing lifts the dirt
of neglect creased into saucer rims and
the delicate feet of her bowls, but not
this ponderous sadness that blindsides me
sometimes while shopping for cantaloupe or
typing a letter or smoothing the bed

sheets cool on the mattress. All these same things
she did with such ease, quick and unthinking
no time for distraction, I remember
too late. Her teacup falls like a feather,
a golden-edged bird who lost her way home,
sparkles in sunlight then shatters like bone.

1888–1988

I wash my hands with the soft cake
of Ivory soap in my sister's bathroom
and for the rest of the morning, smell
the way our grandmother smelled.

The girl I was dances in her red Formica

kitchen, the white soap fragrant as it drips
into the rust of the metal drainboard.
Even on Christmas Eve when her table
is heaped with peanut butter candy and winter
oranges, coffee and cashews, the clean
scent of soap sings loudest of all.

My daughter's baby clothes smelled
like this too. Her little cuffed gowns
and undershirts with snaps perfumed
the house as they clicked against the dryer
drawing circles around our lives.

One hundred years pass between their births.
Riding the cusp of a crescent moon they roll
over one morning to a new century
and bloodstained bedclothes. Plasma
and platelets flow forward like time,
their girlhoods left in an old world, their stains
rubbed clean with a bar of soap.

FRANCES NICHOLSON

On Motherhood

My daughter has never seen a firefly,
never spent the leeward end
of a slow summer evening running
through a field, jar in hand, to catch
a moment of wonder to carry home,
examine up close. The thing caught,
no flame present in the glass, she
has never studied the treasure's lack
of incandescence, then let it go again
to pinprick the night with its glow.
Still, each time I stand aside, let her
walk out the door—combustible—
I unscrew the lid on the jar.

My Grandmother's Favorite Book

On Discovering a Copy of the *Selected Works of Edna St. Vincent Millay*

Deep in an old box, a slim blue volume.
Yours, of her poems. Mine now, to take home.
I can imagine you two, of an age—the author
flying down the streets of the Village
laughing boy in pursuit. You breaking
rules more quietly, her sonnets the anthem
of your revolutions, in that time you always
called *the long ago.* We share that song as spark,
element of the passion, which filled your house,
your daughter's, mine, with shelves of words—
our beloveds. Now, as I pack that daughter's
things for sale, I find this book. On the flyleaf,
only your name, your script. Inside, the poet
speaks her words. I hear them in your voice.

On Violence & Survival

EILEEN McDERMOTT

The Angry Girl at the Funeral

In front, a casket; behind, the past. We sat side by side—sisters—stiffening.

We had come to support our mother. By now, the anger was little more than a confused memory. Still, the words being spoken stirred something deep. There was a comparison to Jesus, to Joseph, a line about how much he cared for his family. How funny he was.

He was. But reaching back through the decades, I felt I was trying to recall the story of someone else's life—a story I'd been told while drunk. Searching for empathy, all I found was a blue hot anger simmering deep, threatening my adopted pragmatism: "He is so old now. It isn't worth it. He is still my mother's father."

We do this.

I had exploded into adolescence like a suicide vest. The anger boiled so deep then that I could not speak to the people closest to me. Rebellion is natural, but when provoked by the poking of an unacknowledged wound, it expands into warfare.

The anger saved my life: every seemingly unfounded act of vitriol wielded at my parents or sister was a day that I avoided self-destruction.

I was a ghost to my family. They could not see me anymore.

There had been a moment, at sixteen, on a family trip. My little sister, only nine, had left her diary unlocked in a suitcase.

I saw it there and my heart erupted in my ears. My throat squeezed tight. A force unknown compelled me as I flipped from page to page.

The words were not surprising. I had written similar ones dozens of times, only to later shred the pages so thin that not one letter could be discerned.

But the words were not about me now, and I could not unsee them. I sat, choked by inaction, overwhelmed by the inexorability of my next move. I grasped for the anger I carried deep—a crutch to propel my body into battle, as my mind shut down.

"Mom, what the fuck! Read this! Come here and read this!"

I disappeared as my parents called to confront him. There was no avoiding it now—the truth was hanging in the air like a poisonous gas.

My father cried to me in the car. I stared ahead. Said, "It's okay."

I wanted it to go back to the way it was. Silky, anesthetic silence.

Did I speak to my sister about it? I don't remember.

❧

At the funeral, we still sat side by side. The air smelled of flowers and sterile rot. The minister spoke. The comic irony of his words was lost on him, and on many there. "Joseph touched his family each day."

In another life, I would have burst into maniacal laughter, a scene from my own personal rock video. Spit on the corpse. Pushed the minister into the coffin and slammed the lid shut. Grabbed my sister's hand, my mother's, and rushed the door. I would suddenly have been wearing a puffy, pink taffeta skirt and a leather vest. We'd have run until we were somewhere that made sense. A guitar would be produced. We would all scream and bang our heads.

Instead, I sat, soundless. Burning. Watching myself from above shovel the anger into a hole.

The minister asked the grandchildren to pay their last respects.

❧

Heading to the cemetery, my mother joined her brothers—his sons—in the limo. I walked with my wife and sister slowly to the car.

He was given a military funeral: soldiers, a flag-folding ceremony, a tribute to his service. We all placed roses on the casket, one by one.

For the first time, our mother cracked into tears. We hugged her, but only for a second before she composed herself, lifted her head and said:

"Are we ready?"

PENNY PERKINS

A Girl's Mouth

At some point, all girls have to make peace with their mouths. The things shoved into them, the words kept out of them. At some point, all girls have to make peace with their mouths.

Soap.

She remembers once having her mouth washed out with soap. Her father did it. He shoved a cake of soap into her mouth and ordered her to bite down. She can't remember, of course, what she might have said to have warranted such a punishment. What can a young girl say that is so filthy to her father—or even in his presence—that she would be made to masticate a meal of soap cake?

The taste of soap is bitter. Like the experience of growing up as a girl with a mouth.

All girls have mouths. All girls regret mouths.

The mouth of a girl is an entry, a sentry, and an exit. What goes in and what comes out are not always under her control. Like soap. Like protestations at her place in the world. Like outrage at the indignities she and her mouth undergo. But, sadly, this is just the kind of honest expression that gets met with resistance and punishment, like soap.

Other things come and go in a girl's mouth. Repeated forced entries that, over time, force her young teeth to cave inward. She believes the word for that is *concave.* All the young girls with mouths full of concavities. In contrast, convex is the motion of the teeth leaning forward, trying to escape into the world and out of the confines of her mouth. This condition is often caused by repeated vomiting. Projectiles of mushed emotions, fleeing outward, into the world and into the porcelain containers that hold the secrets of girls with mouths.

Here is one of those secrets: what the throat cannot cough up, the mouth cannot utter.

And another: what the mouth cannot in good faith pass, the throat cannot swallow.

Things get stuck in a girl's mouth. Bitter things. Food particles get caught between crooked teeth. Teeth that, through neglect and poverty, parents never bothered to have straightened. There is so much in a girl's mouth that isn't straightened. So much that isn't straight: the whys of existence. The how-tos of pain. The repetition of Daddy's insertions and the repetition of Mommy's averted eyes. There is so much in a girl's mouth that is left unexplained, left to rot, caught between yellowed, crooked teeth.

Decay is a process. Death is decay gone on, unending. Death and decay fight it out in a girl's mouth.

A girl's mouth is always decaying and dying. Brushing up doesn't help. The decay in a girl's mouth is of the soul. Cavities of the soul. And that's a space that pointed, metal instruments can't touch, let alone scrape clean and straighten out.

There is great work to be done in the mouths of girls. Great excavating. Great drilling. Great packing and great healing. Girls must learn to rinse and spit all over again. Spit out the toxins and stop spitting on themselves. Girls must learn that their mouths were given to them, preordained and sacred. Girls did not make their mouths, and certainly did not make the mess within them. Girls did not ask for the objects forced in. Girls did not agree to the mountains of words, of feelings, of truths, of witnessing, to be kept out. Girls did not ask for these things. Girls are merely the temporary keepers of their mouths—mouths given to them by Providence, but molded and shaped by others who fill their lives and their dreams and their thoughts and their words and their private, inner cavities.

It is time for girls to make peace with their mouths—and to take ownership of them.

It is time for a girl's mouth to be her own.

MARY HEATHER NOBLE

Things I (Shouldn't) Have to Tell My Daughters

I was in the third grade when I learned how it was done.

The mechanics of it, I mean. I'd had an idea before then, taken clues from the movies and soaps. Bare-shouldered people in silky sheets, kissing with open mouths. I used to strip my Barbie and Ken dolls down to their plastic Malibu flesh and then tangle them together to pretend they were "making love." That's what they called it on TV.

The truth is, I learned it from a naughty playground song.

One day my mother found Ken and Barbie in a corner of our basement, still tangled in a nude embrace. She turned to me with eyebrows raised: was there anything I wanted to ask? "No," I muttered, and scampered off with a prickly heat in my face. I thought I'd been caught knowing something I wasn't supposed to know.

It sounded innocent enough at first . . .

But I didn't really know. I didn't really know until the third grade, when the girl whose name I forget taught us that song in the little girls' bathroom. She repeated the words for us again and again, and our voices echoed against the cold marble stalls, the thick oak doors. We sang as we washed our hands with pink soap in cast iron sinks with streaks of rust around the drains, our eyes fixed on the holes in the tile where the mirrors used to hang.

. . . unless you were paying attention to the words.

The next year, at my new school, I had a crush on a boy named Mitch. He couldn't pronounce his *R*s, but he had shaggy hair and clever eyes that made my heart stir when they locked with mine. Mitch liked to chase me on the playground, and sometimes I allowed myself to be caught.

It was the boy next door . . .

I secretly enjoyed his arms around my waist, the thrill of our bodies panting in sync. Then I'd work my fingers against his grip and run away. One recess, though, he pulled me into the tire structure while his friends blocked the tires' open mouths. Memory holds the taste of fear, an acute scent of rubber.

. . . who pushed me on the floor.

We had a middle school teacher we often wondered about. He liked to seat the girls in the front of the room, touch the lockets on our necks. "What a pretty necklace," he'd say. He wasn't fatherly like the others, laughed a little too hard at our jokes. He had olive skin and a piercing gaze, wore cologne that liked to linger. Once, during truth or dare at a sleepover, someone confessed that he'd appeared in a sexual dream.

He lifted up my skirt . . .

That's when we started to wait for each other outside the classroom door, if one of us was ever asked to stay right after school.

. . . and said it wouldn't hurt.

Don't ask me how we knew that this is what you ought to do. Or that showing up all by yourself would seem like wanting something bad to happen. It's like my father told me when he gave me the key to our house. "Always keep this hidden," he said. "Don't lose it, don't play with it, don't ever dangle it in front of others." Here's the lesson I heard: even if it's stolen, it might still be your fault.

He counted, "One, two, three" . . .

A few years later, during high school gym class, as we were jogging on the track, we caught up with Christina, who had stepped aside to cry. *What's wrong?* we wanted to know, and gathered around her like a cloak. *My boyfriend*, she could barely say. It had happened in the basement.

. . . and stuck it into me.

Except she wasn't sure, and it became a matter of internal debate. Something in us had been trained to wonder: was it rape or just regret? We didn't know her well enough, couldn't tell by what we saw. She didn't have any bruises. She had no black eyes, no scratches like the victims on TV. Wouldn't a good girl have put up a fight?

My mother was surprised to see my belly rise.

In college, during the winter, we used to swim laps at the rec center and then go back to the dorm to smoke cigarettes. The nicotine felt more potent after a workout. We savored the menthol in our chests. But on that particular night, our friend Faye never showed. *Fucking lazy Faye,* we said. What we didn't know was that while we squeezed the water from our ponytails and formed our mouths into *Os* to blow little rings of smoke, Faye was in a shadowy part of campus, being forced to open her mouth for something else.

My father jumped with joy: it was a baby boy!

No ambiguity there. At least I didn't think there was. When I told my parents what had happened, my father seemed perplexed. Why didn't she fight back? he asked. Did she actually *see* the gun?

GAIL C. DiMAGGIO

Foundation

My mother never wore it.
Daddy said: You are more beautiful
bare faced. What
are you trying to hide? Daddy said. So the first secret

was the clam-shaped compact,
its icy sponge. That morning—
sometimes it's winter, sometimes

it's spring—and she calls me
to the bathroom, case open, water running.

I dream
that room, her oval face, the mirror watching.
The way we are afraid.

She wipes cold on my left cheek, at the base
of my throat above my collar, my right arm, left wrist.

The garland of his fingermarks dims,
paste stiffens at my throat.
The mirror-face lifts her chin, smiles. Promises.
I will live

in a casket of ivory beige, and be
her good girl.
She will love me
for telling their lies and never again

my own. The face in the mirror
has blank, black eyes, a hooked beak, a predator's
sneer. It looks at me.
Someone is a monster.

CADE LEEBRON

Fuck Us Harder

the prequel

Survivor. I don't feel like a survivor of anything. Sometimes I think that one girl died on a bed in a dorm room on her third day of college; she died in his bed while he was fucking her, raping her, whatever. Another girl was born in her place, and she rose, gasping like a phoenix, and ran from the room. She was a virgin. Nobody had ever fucked her, raped her, whatever. She was brand new, and she stumbled to a different dorm room and collapsed on the floor and then eventually crawled into the dead girl's bed and fell asleep, and in the morning, she took a shower.

testimony

Three and a half years later, in April of my senior year, it still feels like a lie to call myself a survivor. I still don't feel like I survived at all. I'm sitting on a carpeted floor, the institutional carpet leaving an imprint of its texture on the bottoms of my thighs, and I glance around and start to speak to the people on all sides, unsure of which way to look. It feels wrong to start my sentence with *as a survivor,* but I say it anyway.

We are here, at this meeting of the Wesleyan University Student Assembly, to have a community discussion regarding sexual assault on campus and the role of fraternities, if fraternities should be dismantled or coeducated in order to combat rape culture, and if fraternities contribute to rape culture at all. I turn to look at the back of the room and see rows upon rows of massive men: fraternity brothers. They are just so much bigger than me that it is shocking. Why do they get the chairs? How did they get so big? I have seen them in the dining halls, their plates piled high with what would be several meals for me, but they didn't seem so large then. Now, here, they are: massive men sitting in comically small chairs. Perhaps those chairs were meant for small and fragile people like me who are instead down here on the floor. I don't usually feel small. And I do know why they got the chairs: it is because they got here first. And I know what this must look like: they care more; we the women don't care enough, we showed up a little late. The truth is that we didn't show up late, we were here, wandering around the student center and avoiding entering this particular room, getting coffee and pretending to text, doing anything not to come here until the last minute. We were hesitant, maybe a little afraid; they were not. But we are here now. I am here. And so I say things, I add my voice to this war that's happening very politely in this room. I say, according to the transcript, *to the members of fraternities: if you care about women, why don't you want to share this with them?*

I'm sure that's not how I said it; I know I said something about how *siblinghood* can be just as meaningful as *brotherhood,* how *coeducation* is a viable option, and something about how *as a survivor, I feel safer in coed spaces,* but I don't remember exactly how I said it, and the transcript is available online. It's accurate enough.

I know that in the context of the world, a big place almost entirely full of crime and genocide and war and hatred and dead or abused children and terrorism, if you believe CNN, this is a very tiny little battle in this carpeted room. This is a group of college students at an extremely liberal arts college arguing over whether or not men get to have clubs and call them fraternities and not let women join. And if we the women don't fight against it, if we let these fraternities continue to exist, let men be together in this way, are they more likely to rape us? And are there enough of them for it to matter? Only three campus fraternities own houses. This whole situation feels artificial and surreal. We are having a conversation facilitated and policed by members of the student government and the administration. We are not allowed to laugh at each other or speak out of turn. A woman speaks. She says that the president of a fraternity called her a *slut* at a party recently. In response, the president of that fraternity introduces himself and then calmly attempts to explain it away. He says she was dancing inappropriately at his fraternity and that's why he called her a *slut*—she was just dancing that way, dancing like a *slut*. As if this is justification. As if we should not notice that he is white and she is black and he is policing her body and the way it moves in his privileged space. We are shushed by student assembly members for booing him, and then we sit quietly, chastised, waiting our turn, as the meeting continues. The minutes make no mention of this incident. The administrators, the supposed adults here, sit in a row of chairs against the windows to the right; they are silent. My campus therapist is among them; sometimes we make eye contact and then look away. This is a very orderly kind of pain. And it has become the reality, the vocabulary of my life. I've gotten so sucked into it, using these words—*triggered, survivor, rape culture*—so easily that someone might think it's what I actually mean.

new language

And do I feel *triggered*? No, I really don't. I am not a gun or a bomb or any other instrument of destruction, and I have no triggers. I feel fear—I know I feel that. I am afraid of massive men sitting on tiny chairs looking so barely contained, saying things that they might not realize scare me. Looking at me with eyes that seem to burn with rage, or maybe it's all in my head. Maybe it's in all of our heads, all of us girls in the room, on the floor, trying to say things to make them understand, and we are all just talking talking talking, trying to convince massive men that tiny girls are scared of them, or we are massive men trying to convince tiny girls that they have nothing to be scared of. And I know that it's not so gendered as I'm seeing it—there are women speaking in favor of fraternities and men speaking against them. But it does feel as though those women are traitors and those men are miracles. It shouldn't, maybe, but it does.

Afterward, when we've run out of time and have been politely dismissed, I make an effort to casually join a group of first-year women leaving the meeting. These girls didn't have much to say at the meeting, though they did snap their fingers in support when *survivors* spoke. They chatter cheerfully about *feminism,* and I am glad not to be wandering out into the darkness alone when we know that there are massive men out here, angry and freed from their tiny chairs and scolding bureaucrats. Everything we, the women, said was so falsely *polite,* so hollowly *cordial* and *respectful.* We're doing as we're told; we're pandering. They don't bother. Shouldn't we know that this is not the time to be *professional?* I feel old. I feel tired of referencing one night almost four years ago. I feel frustrated and ecstatic and scared about graduation. I will be happy to leave this little war but worried about leaving my side of it in the hands of girls who sometimes talk about rape like it's something theoretical—they talk about it as *oppression, systematic, misogyny,* as if those are the words you feel as you are being held down in someone else's sweaty bed being fucked after you said *no.*

No, I know to some of them, rape is more than hypothetical. I'm not delusional enough to think that I was the last woman raped on this campus, but I'm sometimes just tired, just exhausted, just on the edge of asking all the girls who don't know what they're talking about to sit down and let those of us who know this pain stand up and talk. Untouched girls fall back, *bros fall back*—aren't you rubbernecking to hear about the real thing anyway? Don't you want me to say something about penetration, don't you want me to mention sitting in a large and dimly lit building with other unknown people, all trying not to look at each other, waiting to get tested for STDs after it happened? I could tell you about peeing into a cup while resolutely thinking *this is not my life* and then realizing that in fact I had started a whole new life and everything from the last one was an utterly meaningless blur.

So no, I don't feel *triggered,* I feel fear and anger, and sometimes I see things that remind me of that past life: bottles of *cava* from Spain, sure, but also girls wearing crop tops out at night, girls walking alone at night, girls looking up at stars while walking alone at night, girls laughing, girls swaying to music and their hair flowing out behind them.

I am in love with all of them, or I want to be all of them; why wouldn't I? Don't I want to go back to that dead girl and wake her up and unrape her and make her whole and be her for a little while? Aren't I tired of thinking about whether fraternities are bad and how to define my feminism and whether I should be afraid of men? Wouldn't I love to go to college all over again and not be a *survivor,* a *victim,* a *liar,* or just a plain *slut*? Don't I wish I'd never let a previous version of myself die, only to be resurrected as a scared and pathetic little thing?

A scared and pathetic little thing translating her feelings into the terms that those around her will understand, saying *triggered* when I mean *scared, angry, nauseous, reminded, uncomfortable, weak.*

sisterhood

I can't remember when I stopped thinking that I had something in common with other women who'd been raped here. I can't remember when I started scoffing at any notion of *solidarity* or *survivor community.* It might have been going to Take Back the Night sophomore year and watching a girl get up in front of us and agonize about whether the time her best friend kissed her in a basement when they were lying on a couch together watching a movie was sexual assault. It might have been sitting in the grass looking up at her and thinking, *well, to me, that actually sounds pretty fucking romantic by comparison,* and then instantly feeling nauseous and horrified with myself and standing up and leaving. It might have been senior year in the fall when a girl, whose name I remember but who I have never met, identified herself to the media as the girl who'd been raped at a frat party on campus and people saw it as scandalous that she'd dared to connect *rape* with her name. It might have been when I realized that so many people on campus just didn't get it, didn't get that these men strive to make us nameless faceless *whores, sluts,* and that the real scandal is that we have gone along with it and pretended that this anonymity is necessary to our *survival.* It might have been when I noticed that the media never shies away from identifying victims of any other crime. It might have been when the *survivor community* took a supposed stand and started a website called Silence Is Violence where *survivors* could speak out about *rape culture* and wasn't it so fucking radical and exciting that we could post things anonymously online in this empowering forum and wasn't it so great and meaningful? It might have been when I thought about the time, freshman year, when things had been posted anonymously about my rape online, on the campus Anonymous Confession Board, when his friends called me names, and my mom found it and she saw all of it, saw all those words. How do you talk to your mom after she sees all those words?

And it wasn't that I was unique or special or the perfect *survivor* or the perfect *victim.* It was that there were just so many of us, and our stories were so different, and it is so hard to feel a sense of community when everyone has a story of *that one time* and they call it different things, they call it *a bad hookup,* or they call it *rape,* and maybe it was a stranger or maybe it was their boyfriend, but this feeling of violation can't be unifying when it is felt by at least a quarter of the women I have met. I do not feel a sense of community when I meet someone else who bites nails or watches bad reality television. I do not feel a sense of community with other people who are sixty-six inches tall, or people who have tattoos, or people whose parents are still together. *Survivor* is just yet another overly common characteristic.

rage

On another April night, after yet another *campus forum* to discuss this *important issue,* I sit in the lobby outside the classroom where the forum was held, leaning forward, on the edge of a bench. Brian,[1] the vice president of the student assembly, comes to sit beside me. He asks if I'm okay. I don't remember how I respond. We're both silent when Edmund, an acquaintance, approaches.

"My dad was in a fraternity," he begins, and then there is a blur of him insisting that though he isn't in a frat, he believes his dad is a nice person, and so are other men in fraternities. They don't hate women. They are good guys.

I think about how Edmund seems like an old-fashioned name.

"But why aren't you in a frat?" I ask.

"What?"

"What she's asking you," Brian says, "is why you aren't in a fraternity if they're so great." He sounds tired.

Edmund says something about how we are being close-minded. I remember that his girlfriend's name is Ruth, and in my head, I am amused at the thought of them together, sounding like someone's grandparents.

I remember a night back when Edmund was my physics lab partner, sophomore year, and he and Ruth had gotten into an argument before class, and he slammed some piece of equipment down onto the lab table in frustration. I remember looking at him and quietly finishing the rest of our report by myself while he texted her furiously, him sighing heavily after he sent a text and waiting for her to respond, his finger tapping too hard on the edge of the table.

That feels so long ago.

I tune back in as Brian is saying something about how people like us are trying to say something real and maybe Edmund should stop talking and just listen. It shouldn't feel so nice to be included, to be a part of something that might matter.

Jessica, the student assembly president, comes over to us and asks if I'm leaving. She glances at Edmund in an annoyed way. I smile at Brian and stand up, and we leave.

I walk Jessica to her meeting across campus, and then I just want to keep walking. I go to the campus grocery store and get an overly expensive chocolate bar with

1. Names have been changed.

potato chips in it and a lemon soda. Both of them have shiny yellow packaging. I marvel at how the potato chips are still crunchy inside the chocolate. The soda is perfectly sour. The air is a good temperature—it surrounds me and holds me up in its humidity. I want to break things. I want the license to slam fancy physics equipment on metal tables and have it be loud and have nobody comment. I want to be bigger, to have a big muscular body to run around in and burn up all this energy. I want to be allowed to be aggressive, to smash some stuff if that's what I feel like doing. I think it must be nice just to get to combatively approach vague acquaintances and express loud opinions. I think it must be nice not to be afraid. I think about how shitty it is that rapists rape people and leave bruises and then they graduate and get high-paying jobs and long-legged girlfriends and yet it is somehow considered *radical* that I tap my fingers so quietly on a keyboard in my bed at night to tell people about it. Fuck us if we're quiet, fuck us harder if we try to speak.

the end

In my head, I'm still sometimes lying on the floor of my freshman dorm room with my clothes half on, looking up at my bed like I can never climb that high, it is impossible.

But these words, these nights, these feelings, they are things I could shed and leave behind. It is May. This life of college is ending, over, now. Graduation marks another ending; after graduation I no longer have the option of pursuing charges against my rapist within the university's system. This should feel like impending doom, but instead I feel almost relieved. This ending has been a long time coming, a long time spent eating in dining halls, attending classes, showing up to meetings, walking the same neat paths in the same purposeful directions, describing myself as a *survivor* who can be *triggered* so that people will understand that though I am not an instrument of destruction, I have lived through it, I have been so close, I could tell you such sad and awful things, but this is such brief education, and here we are at war until we are politely dismissed with our fragile diplomas, and then we are gone.

epilogue I

In July, Michael Roth, the university president, writes a blog post asking for thoughts from the community on what to do about fraternities. I send him an email. It begins:

> I was raped by a classmate on my third day at Wesleyan, in the fall of 2010. He was also a freshman, and thus not involved in any Greek life at that point, but he had made friends with a few brothers of one fraternity, and the rape occurred after we had left a party at that fraternity. He later went on to pledge (though not initiate, by his own choice) that same

> fraternity. It seems to me that sometimes when we talk about statistics of rape on campus, specifically whether they occurred in a fraternity house or not, this is what gets left out. I have heard several female friends describe being sexually assaulted or harassed by a fraternity brother on campus in places other than inside fraternity houses. I have also heard stories of women who were assaulted after leaving a fraternity party (by someone, not necessarily a fraternity brother, who was also at the party). I think that fraternities perpetuate male domination and the objectification of women, and that this attitude is not contained within the walls of the fraternity houses. Men in that space (whether they are brothers or not) are allowed to view women as "others," which is at least partially because they could never be brothers. Men explicitly have the power in these spaces, and fraternity brothers seem to have a particular respect for each other and for other men.

He responds, thanking me for my email, saying that he has taken everything to heart. I try to believe him. I also try to believe it's not a form email, with my name just inserted into a slot at the beginning, but it probably is. He's probably received hundreds of emails just like mine, but in different words. I think that's a good thing.

epilogue II

In late September, it's announced that Wesleyan's Board of Trustees has mandated coeducation for residential Greek organizations within the next three years. This is amazing—it really is. I send all my happy thoughts to campus from grad school several states away, but I also wonder: did they do this for us, because we asked to feel safer, or did they do it for their own reasons, because the frats were becoming a liability? Does it matter, when both have the same outcome?

Some of the frat boys are enraged, as expected. I just don't care, don't give a fuck if they're feeling upset or inconvenienced. The safety of women on campus will always mean more to me than their hurt feelings or whatever loss they're experiencing. I want to ask them to come lie on the floor with me, to feel really low with me, to understand that because of the actions of one boy four years ago I still sometimes stay up until five in the morning doing absolutely nothing other than lying in bed hating myself. I want them to know that he didn't go to therapy; I did. He didn't think about dropping out; I did. He didn't drink himself to sleep for months; I did. Even now, I am constantly monitoring myself, interrogating myself, trying to make sure that I don't fall into those bad habits again. I'm still reminding myself to practice whatever self-care I can manage. And we both graduated in May, both wore red caps and gowns, and when they called his name to give him that diploma, I heard one lone voice rise up to cheer for him, and knowing that only one person in a crowd of thousands loved him, knowing that when my name was called I would hear a chorus of voices cheering for me, even though it was mean and it was hollow and it was selfish, I felt finally somehow victorious.

KATHARYN HOWD MACHAN

My Brother

My brother lives in a box of cigars.
Each day every day
he lifts the lid to peek at the world
and hopes the world won't notice.
Bristles grow on his face and throat.
He smells, fears soap.
He never throws his loose hairs away
but carefully keeps them, dirty and dark,
in the teeth of a green plastic comb.

Long ago he spent years committing incest.
I survived but we never mention it.
He's thirty-five now and still lives with our mother.
My favorite joke when I visit is to talk
of the time I stabbed his thigh with a fork
and sent him screeching around the table
for ruining my first perfect crayoned picture.
We pretend to laugh and the scar
does not go away. Migraine headaches
take me back to the fork, to the fort
he built under cool pines
where he wouldn't let me visit
unless I would . . . and I did.

Now he does his best to repel.
He rots his teeth, sucks his cigars,
growls and belches and grows fat.
Each night every night
he grows a little smaller inside.
One morning my mother, weeping,

may find he's flickered out at last,
a small gray heap in an ashtray.
I'll visit, leave the jokes behind,
bring instead a perfect crayoned picture
to wrap around his coffin.

SIOBHAN HARVEY

When My Best Friend Came to Stay; or, Corporeal Minimalism: Composition in Twelve Parts, Inspired by Philip Glass

There is no sincerer love than the love of food.

—George Bernard Shaw

1

After my best friend disappeared, my counselor asked me to describe her.

"Thin," I said.

My reflection stained the window. Outside, beyond my ghostly image, strangers crammed in red London buses idly stared out of foggy glass. Strangers on foot bustled through the city, moving shadows across department store windows.

The counselor noticed my inattention. She looked up from her notebook, caught my eye, inquired, "Did your best friend have a name or distinguishing features?"

"Thin," I replied. "Thin."

2

An early spring morning, 1987. I was fourteen years old. The sun was a shard cut between grey stratocumuli. Frost pricked earth and air.

I changed into my sports clothing for my first class: gym. When I ran onto the field, a girl from remedial class, Billie Harper, pointed at me and brayed, "Fat features!"

Like many caught on the cusp of puberty, I carried puppy fat on my jowls and cheeks. It's toward this commonplace misfortune that Billie directed her cruel intent. Girls peeked at me, huddled and gossiping. They could have joined in. They could have cackled and finger-pointed and sneered, but they chose not to. Perhaps they were tired, bored, or simply aware that Billie's jibe was weak. After all, it carried little of the bile and barb prepubescent children traditionally throw at each other, such as *Dumb, Weirdo . . .*

And yet . . . and yet . . .

My best friend, hidden perhaps behind a slight-trunked poplar nearby, witnessed the slur, felt my jag of pain, and knew she could offer me her secret companionship and solace.

3

The day after Billie's taunt, my best friend arrived on my doorstep. I was in the kitchen alone, cooking boiled potatoes, tinned carrots, and fish fingers for my absent family. There was something about the kitchen, its steam, fire, and stricture, and about the abandonment of my chore, Father asleep upstairs, Mother working all day, and my twelve-year-old sister Sarah supposedly playing Cabbage Patch Kids at her friend's house. (Though, later it would transpire that she and her friend were smoking, experimenting with makeup, and poring over posters of Wet Wet Wet's Marti Pellow). Yes, there was something about all this that made me invite my best friend to move in.

It's strange how my best friend traveled so light. No suitcases. No clothing. No possessions whatsoever. Like an angel of abstinence personified.

Each day thereafter, my best friend and I walked to school together, sat side by side in class, and then trekked home. We communicated all the time. Our favorite topic was food.

"One hundred grams of apple has 47.5 calories," I told her. "That's as much as ten grams of Edam."

She knew, of course. She was an authority on how many calories every item of food possesses. So, at lunchtimes, while we walked around the yard, me nibbling on a wafer of cheese or morsel of apple, we recounted how little we'd eaten and took pride in discovering who'd consumed the least amount of food. Naturally, my best friend always won this contest. But increasingly, I ran a close second.

4

On Sundays, while our neighbors were at church, Mother washed, scrubbed, and brushed our uncarpeted tenement. As she worked, a chicken roasted in the oven and the Carpenters spun on the stereo. *Close to You, Now and Then, A Kind of Hush, Passage.* Mother owned them all. Sometimes, as Karen Carpenter's somber voice undercut her brother Richard's cheery lyrics and piano, Mother, on knees before the black grate, paused over ashes accrued from a week's worth of blazes, then burst into tears.

5

Father kept different habits from us. Every morning, his face haggard, his eyes bagged, a dust of metal upon him, he arrived home from turning a lathe just as Mother left for her job. My sister Sarah, my best friend, and I headed for school.

This routine shaped others. When my best friend and I returned from school—piles of books, reams of homework, and Sarah in tow, I was laden down with the knowledge that I must prepare Father's lunch box and flask of tea, reline his shoes with cardboard, make dinner for the family, then awaken Father from his slumber. Later, the dishes washed, Mother came home to a dinner turning hard in the oven. As I pored through revision texts, my parents sat silently over a pot of tea, the television broadcasting news of election rivalry, factory closures, and increased unemployment.

There was another routine. It began once Father's car lights disappeared from view. Mother sprawled on the sofa, cradling a quarter-pound of rock candy, and cried. Always she spoke of her thirteen siblings, her jobless father gambling away the housekeeping funds, her jaundiced mother working four jobs to support the brood. She mentioned her own top marks in school, her removal from education when she was fifteen in order to keep house for her younger brothers and sisters, her escape by marrying Father. She talked about how I arrived too soon and about my sister's birth two years later, the only child Mother planned.

All these routines made the house dusty. School clothes and overalls went unwashed. So, with my best friend's silent approval, I stayed up long after Mother went to bed. I polished furniture. I washed and ironed clothes. At first, I expected Mother—or Father, even—to notice how the coffee table shined and how their clothes smelled fresh. I yearned for praise. But they carried on as before.

It was my parents' blindness that gave my best friend and me our next brilliant idea. Having made the best I could from a tin of marrowfat peas, a packet of dehydrated mashed potatoes, and slices of liver, I served the meal to my family, then slipped away to my room. There, my best friend and I delighted in the fact that no one noticed my absence.

6

All the time, anger, searing and volatile, inhabited our house.

It arrived at unexpected moments. Like the time I was washing the dishes and Sarah was drying them. To remove the condensation from the kitchen, Sarah opened a window. A gust of wind caught the glass, swung it wide, and smashed it.

Her wooden-soled Dr. Scholl's sandal in hand, Mother tore into the room, shouting at me. Again and again, the sandal landed upon my back and arms.

When Mother's screaming and sandal-beating stopped, my teary-eyed sister confessed, "I broke the window."

Mother pointed to me and roared, "She's the eldest. She should have stopped you from breaking it."

Later, in my bedroom, I selected school clothes that would hide the bruising.

7

A month later, as winter hardened and the late afternoons coalesced into darkness, Mother returned home early from work. She looked me over as if encountering a stranger. She switched off the television and demanded that we sit at the dining table to eat our meal. While I scrambled to make a meal for three stretch across four plates, Sarah set the table. When I brought out the food, Mother settled at the head of the table, her eyes stern upon me. We sat in silence, my best friend quiet and uncatered to, Sarah and Mother eating. I moved a fork around my plate. Soon Mother was out of her seat. Her plate upended. Her knife and fork flew toward me. Hard, loud words rained down: "You bloody idiot! How dare you shame me in front of my friends!"

Suddenly I was water. My calm, composed skin, the one which presented a smart, diligent child to my family and teachers, broke. Ripples, born of an energy I was too young to name rose and retreated in me. They built. They fell. They built. Until tears and sobs streamed from me, and I ran to my room. In my wake, Sarah and my best friend looked on.

8

A glance. That's all it took to unravel me.

The events that exposed my lie unfolded once Father rose from his slumber and Mother started to yell.

It was her workmate Mavis who was responsible. She bumped into my best friend and me on our way to school that morning. She peered at me and asked me how I was. Then she bustled into the decorating store and demanded to know of Mother, "What's wrong with your daughter?"

Of course, Mother was her usual defensive self. "What do you mean? There's nothing wrong with her."

"She's a skeleton," Mavis observed. "Is she ill?"

9

The next morning, Father returned from work looking unusually drawn. He escorted me to Dr. Longbotham. As we sat in the waiting room, Father dragged on a smoke.

The burning silence between us made me feel sick.

Eventually Dr. Longbotham called us into his consulting room. The place was cold and, except for a snatch of an old railway bridge traversed occasionally by a train clattering out of town, afforded little perspective. At the doctor's prompting, Father explained in clipped sentences. Dr. Longbotham asked if there were any reasons why I hadn't been eating.

Father stared ahead as if the question didn't concern him.

Too many words clogged my throat—I felt as though I were drowning.

Eventually, I replied, "No."

I was ordered onto the scales. My height was checked. Addressing the notes in front of him, the doctor said, "Go home and eat. Come back in a month's time. By then, I expect you to have put on weight."

At home, Father retired to sleep, and I returned to schoolbooks, the expectant kitchen, and the grimy furniture.

10

I attempted to eat. Food, huge plates of it, were given to me. Mother, her Dr. Scholl's sandal in hand, ordered me to eat it or face punishment.

A few weeks later, I returned to Dr. Longbotham. After hearing the news that I was heavier, my mortified parents told everyone they knew that I was better.

I never saw Dr. Longbotham again.

On top of my unrelenting household duties, academic and familial pressure built as forthcoming exams drew near. Everyone expected me to be the first person in my family to attend university. Father's night shifts, Mother's criticism, and the regular incidents of violence continued. And I, consuming food in front of my parents at dinnertime, started to vomit and deny myself breakfast and lunch.

11

The day I was to receive my exam results, I rose to discover my best friend standing over me, her body a shadow falling across my face. She walked me to school where I collected my marks: three A levels. More than confirming my place at university, such achievements meant escape. On the way back, my best friend lagged behind. She seemed to be fading slightly, her body a poem subject to erasure:

best *friend*

body

poem

subject *erasure*

As I entered the kitchen, I felt suddenly refreshed, cleansed of any desire to vomit or starve. Instead, I fed my body bread, peanut butter, chicken, chips, and chocolate, all the foods my best friend safeguarded me from. As I ate, my best friend glared on from the corner of the room, her edges fracturing like a kaleidoscope.

As the following months counted down to varsity, my days became framed by three meals, each fixed to a certain time and foods more extensive than previously but still limited in range. The strangeness of such consumption disturbed my body—I was so sated by eating previously forbidden delights like fat, that I was tired constantly. I slept, like a newborn, fifteen hours each day.

As I gained weight across my thighs and breasts, these same parts of my best friend's corpus became gaping expanses of empty air.

When the day came for me to go to university, my best friend was a sliver of ash. When I departed, she floated from me, propelled by a strong breeze toward the sky.

12

It was only later, once I settled in a big city, began my studies, and starved all communication with my family, that I sat down with a counselor to discuss my best friend and my years as an anorectic. Each time I spoke, a story opened up before me: a postmodern plot; a small-town setting; a young protagonist raised by impoverished, violent, poorly educated parents; her ghostlike buddy, corporeal despite her slenderness.

Those were the years my best friend returned during my sleep. The house I grew up in was a hall of mirrors. Glass enlarged, extended, and squashed my body. There was also a two-way mirror, which briefly revealed the shadow of my best friend on its other side, a fragment of light distilling our essences just as the past often reflects the present, especially in memory, especially in song. Then the light was extinguished, and I was separated from my best friend, my other self. By such frail darkness, I awoke.

KATHARYN HOWD MACHAN

Les-Salles-du-Gardon

And what if you hadn't hit me.
Hadn't swung your arm backhanded
against the curve of my eyes and mouth,
your blind father right across the table
confused: what did I murmur wrong?

And again, later, back in Marseilles,
after my broken French had explained
you could never, never do it again,
simple candles and the harbor lamplight,
wine in strong clear glasses—then

your rage uncoiling like a creosote rope
within the storm of midnight. What
if you hadn't opened that drawer
and pulled the gun from its careless corner,
in your other hand the unsheathed blade—

you sneered you could easily kill me,
but I wasn't worth it, a woman.
Two weeks pregnant with my daughter of roses,
the child you'll never know we made
because I fled through winter rain

back to America, to silence.
What if you'd hidden the fist
of your laughter till later, longer
in love's warm rooms, and I
had stayed behind time's doors

and learned to believe you were God.

On Silence & Subversion

LOIS ROMA-DEELEY

Apologizing for the Rain

I'm sorry   The sky wouldn't listen to me   /the bakery was closed
sorry I bumped   into your shoulder   stepped on both your shoes/
I'm sorry//the wind gets in your eyes/some voices like to screech//
sorry//really/so sorry I didn't think to cook your bacon/ the lawn
is still   unmowed   And I inconsiderately was taken with an urge to let
it go   sorry   I use up all the air   sorry   I take up too much space
I/am/sorry/your mother didn't love you and your father was a jerk so
very sorry   that   car   ran   through   the   red   light/sorry/that
salesman knocked on your front door/   sorry   /those kids chalked up
the sidewalk/a nun came collecting for the poor   sorry   you're still
yawning   that the water isn't cold   that the world owes you a living
and I didn't even know.

CHERYL DENISE

Swallowing

In Mrs. Ellis' class when it was time for our test
with that giant clown poster with all the colors
we were supposed to know
        I got stomach sick
        that easy-to-slip-into sick
            that struck again in nursing school,
        the 6 A.M. vomiting
        then walking erect,
blue pinstripes, that white starched cap.
During med pass my hands shook, breaking
the glass vial of Dilaudid
cutting my palm.
In peds all those tiny calculations
and that boy with his gangrenous foot,
me mixing powders and solutions,
hanging little IV bags, counting drops,
questioning my math, interrupting my sleep.

When I was twenty-five and freshly engaged
my future aunt asked *lemonade or iced tea*?
and I turned to my fiancé for the answer.
Drank the tea I did not like.

After the open-mic reading
the poet I love danced
right in front of the guitar man.
My legs ached to join her but stood
like pillars immobile before the whiskey-
breathed professor, criticizing my poems, standing so close
like he might kiss me while I swallowed
the words I wanted to scream.

SWALLOWING

At forty-five, I was going to be the only
nurse in the county making home visits by motorcycle.
On a tiny toy Honda I drew

giant figure eights in the field, then graduated to dirt
roads but I imagined men in pickup trucks laughing
at my efforts. And then that slight incline, that rose
like Everest, while I whispered *fuck, fuck,*
fuck, under my helmet
before placing an ad in *The Trader*: "*One slightly used Honda 200.*"

Someday I'll be ninety-five, a porcelain-
skinned nurse will enter my room without knocking,
hand me a small paper cup with two oval pink pills and one blue.
        I will think
        these are not
        mine.
She will hand me a glass of water, confident
in her white uniform, shiny name tag,
shimmery smile. I will hesitate.
            She'll nod.
            I'll shake
            the pills onto my tongue,
        swallow.

SHLOKA SHANKAR*

Invasion

It's almost an infectious disease
for us Indians to play the dutiful host
that we sometimes just pretend to be.

Relatives thrice removed from us
now occupy the same living space as me,
use my hairbrush without permission,
close open windows and files
on my computer, and kick me
out of my own room.

I politely smile and lend
a helping hand in the kitchen;
suddenly, we've morphed
into *Bakasura*'s household
with meals and beverages
being served every few hours,

and of course, the *khaatirdaar*
has to be impeccable, since so much
of our honor depends on it.

What will they say?
Do you think your room is too small?
Are they comfortable?

I've been reduced
to an invisible speck,

* *Bakasura*: In Hindu mythology, Bakasura was a great Asura who lived near the city of Ekachakra and forced the Raja to send him large quantities of provisions, which he devoured every day. He epitomizes gluttony. *khaatirdaari*: A Hindi word for "hospitality."

forced to fuss over my clothing
as I dare not look *too modern.*

A secret contest wages
between the ladies; which of them
can mudsling the most?

Inquisitive eyes bore into me,
prospective alliances
discussed unabashedly
before perfect strangers.

But that's how it is with us,
an overzealous lot
who have not the slightest clue
of when to back off,
but are well-meaning nevertheless.

ANNETTE SNYCKERS

Clipped

On those days
I ran about the garden
like a wild foal,
my father was convinced
that little devils nested
in my mane.

White sheet draped
over small shoulders,
I was made to sit
so he could snip
and exorcise these sprites
who whispered in my ears.

I emerged bobbed,
cut straight,
in step.

The Final No

Many years ago,
when my father feared
his youngest daughter
would fall in love
with the spotlight,
he cleared his throat
and despite my tearful pleading,
finally, definitely, said no.

I was too small,
I did not have the words
to sway him.
All I could do
was climb the *koppie*
behind the house
and sob for hours
in the tall dry grass,
until the *kiewiet* called me back
from Swan Lake to the winter veld.

No ballet pointes
to help me on my toes,
no diaphanous tutu,
no soaring music to lift me up.
How I would have flown.

But I am earthbound.
I'm toeing the line.

~DREAMA PRITT

eggshells

tip-toe or

stomp

will crack

the façade

so i

dance

PAULETTA HANSEL

Girl Villanelle

She's still there, that girl,
the one I was and hoped to leave behind.
I am forever loosening the ties.

The only life she could imagine for herself
was one she'd heard already in a song.
She's still there. That girl

took more than her share and left scattered
on the table all that could have fed her.
Hell-bent, she was, on loosening the ties.

I am not ready yet to claim her as my own.
She thought her body was the price of being seen.
She's still there, that girl,

bound and shivering inside her own smooth skin.
I'll say for her what she could not; that's how
I'm loosening the ties

and slipping through the doorway
from the past—I won't return alive.
Though she's still there, that girl.
Me, I'm loosening the ties.

SHOBHANA KUMAR

Brown

my darkness was dark enough
for unkindness that flowed
from fellow adolescent tongues,
from teachers who never picked me
to offer gifts and bouquets
to visiting guests,

even when i stood first,
in every subject,
broke into ribbons at finish lines,
danced, sang, debated and won.

my dark skin turned me away
from many suitors,
misguided by poetic metaphors
to moon-skinned damsels.

but in the end,
it was my surgeon's hands
they all turned to.
even before they called out
to their dark-skinned gods.

LLEWELLYN McKERNAN

Getting Out of Bed at Dawn

You feel for your artificial limb,
put it on with your second nails. Your
fake eyelashes flutter
like stuck flies.

You struggle blindly.
Inch by inch
the girdle envelops
your unreachable
thighs. You pull

your jelly-roll waist
taut, squeeze your belly button
shut.

You become a size five: an uplift bra
jells your mush-meal breasts, little shelves
where you store your breath.

You smile, the bloody fist
of your heart gloved now in the simile
in the mirror: the slow rich
waltz of your best
dress, silver grazing
the ripples.

So you get high on
dagger-thin unreal heels,
bruised toes jammed like
berries in a patent-leather
shine—you feed

on this height. You put on
plastic eyes: bright-as-gold irises
the dim slits of your pupils swim
behind.

You fluff the pumpkin-colored wig
hiding your head: its sad
bones hold the endless
dark brainwaves swelling there. Your

surgically altered words
trip lightly on
your tongue, thick
with its own unexamined
life, as you greet

the day, prepared for all
possible visitors: *Welcome,*
welcome, welcome, you

cry to the doctor,
the divorce lawyer,
the
undertaker.

RACHEL A. HICKS

Paper-Thin Girls

rip in dark waters, tear to time in threes.
She tells me burnt hair has a funny smell.
Paper girls hold hands, if cut they bleed.

Their blood was once blue. Did you know
that your blood starts out like an ocean too?
Red seeps quickly into paper, newsprint
more than others. Headlines & conversations,
horoscopes & weddings, all fall apart in tiny hands.

No more papier-mâché today, please,
I think the masks are finished.

MARY HUTCHINS HARRIS

Postscript

I want the lining of the yellow coat to be enough.
I want to never have to ask for extra helpings.
I want to learn to speak saxophone. I want to run
leaving no footprints. I want a tongue full of yeses
to seep into your good ear. I want the wisteria to appear
larger in their reflections in the mirror. I want arguments

in my belly to be quiet and go to their own corners. I want
the hole in my cheek not to fit perfectly to my teeth.
I want the mockingbird to sing only in whispers.

I want lemons to peel away the wrinkles around my mouth,
to leave the fullness of my lips maroon. I want my tears
to magnify enough so I won't need glasses. I want to say

thank you when you knock me to my knees and *fuck you*
when you pull me up. I want your words to undress me,
one piece of clothing at a time, from half a world away.

I want to taste the frayed edges of your shirt cuffs
but not their echoes. I want to silence the clock ticking
with a sideways glance but not the breeze its hands make

waving goodbye. I do not want to be in the story the ants tell
their children. I do not want to be the corona around the moon.
And when you are the last name on my dance card, I want

to take off my gloves, leave them on a chair by the open door.

PAULETTA HANSEL

On Faith

I never found a church I
could enter holy—heart, mind,
and body safe on hard-worn
pew. I wanted mystery
I could swallow whole, no catch
inside my throat. I wait, small
bird, eyes and mouth wide open.

On Pregnancy & Birth

M. J. IUPPA

Between Worlds

Submerged in an aboveground swimming pool. The water is perfection—chemically balanced, a clever blue—ear-to-the-world ignored. I hear everything: the swallows rev and swoop inches above its surface, the Kreepy Krauly's lub-dub scrub along its smooth lining; heartbeat echoing in my ears. I float motionless in the center. Eyes closed. A single thought imagines the threshold between worlds depends upon water. One's being seemingly spills into being everything, and, in an instant, spills over.

La mer, the sea. Blue. *Ma mere,* my mother. Pink. Two inscrutable bodies. As a child I confused the colors, calling pink blue. My mother, the sea. Now I've become both. In their vastness, I've known possibility. In the swimming pool, I'm defiant of gravity. When I rise out of water, my body lifts refreshed, withstanding. I'm not my age. A puddle collects around my feet.

Begin again. This time a scene that's memory. A young woman, with brown eyes, brown curls, wearing baggy corduroys comes to the doctor's office certain she's pregnant. Her three-year-old hides behind her slimness. She smells of patchouli and tobacco. I ask her a hundred invasive questions. She answers in few words. Mostly yes and no. This record is private. I tell her she can't clean the cat litter box; she can't smoke or drink alcohol or caffeine. These are the doctor's orders. She nods her head and takes her fistful of papers home. I tell her to call if she has any questions, any questions at all.

Three days later, she's waiting at the front desk with a small plastic container that once kept margarine, with its name "Promise" on the lid. I smile at her and she smiles back, sheepishly handing the little tub to me. She follows me back to the lab, where I routinely dipstick urine for albumin and sugar. I set the tub on the counter and pry the lid off gently, not wanting to spill her specimen. She watches me tentatively.

Not urine, but a fetus no bigger than the pad of my thumb, a translucent cameo nestled on a bed of cotton balls. Small hand crossed over mouth, body tucked in the shape of C, eye buds, nose—all the fine details made by twelve weeks—she asks me if the doctor can keep it alive. I hear water in her words rushing to care for what spontaneously spilled from her—fetus, saltwater, roar of the sea.

Begin again. My mother sleeps in a fetal position, floating between worlds. All the windows open. No wind tonight. The sound of waves rubbing small stones together. Her breath uneven. I touch her cool skin and feel water beneath my fingertips.

Looking up through the ceiling of water, I see a dome of sky glowing incandescent pink. I push to break through its glittering surface, gasping at first breath, then the next. My vision blurs in the sting of water—sound spills everywhere at once.

MELISSA HELTON

Gravidity

So much like gravity, the sound
of weight, of still, solid mass, sliding
forces, fluid down through bedrock vein into a secret—
so much like a woman with her rift
and blood aquifer to fill with water in the dark.

To ask a man to give you a child is irrevocable
and scouring, a slow feeling of grains flayed
by a steady drip, hand on the divot between
hip bone peaks. An immediacy leaches
into that vein—minerals from a pea-sized gland.

I've asked him to fill the dark with fluttering noise,
and the water table rises, postponed.

SUSAN RICHARDSON

Mother and Child

When we bring you home from the incubator
after 18 days, your head a perfect cantaloupe
unpummeled by birth canal,
lips on loan from Betty Boop, hunger rules.
We battle it out in a dark room.

In between feedings I lie on my back.
You lie on your stomach on my gut.
Gut to gut, invisible pouch of the kangaroo
holding us in place,
we're the two halves of a whole egg.

On the other side of the door,
Dad watches *Star Trek.*
Nana wrings out diapers,
stocks the cupboard with jars.
Any other world has no pulse.

When you wake to feed every couple hours,
we roll as one from right breast
to left, 180 degrees,
a rotating spotlight seeking home,
sprinkler creating rainbows on the lawn.

Then, we sleep,
all we can do till the milk gels
into tissue and bone, fattening you up enough
to support your own head, crawl, sit,
and pull yourself up by the furniture—

But for now you're mine,
little walrus, little honeydew,
your lips a bright Christmas bow!
Dependent on my body for food,
your body a miniature blanket warming us all.

MARTHA CLARKSON

She Decides about the Baby

It was the way they latched the door
behind her. Things sliding into place.

She unbuttoned and unzipped and held out
her arms like a sleepwalker, to accept their gown.

A hammering on the other side of the wall.
How you could count on day labor.

As she hung her clothes thought of how
a bath of blood would leave a ring.

A cousin took her sleeve but not her arm
like she was contagious with poor decisions.

How wrong it seemed when she woke craving
chocolate cake, so she asked for a red apple,
skin sticking between her teeth.

In the morning there was so much less of her
she tried not to wake up.

LUCY PALMER

Post-Natal

Once, I held your bones within mine,
grew you as I grew as I bloomed
with the life inside me, golden limbs
burst within, your kicks keen reminders,
not that I could forget. I waited for you
like a lover counting eyelashes.

You arrived one spring afternoon, lark song
lazy outside my window, chorus oblivious
to my screams as you scrambled into the world.
I wanted the world to be yellow, wanted
the bond promised in books, but all I could see
was the blue of your eyes, black puzzle
of your hair and pain, pain, when I realized—
                    I didn't know who you were.

There were days when I wondered if I'd been
handed the wrong child, a tiny dictator with cashew
feet and starfish fingers, beautiful angry bones
a mystery to me. You cried enough to fill
drought-destroyed rivers. I loved you fierce
and wanted you gone.
On certain dark nights when my mind
threatened to break like glass, I sobbed
as I thanked a god I didn't believe in
for placing us in a ground-floor apartment.

But I studied you close as poets study the beauty
of stars. Each finger and toe that I kissed
turned familiar under my lips; I came to know
each pore as if it were my own. The petals

of your skin became a joy that scoured away pain,
and as your tears turned, as a starless night
became day,
I learned how to love the bones of you.

WENDY BESEL HAHN

Where the Sexual Meets the Sacred

I reclined on the obstetrician's examination table and stared at my exposed stomach. My white skin was taut, but soft. Weeks earlier I had announced my pregnancy to my colleagues and my students—seventeen-year-olds in my junior-level English classes. Since that time my department chair had taken to cheerfully greeting me each morning, making eye contact, and quickly lowering her gaze to assess my "progress." A male student in my eighth-period class had blurted out, "Mrs. Hahn, you didn't look pregnant before break—what happened?" Weeks later, a female student had whispered, "I can see your belly today." She smiled so hard that she squinted. I tried not to feel insulted by the attention—it wasn't my glowing personality or wit that garnered these outpourings.

As the doctor looked at my chart, I thought of the maternity clothing catalog. Its bikini-clad swimsuit models reminded me of *Vanity Fair*'s August 1991 cover picturing Demi Moore in a scandalous combination: pregnant and nude. In the photograph, she stood nearly in profile, partially covering the breast closest to the camera with her left hand to show off an enormous diamond ring on her middle finger. Her right hand cupped the underside of her belly as her eyes looked away, revealing three-quarters of her face. The lighting emphasized her pregnant abdomen, perfectly smooth and free of stretch marks. She looked incredibly sensual, a modern-day twist on Botticelli's *The Birth of Venus.* On first viewing the magazine cover over ten years earlier, I had judged it critically—it hadn't seemed appropriate to depict the pregnant form as sexy, yet it had become an image to emulate in American culture. I hadn't ordered a bikini for the upcoming summer months, but I diligently applied cocoa butter to my growing abdomen daily to keep my options open.

After asking about the baby's movements, my doctor produced a tape measure. She must have seen the face I made, the same involuntary wrinkling of my nose that happened as the nurse adjusted the scale at each visit, because she smiled.

"Just remember that you are a walking miracle," she instructed as she stretched the tape measure from my pubic bone to my navel.

I smiled blankly at her, unsure of how to take that remark. Several million "walking miracles" inhabited the planet with me, contributing to overpopulation. My major life accomplishment seemed to be getting knocked up.

While I fastened my pants, I thought about our high school's upcoming commencement for our graduating seniors, at least two of whom were pregnant also. Did their doctors call them walking miracles at their visits? I had a license to breed on my ring finger and had reached a respectable age; therefore, I received congratulations.

Despite my cynicism, I had felt like a walking miracle at times. In the early morning or late at night, while I sat still, I felt the flutter of something moving deep inside me. My uterus was an opaque fish bowl containing a tiny fetus that occasionally bumped up against the glass so I could feel her. For several weeks, my husband, Pete, placed his hand on my belly without feeling the movement. These quickenings were private moments, like kneeling to pray in an empty sanctuary. I was the only one who could detect the amazing communication from within.

In biblical times, pregnancy was a sign of God's favor, and barrenness, conversely, a curse in response to some wrongdoing. Each of the Old and New Testaments contains a story about God intervening to bless a husband and wife who are well beyond their childbearing years. In Genesis, Abraham becomes the father of all nations when his elderly wife, Sarah, bears a son, Isaac. In the Gospel of Luke, the Angel Gabriel announces Elizabeth's pregnancy to Zechariah while he works in the temple. In their old age, husband and wife become parents to John the Baptist, who prepares the way for Christ.

The Virgin Mary receives a similar visit from an angel, who explains that God has found favor with her and wants her to carry the Messiah. When Mary questions how this could happen to a virgin, the angel responds, "The Holy Spirit' will come upon you, and the Power of the Most High will overshadow you" (Luke 1:35 NIV). This divine conception is a spiritual rather than sexual experience. Interpreted literally, these stories describe miraculous births.

Although the biblical account of the Visitation, found in the Gospel of Luke 1:39–45, has Mary only three months pregnant at the time, many painters have exaggerated her swollen abdomen to make her look further along, closer in shape to her cousin Elizabeth, who is at least six months pregnant with John the Baptist. These works of art commonly depict the sacredness of pregnancy with halos around the women's heads or the placement of hands on one another's extended abdomens.

The women are typically located at the center of a scene, sometimes with men pictured off to the sides.

A reverence for pregnant women predates the Bible. Archaeologists have discovered statues of women with swollen bellies alongside prehistoric remains dating back to the Paleolithic and Neolithic periods throughout Europe and Asia Minor. These icons represent the origin of all life: sexuality and spirituality united in the pregnant form.

I never did get used to grown men calling me "mama" during my pregnancy. These were not construction workers yelling "hey, sexy mama!" but rather men with graduate degrees who were old enough to be my father using what they perceived to be a term of endearment. "How's the mama doing today?" one male colleague inquired.

With another, the talk of my pregnancy took on a more sexual tone. "You're looking very ripe today, Mama," John commented as he sipped from his coffee cup in the teacher's lounge. My checks felt hot as I noticed his gaze fixed on my cleavage.

"Pete thinks I'm getting that pregnancy glow."

"Oh yeah, I can see it in your cheeks. You're radiating," he smiled as he held the door to the faculty lounge open for me.

"I'll be radiating all over the place by June," I quipped.

Strangely, I did feel sexy for a while during my second trimester. It seemed odd to feel desirable. I could remember cringing as a teenager when my pregnant religion teacher informed our all-female class that it was possible and even pleasurable to have sex during pregnancy. I would never divulge such personal information to my students, yet I understood how being pregnant could make a woman feel confident and daring while still safe. My body testified to my sexual experience, inviting a sort of eroticism at the same time it was supposed to symbolize something miraculous and pure.

An Episcopal priest once told me how strange she had felt celebrating the Eucharist while pregnant. She could never shake the suspicion that the members of her congregation were staring at her, thinking, *She had sex.* Aside from the biblical exceptions, pregnancy attests to sexual intercourse. Sexuality and spirituality remain problematic even in contemporary Christianity.

According to a Platonic view of the world, in which the body and the soul were separate and competing entities, women were thought to be more susceptible to bodily appetites than men. Yet our culture had reversed these roles somewhere, making the male libido acceptable and celebrated, while women were assigned one of two roles: temptress or virgin. As a pregnant woman living in the twenty-first century, I could, at least for a few months, feel like both.

Being pregnant during my third trimester was far removed from the glamorous *Vanity Fair* cover. My stomach changed shape as the fetus kicked or moved. In adhering to fashion of the day, I wore more tailored clothes that sometimes made my belly button look like a doorbell waiting to be pushed. I bumped into desks in my classroom when I miscalculated how big I was and got chalk on my belly from brushing up against blackboards. Although the cocoa butter, or maybe great genes, warded off stretch marks, I never did work up the nerve to parade around at the pool in a bikini.

Although I felt clumsy in my own body, people seemed drawn to me. A woman at church gave my stomach a "Buddha rub" for good luck. A neighbor's mother apologized for placing her hand on my stomach when I recoiled at the touch. While I wore increasingly larger necklaces to draw attention upward, I felt the gaze of men, women, and children focused on my protruding belly.

Supermarket tabloids have long used protruding bellies to garner readership. In 2002, the disappearance of Laci Peterson, then eight months pregnant, captured national headlines. A picture of her wearing a sleeveless, crimson dress that accentuated her pregnant form appeared in the media long after her body had washed ashore in California and her husband was captured and convicted. Somehow, her pregnancy made her murder all the more tragic, as if hope and goodwill for the future had been extinguished in her form.

It would be easy to dismiss her murder as the work of a psychopath; instead, her case highlighted an alarming trend. A variety of sources attribute 20 to 25 percent of deaths of pregnant women to homicide, with the father as the most likely suspect.

Would-be fathers who murder their pregnant wives are not the first to view the pregnant form or women's reproductive capabilities as something sinister and threatening. Hippocrates, the father of modern medicine, viewed women's wombs as the source of disease, able to travel throughout a woman's body, creating instability. Hysteria (wandering of the womb) became a malady attributed to many female patients. Medieval scientists, who rarely conducted autopsies, especially on pregnant women, believed that the womb was permeable. Barbara Duden, a seventeenth-century doctor, regarded the female body as fluid.

Three years after giving birth to my daughter, I succumbed to a fascination with the pregnant form as I sat in my friend Karen's living room surrounded by pink and blue streamers, watching her open gifts. Toward the end of her shower, she stood up to let us inspect her physique and offer our guesses about the baby's sex. I thought about the card I had selected for her depicting a cartoon pregnant woman standing in profile. Actually, it wasn't a woman—just a headless, legless, pregnant torso whose curve formed the edge of the card's front. The inside read, "Some miracles happen instantly, others take nine months." Rather than conveying a saccharine sentiment, I intended the card as a parody. I hoped that Karen would have a sense of humor about it, and that she knew me well enough to realize I found the attention that a pregnant belly received rather bizarre and insulting. As I watched Karen model her form, I couldn't tell whether she genuinely enjoyed the attention or did it to mock people's propensity to look.

As I studied her profile, I thought about my other friend, Elaine, whose doctor had told her she could never carry a child. Her baby was due the same day as Karen's, except her son resided in the womb of another woman who lived a thousand miles away. That card with the pregnant torso would have been entirely inappropriate for Elaine. Yet her situation seemed far more miraculous.

Several of the guests at Elaine's shower were former colleagues she hadn't seen recently. They had arrived in my living room anticipating the sight of a swollen stomach but politely refrained from asking questions until Elaine brought up the subject of her surrogate. As the hostess of the shower, I hung back and watched Elaine expertly educate them. She explained that doctors had used her egg and her husband's sperm to create the embryo that they then implanted in another woman's uterus.

For several years, I had talked with Elaine about all of her options for having children. International adoption had become a costly and uncertain proposition that often put prospective parents at the mercy of corrupt government officials or changing political attitudes toward Americans. I had watched my friend, an intensely private person, cry on numerous occasions as she relayed details of failed IVF cycles. Even though we were extremely close, Elaine had approached me cautiously about her decision to try surrogacy, afraid I might disapprove.

Once the process was under way, she had shared that her surrogate suffered from migraine headaches pregnancy alleviated. From Elaine, I had learned that participation from all parties involved a complicated legal agreement. When I mistakenly used the term *birth mom,* she had patiently taught me new vocabulary: *surrogate.* She understood that even well-intentioned people like me didn't have a frame of reference for this new process of motherhood. The year Elaine and her husband began their journey to parenthood, an estimated two thousand babies were born to surrogates in the United States. I admired her not only for doing something that society and certainly her Catholic faith did not readily accept but also for having the patience and confidence to explain to a roomful of people how surrogacy worked.

How different it was to watch her sit on a couch and open gifts without an enlarged stomach to monopolize her lap or the conversation. Her impending motherhood was abstract, leaving me to think about a pregnant woman somewhere acting as the incubator. This married mother of two teenaged children was experiencing pregnancy without preparing for motherhood. Elaine had assured me that the fear of this woman becoming attached to the baby was unfounded; the surrogate had done this several times before. Yet I wondered how it felt to have someone else's fetus pushing against her uterus. Certainly, it didn't physically feel any different than what I had experienced, but I wondered if there were some psychological ramifications in parting with a baby who had shared her body for nine months. As a woman who had experienced the public response to pregnant women, I could imagine strangers approaching her in public to ask her when her baby was due. How would they respond if she told them that the baby wasn't hers?

Once Elaine concluded her explanation, one guest commented on how lucky she was not to experience morning sickness, labor, and delivery. Elaine smiled and went along with the remark. She had received similar congratulations for not getting stretch marks or droopy breasts. People who tried to emphasize the negatives of pregnancy intended to make her inability to carry a child into a positive. They meant well. Yet they knew, as Elaine and I did, that she had missed out on experiencing certain facets of the miraculous. Even so, Elaine and her husband would have a biological child—something that would have been impossible a decade earlier.

❦

I was nearly three months pregnant with my son when I went to an Annie Leibovitz exhibit. Next to the portrait of Demi Moore that had graced the cover of *Vanity Fair* hung a plaque explaining that the actress had been pregnant with her second child during the shoot. The nude photographs had been initially intended for her and her then-husband, Bruce Willis. Leibovitz had convinced the couple to allow her to use the photograph for a cover, forever committing Demi's pregnant form to the public domain.

Across the room, I found a photograph of a pregnant woman's nude torso. Leibovitz had shot the image with the model facing the camera. A pair of hands intertwined over the woman's stomach clearly belonged to a man with a wedding band who had stood behind the model, embracing her. The plaque explained that this was Demi Moore with Bruce Willis. The work had a much more intimate feel than the famous magazine cover. It more closely resembled the candid portraits that Leibovitz had captured of her family members and partner, Susan Sontag. While Moore and Willis were posing, this posture seemed natural. Moore exposed her nipples and let her plentiful breasts repose. The image's beauty had less to do with Moore's amazing physique and did not even include her attractive face or sleek, short haircut. Everything about the photograph made it more accessible and less glamorous than the *Vanity Fair* cover. Pete and I might have been that faceless couple captured in black and white for an instant. Yet I found myself retreating from the image rather than studying it. Viewing it felt slightly voyeuristic—as if I had caught a glimpse of some private moment through partially opened window blinds.

In the museum's gift shop, I found a postcard with a replica of Demi Moore's *Vanity Fair* cover. I looked in vain for the second image—the pregnant torso unadorned. I admired the woman in that second photograph, who was comfortable in her body. It reminded me of a pagan goddess statue and my own body's impending transformation.

I debated purchasing the *Vanity Fair* cover postcard, but finally did so knowing that the iconic image would forever evoke its companion. Together, they constituted a complete image.

On Late Life & Death

JACQUELINE DOYLE

Mirrors and Reflections

I stop by the restroom after my first class and catch a glimpse of my stark reflection in the mirror. Under the fluorescent lights my reflection looks unfamiliar—the color of my hair lurid and artificial, my face pale and drained of life. Is this what I look like in the classroom too? Lately I'm startled at how much I've aged. Puffy circles under my eyes. Broken blood vessels on my cheeks. Crepey jowls under my chin. Jowls, who could have imagined that? But then, who could have imagined that one day I'd be sixty, with a long-term marriage, a son out of college, a thirty-year mortgage, and a full-time job that I often resent.

There's no time for lunch between classes, so I gulp down a yogurt at my desk, trying to read my e-mails at the same time, flipping through a stack of student papers I'll need to grade tomorrow. I tell four students that they'll have to come back during my office hour for advising. I try not to be annoyed when two of them delay me in the hall. I like my students, working-class kids at an underfunded public university. It's not their fault that there aren't enough advisers, or enough courses, that the waiting lists are so long, the state budget so abysmal. I check my watch and rush off to my second class.

Today I'm teaching a series of mirror scenes in Edith Wharton's novel *The House of Mirth.* They can mean different things, I suggest. You might look in the mirror to admire yourself. (I think of Milton's Eve, and Narcissus. Vanity is apparently dangerous.) You might look in a mirror to check on your appearance to others, put on your public face. (I think of an old woman admiring a sultry movie star as she blots her bright red lips—oblivious to the wrinkled crone with garish, crooked lipstick whom others see. Already my imagination is falling into the cracks of our discussion of the novel. There are a lot of things I'm not saying, including, of course, how I feel when I look in the mirror myself.) Wharton's Lily Bart adjusts her hat and veil in the mirror at Lawrence Selden's apartment, ready to sweep out into public and dazzle the world with her beauty. That night she checks the mirror and worries about the fine lines around her mouth. Is it so apparent that she is getting older? Determined to marry a wealthy man, Lily depends on her beauty to achieve that end and becomes progressively more anxious, as this commodity-driven novel unfolds, about her chief asset. Mirror scenes may go even deeper, though, beyond appearances. You might look in the mirror to confront who you are. After the reckoning with Gus Trenor, Lily feels a kind of moral horror. When she looks in the mirror she sees something monstrous.

I stay focused on Wharton in the discussion, but I'm reflecting on other mirror scenes. Snow White's wicked stepmother gazes into the glass and can't refrain from comparing herself to other women. "Mirror, mirror on the wall, who's the fairest of them all?" Not a good question; sooner or later you're not going to like the answer. Virginia Woolf calls the early guilt she felt in front of the mirror her "looking glass shame," a shame that lasted her entire life: "I must have been ashamed or afraid of my own body." Woolf was molested, also anorexic. Do all women feel shame at some point, or do some take lifelong delight in their bodies? Not me. I bring my straying attention back to class. Discussion is animated in the front and on the right side of the room, but there's a student text-messaging in the back row, another surreptitiously reading a textbook for another class, another checking her makeup in a lipstick-compact mirror, and I wonder if they've been listening at all.

I rush to yoga after my crowded office hour and arrive home feeling calm and pleasantly spacey, my senses heightened. Dinner by candlelight with my husband is an oasis, though I can't refrain, it seems, from talking about work. He's better at shedding the day than I am. I wonder what my life would be like, our lives would be like, without the warm reflections of ourselves that we see in each other's eyes. In the waning light after we finish up the dishes, I go outside to break off a deep pink camellia from the small tree by the front gate, and a small branch of fuzzy yellow flowers from a tree by the driveway—I don't even know what the tree is called. I spend some time choosing a pottery vase, and put them on the windowsill in front of the sink. The immigrant mother of a school friend of my son's said the trees were all over Ukraine. She remembered gathering armfuls of flowering branches as a girl. They always reminded her of her homeland, she said. The woman's memory has created a kind of nostalgia for me, though I have no girlhood memories of this tree. I've come to appreciate the tree's bounteous beauty, to feel a kind of celebration and mourning of my own youth when it blooms each year now.

I look in the mirror as I brush my teeth for bed. The dim bathroom light softens my features. Even with toothpaste foaming out of my mouth, I don't look so bad. I smile to myself when I think of the students in my classes today, faces lit up during the lively discussion, and the students in my office hour later, who left feeling better about their problems or their futures. I think about how close I've become to my son, despite our geographical distance. I think about what I'm teaching and writing, and how much I share with my husband. I think about the flowers on the windowsill in the kitchen, already dropping their petals, but beautiful just the same.

MARY IMO-STIKE

Old Women

I am one
with the old women,
like Mrs. Finney,
in the back pews for
weekday Masses,
loneliness at last
taking the outward form of decay.

As children we dismissed her,
called her "The Finneys' grandmother."
She was defined by who she bore;
her life was a buried name
and time passed
in endless maternal service.

We old women wait,
when we want to wail.
We are the cinders in God's ash can.
The nuns reach in
and spread us on icy sidewalks
in hope for purchase on their way
to early morning Mass.

In my dream, we ride
on shaggy royal llamas
up the center aisle
of church, floating like
queens of restoration,
purity and strength unbridled
to occupy the main altar
in our benevolent seniority.

We glorify the Host,
and the wine reflects
our vital blush.

At Last Blessing,
the congregation recesses behind
Mrs. Finney,
in awe of her majesty.

JESSICA LAWRENCE

I've Spent My Life

I spent a lot of time looking at the bright
plastic promises, each on a shelf of
rows of hope—stacks of beginnings.
I've spent a lot of time reading
other people's stories, reading
other people's books—
Withering from twenty to thirty-five
to forty-five, fifty—older.
My three-year-old daughter stepped into the house,
and didn't look back as I rushed to catch up.
Moments later, she was twenty, stepping
into a new city without me. I was not there.
The window by my chair is a measure of seasons, frosting over,
thawing, wet with rain then dry.
I read by that window.
The poets were here, too—they saw me,
saw my life slipping away like a first spring breeze.
When my life slipped away like cold winter,
memories stacked like firewood and burned.
There were milestones captured in frames, in phones.
They collected in rows—on shelves—like promises.
Every day of it was a new, plastic promise.
There was work and then home,
work and then home.
work and then home.

CAROL GLOOR

Your End

So you will end in a bed
you never made, spittle running
from your cracked mouth's corners.
The world—
brick light from
aluminum-framed windows, the hiss
of cars through rain but
still your body beating through
the tangled sweaty sheets.

So you will end treated by white coats,
sleek with arrogant youth, people
you don't know, people who believe
they will never let their toenails grow
to claws, never let oatmeal
slip from their mouths,

people who don't know that you
once lived an October afternoon

under trembling leaves,
under fat scarlet berries taut
with the juice of Wisconsin's hottest summer,

your orgasm pulled from you
like an uprooted tree, the hot dirt
clogged beneath your fingernails,
your body beating,
beating still.

PAULETTA HANSEL

All I Know of Death

I know from this side of the doorway.
Click of the lock. The body
without breath, an empty room.
I know a boy who drew the cave
he'd lived in, girl-child of Tibet.
My mother, eight years from
my father's death, still lives
as *we*. The hospice nurses rest warm
palms against their patients' calves,
then thighs to track death's chill ascent.
Feet first, we leave this world
headed nowhere I know.

GINA VALDÉS

Between Worlds

My sister decided to leave
hospice for home.

On her nightstand glared neon-colored pills
sorted in an ice-cube tray. Each pill
was a blessing, a curse.

Daily for one week she asked,
What am I?

Each day in a mirror a woman warrior appeared,
dimmed.

In her dreams she saw a bird
in flames swirling to smoke, ashes.

I'm between worlds, she whispered,

Offered agua fresca and mangos
to las abuelas who arrived
dressed in brilliant indigo light.

My sister stepped out of her house
of fire and ice, tissue and dreams,
terror and bone

and followed las abuelas' blue trail
to another star.

About the Contributors

Ellen Bass is a chancellor of the Academy of American Poets. Her most recent poetry collections are *Like a Beggar* (Copper Canyon, 2014), *The Human Line* (Copper Canyon, 2007), and *Mules of Love* (BOA, 2002). She coedited the anthology of women's poetry *No More Masks!* (Doubleday, 1973) and is coauthor of *The Courage to Heal* (HarperCollins, 1988; 2nd ed. 2008) and *Free Your Mind* (HarperCollins, 1993). Her poems frequently appear in the *New Yorker* and *American Poetry Review* as well as many other journals. Among her awards are three Pushcart Prizes, a Pablo Neruda Prize, a Larry Levis Prize from *Missouri Review,* a New Letters Prize, and an NEA Fellowship. She teaches in the MFA program at Pacific University.

Michele Tracy Berger is a women's studies professor, a writer, a creativity expert, and a pug lover. Her main love is writing speculative fiction, though she is known also to write poetry and creative nonfiction. Her creative writing has appeared in the *Chapel Hill News, Glint, 100 Word Story, Thing Magazine, Oracle: Fine Arts Review, Flying South, Carolina Woman, Trivia: Voices of Feminism, Ms.,* the *Feminist Wire, Western North Carolina Woman,* and various anthologies. Her sci-fi novella *Reenu-You,* about a mysterious virus transmitted through a "natural" hair relaxer, was published in 2017 by Book Smugglers. Michele is completely undone by the sight of pugs and has to restrain herself from collecting any item they appear on. She lives in Pittsboro, North Carolina, with her partner, Tim.

Rachel Squires Bloom writes and teaches in Quincy, Massachusetts. Her work appears in educational journals, literary magazines, and anthologies, including *Meridian Journal of Poetry, Clackamas Literary Review, Hawai'i Review, Poetry East, Main Street Rag, Mad Poets Review, California Quarterly, A View from the Bed, Ars Medica,* and *Chest,* among others.

Lauren Brimmer is a twentysomething writer and bartender living in Portland, Oregon. She writes as a way to examine her own patterns and relationships and, most importantly, to heal.

Ellen Cantarow, a journalist since the mid-1970s, wrote about women's social, political, and economic issues for *Condé Nast* and other magazines, and for decades covered Israel's occupation of the West Bank for the *Village Voice* and other publications. Her book *Moving the Mountain: Women Working for Social*

Change (Feminist Press/McGraw-Hill, 1981) is still in print and has been used since publication in classrooms both in the United States and abroad. Her recent articles on the depredations of Big Oil and Big Gas on grassroots communities have appeared at *Tom Dispatch* and *Truthout* and have been reprinted at *Huffington Post,* the *Nation, Grist,* and many other venues.

Jane Chance published *Only Begetter* in 2014. Her poetry has appeared in *Antigonish Review, Ariel, Dalhousie Review, Icarus* (Dublin), *Ilanot Review, Kansas Quarterly,* the *Literary Review, Nimrod, Southern Humanities Review,* and *Wascana Review,* among other journals. Eight of her poems are featured in the forthcoming *New Crops from Old Fields: Eight Medievalist Poets* (ed. Oz Hardwick, Stairwell Books, 2015), and her new book, *The Middle Ages,* was published in 2018 by Finishing Line Press. The Andrew W. Mellon Distinguished Professor Emerita of English at Rice, she has published twenty-two books on medieval literature and received NEH and Guggenheim fellowships and an honorary doctorate from Purdue University.

Martha Clarkson is a corporate workplace designer in Seattle, Washington. Her poetry, photography, and fiction can be found in *Monkeybicycle, Portland Literary Review, F-Stop, LensCulture, Seattle Review, Alimentum,* and *elimae.* She is a Pushcart nominee, is a recipient of a Washington State Poets William Stafford Prize (2005), and is listed under "Notable Stories," *Best American Non-Required Reading* (2007, 2009). She is the recipient of the Best Short Story *Anderbo/Open City* prize for "Her Voices, Her Room."

Betsy Cornwell is the *New York Times* best-selling author of *Tides, Mechanica, Venturess, The Forest Queen,* and the forthcoming *The Circus Rose* (Clarion Books/Houghton Mifflin Harcourt). After graduating from Smith College in 2010, she received her MFA in creative writing at the University of Notre Dame, and then ran away to Ireland to live with the fairies. She is now a single parent in County Galway, where she writes and teaches full-time. She is also the story editor at *Parabola,* an intersectional spirituality and mythology magazine.

Cheryl Denise grew up in Elmira, Ontario. She is the author of two books of poetry, *What's in the Blood* and *I Saw God Dancing,* both published by Cascadia. Her poetry CD is *Leaving Eden.* She and her husband, Mike Miller, are a part of the intentional community of Shepherds Field, near Philippi, West Virginia. The community raises a small flock of Jacob sheep and sells wool blankets and yarn.

Gail C. DiMaggio lives and writes in Concord, New Hampshire. Her work has appeared most recently in *Salamander, Slipstream,* and the *Tishman Review.* In 2017, her book, *Woman Prime* (2018), was chosen by Jericho Brown for the Permafrost Poetry Prize.

Liz Dolan has published two collections: *They Abide* (nominated for the Robert McGovern Prize) and *A Secret of Long Life* (Cave Moon Press). A nine-time Pushcart nominee and winner of Best of the Web, she was a finalist for Best of the Net 2014 and winner of the Nassau Prize for Nonfiction and Fiction.

Jacqueline Doyle lives in the San Francisco Bay Area, where she teaches at California State University, East Bay. She has published creative nonfiction in the *Gettysburg Review, Superstition Review, Zone 3,* and *Southern Humanities Review* and a flash-fiction chapbook, *The Missing Girl.* Her work has earned numerous awards, including six Pushcart nominations and four Notable Essay citations in *Best American Essays.*

Marged Dudek is a middle and high school teacher and education researcher in Southeastern Ohio. In the past, she has published in journals such as *Red Weather* and the *Adirondack Review,* as well as in an anthology of West Virginian writers titled *Wild Sweet Notes II.* She has published a chapbook titled *Stupid for Dreaming of Alligators,* which was produced by JK Publishing.

Michelle Elvy has lived aboard her sailboat, *Momo,* for more than fifteen years. She is a writer, editor, and manuscript assessor based in New Zealand. Recently, her work has appeared in *New Micro* (2018), and she coedited *Bonsai: Best Small Stories from Aotearoa New Zealand* (2018). She edits at *Flash Frontier: An Adventure in Short Fiction* and *Blue Five Notebook* and is the assistant editor for the Best Small Fictions series.

Beatriz F. Fernandez is a university reference librarian in Florida. She has read her poetry on WLRN, South Florida's NPR news station; was the grand prize winner of the second annual Writer's Digest poetry award; and was featured in the *Latina Book Club* blog. Her poetry can be found at the *Boston Literary Magazine, Falling Star Magazine, FLARE: The Flagler Review, Label Me Latina/o, Minerva Rising, Verse Wisconsin,* and *Whale Road Review,* among others. She received Pushcart Prize nominations in 2014 and 2017. Her latest poetry chapbook, *The Ocean between Us,* was published in 2017.

Jennifer L. Freed raises her teenage daughters, writes, and teaches in Massachusetts. Her poetry appears in *Zone 3, Atlanta Review, Worcester Review,* and other journals. She is a three-time Pushcart nominee. Her chapbook *These Hands Still Holding* (2014) was a finalist in the 2013 New Women's Voices contest.

Carol Gloor lives on the Mississippi River in far northwest Illinois. Recent work of hers appears in the journals *Postcard Poems and Prose* and *About Place.* Her poetry chapbook *Assisted Living* was published by Finishing Line Press in 2013, and her full-length poetry collection *Falling Back* was published by Word Poetry in 2018.

Estela González holds an MFA in creative writing and a PhD in Latin American literature. She writes in English and Spanish about the intersections between class, sexual, and environmental justice. Her work has appeared in venues such as *Ariadna, Solstice Literary Magazine, Barcelona Review, Flyway, Luvina, Revista de Literatura Mexicana Contemporánea,* and Vermont Public Radio. Her piece in *Feminine Rising* is an excerpt from her memoir on being a gay woman of color in Mexico and the United States. She lives in Vermont with her wife and two children.

Wendy Besel Hahn has an MFA in creative writing from George Mason University. Her work has appeared in or is forthcoming in the *Washington Post, CRATE, So to Speak, Front Porch Journal,* and the *Chaffey Review.* In May 2014, she read an original essay, "Sick Mama," during the *Listen to Your Mother* DC show.

Linda Flaherty Haltmaier is an award-winning author and the poet laureate of Andover, Massachusetts. She is the winner of the Homebound Publications Poetry Prize for her debut, full-length collection *Rolling Up the Sky* (2016). Her latest collection, *To the Left of the Sun,* was released in 2018 by Homebound. Her work has won first place in the Palm Beach Poetry Festival Competition, earned finalist honors for both the Princemere Poetry Prize and the Tucson Festival of the Book Literary Award, and been shortlisted for the Robert Frost Poetry Prize. Her poetry has been nominated for a Pushcart Prize and has appeared in journals and anthologies including *Ink & Letters, The Wild Word, Switchgrass Review,* and more. A Harvard graduate, Linda lives on the North Shore of Boston with her husband and daughter.

Pauletta Hansel's poems and prose have been featured in journals including *Kudzu, Appalachian Journal, Appalachian Heritage,* and *Still: The Journal* and on *The Writer's Almanac* and *American Life in Poetry.* She is the author of six poetry collections, most recently *Palindrome* (Dos Madres Press, 2017). Pauletta is coeditor of *Pine Mountain Sand & Gravel,* the literary publication of the Southern Appalachian Writers Cooperative. Pauletta served as Cincinnati's first poet laureate from 2016 to 2018; she leads writing workshops and retreats in the Greater Cincinnati area and beyond.

Mary Hutchins Harris is a poet and essayist. Her chapbook, *A Tongue Full of Yeses,* was selected by Kwame Dawes for publication in the South Carolina Poetry Initiative Chapbook Contest. She has been a featured poet for the Piccolo Spoleto Sundown Series in Charleston, South Carolina. Her work has appeared in *Antietam Review, Kakalak, Main Street Rag, Poemeleon, Pirene's Fountain, Spill-*

way, and *Tar River Poetry* as well as in other print and online publications. She is an interdisciplinary studies adjunct professor in the Lesley University, Cambridge, Massachusetts, low-residency MFA program.

Siobhan Harvey is the author of *Cloudboy* (Otago University Press, 2014) and coeditor of *Essential New Zealand Poems* (Penguin Random House NZ, 2014). She is a lecturer at the Centre for Creative Writing, Auckland University of Technology. Her creative essays have been published in *Griffith Review, Landfall, Blue Five Journal,* and *Segue.* She was runner-up in the 2011 and highly commended in the 2013 Landfall Essay Competitions as well as winner of New Zealand's richest prize for poetry, the 2013 Kathleen Grattan Award for Poetry. The Poetry Archive (U.K.) holds a "Poet's Page" devoted to her work.

Melissa Helton is assistant professor of English and director of the honors program at a rural community college in southeast Kentucky. Originally from the Great Lakes region, she earned her MFA from Bowling Green State University in Ohio and now lives and writes on a subsistence farm in the mountains.

Rachel A. Hicks is a teacher and independent bookstore worker. She enjoys old typewriters, even older books, and indoor gardening. She received her MFA in poetry from West Virginia Wesleyan College and her MA in English from Marshall University. Her work has appeared in the *Pikeville Review* and *Still: The Journal.* She can usually be spotted in Charleston, West Virginia.

Nicole Hospital-Medina earned her MFA at the University of Miami, where she now teaches writing. Her work has appeared in various anthologies and journals, such as *Women Write Resistance: Poets Resist Gender Violence, CURA: A Journal of Art and Action,* the *Acentos Review, Moko Magazine, Barking Sycamores, Linden Lane Magazine, Paper Nautilus, Blunderbuss Magazine,* and the *Miami Herald.* Nicole is a new mom, a surfer, an artist, and a poet-activist.

Amy Hudock, PhD, is a writer, professor, and editor who lives in South Carolina with her daughter. She is a coeditor of the books *Literary Mama: Reading for the Maternally Inclined* (Seal Press, 2006) and *American Women Prose Writers, 1820–1870* (Gale, 2001). In her role as scholar, she has published forewords, chapters, and journal articles on literature and feminism, nineteenth-century American women writers, and the literature of motherhood. Her creative work has been anthologized in the Chicken Soup for the Soul and Cup of Comfort series, as well as in *Blended: Writers on the Stepfamily Experience, Torn: True Stories of Modern Motherhood, Ask Me about My Divorce, Mama, PhD,* and *Single State of the Union.* She is a cofounder of *Literary Mama,* an online literary magazine chosen by *Writer's Digest* as one of the 101 Best Web Sites for Writers (2005 and 2009) and by *Forbes* as one of its 100 Best of the Web (2005). Her work has also appeared in *Skirt!*, *Equus*, the *Post and Courier*, *ePregnancy*, and *Pregnancy and Baby*. She is the assistant campus dean at the Downtown Palmer Campus of Trident Technical College and occasionally teaches graduate and undergraduate classes at the College of Charleston and The Citadel. In addition, she has taught writing, American literature, and women's and gender studies at the University of North Carolina at Charlotte, the University of South Carolina–Columbia, the University of Georgia–Athens, Marshall University, and the University of California, Berkeley.

Mary Imo-Stike's poems venture from the familiar into the bigger world, grounded in her feelings and responses to her Catholic upbringing. Many record her experiences in male-dominated industrial jobs as a pioneer on the front lines of second-wave women's liberation. Her work has appeared in many journals, and her chapbook, *In and Out of the Horse Latitudes*, was published in 2018 by Finishing Line Press. Mary makes her home in Scott Depot, West Virginia.

M. J. Iuppa is the director of the Visual and Performing Arts Minor Program and lecturer in creative writing at St. John Fisher College and, from 2000 to present, has been a part-time lecturer in creative writing at The College at Brockport. Since 1986, she has been a teaching artist, working with students, K–12, in Rochester, New York, and the surrounding area. Most recently, she was awarded the New York State Chancellor's Award for Excellence in Adjunct Teaching, 2017. She has four full-length poetry collections—*This Thirst* (Kelsay Books, 2017), *Small Worlds Floating* (Cherry Grove, 2016), *Within Reach* (Cherry Grove, 2010), and *Night Traveler* (Foothills, 2003)—and five chapbooks. She lives on a small farm in Hamlin, New York.

Marianne S. Johnson holds a BA from Cal Poly, San Luis Obispo, and a law degree from Hastings College of the Law. Her poetry is published in *Calyx*, *Sport Literate*, *New Millennium Writings*, and *Sixfold*. Her work also appears in the anthologies *Lavanderia: A Mixed Load of Women, Wash and Word*; *A Year in Ink*; *The Far East Project*; and *Sunshine Noir II*, showcasing life in San Diego, where she still practices law. Her first poetry chapbook, *Tender Collisions*, published by Aldrich Press in 2015, won a San Diego Book Award, and she was nominated for a Pushcart Prize.

Meridian Johnson (previously Stephanie N. Johnson) is the author of *Kinesthesia*, a full-length poetry collection published in 2010 by New Rivers Press. Her essays and poems have appeared in *AGNI*, *Beloit Poetry Journal*, *Gettysburg Review*, *Bellevue Literary Review*, *Massachusetts Review*, and elsewhere. She is a craniosacral therapist, life coach, mother, dancer, and writer living in northern New Mexico. Meridian loves to celebrate the miraculousness of the human journey.

Michele K. Johnson Huffman completed her MFA in poetry from George Mason University in 2014 and received her BA in English from St. Mary's College of Maryland in 2011. She currently teaches literature and writing at High Point University in North Carolina, where she works with students to integrate meaningful service into an active learning environment. Her poetry has appeared in *OVS Magazine, THRUSH Magazine, Ampersand Review, UCity Review,* and elsewhere.

Elizabeth Johnston hopes that her writing provides a counternarrative to the mainstream representations of women and female sexual agency in literary and cultural mythology. Her Pushcart-nominated poetry and prose appear in many magazines and edited collections, including *The Atlantic, McSweeney's, Room Magazine, Feminist Formations, Women Studies Quarterly,* and *Nasty Women Poets: An Unapologetic Anthology of Subversive Verse,* among others. She is a founding member of Straw Mat Writers and teaches writing in Rochester, New York, where she lives with her partner and daughters.

Shobhana Kumar has published two collections of poetry: *Kolkata: The Voices Never Stop* (2012) and **Conditions Apply* (2014). Her work appears in several anthologies and journals around the world. She has read at several poetry festivals, including in Bengaluru, Chennai, and Hyderabad. Shobhana has authored six books of nonfiction covering local industrial histories and biographies and also writes Japanese short verse forms. She runs the nonprofit Small Differences, working with homeless, abandoned, and transgender communities.

Boutheina Laarif has undertaken a PhD that proposes a postmodern approach to W. H. Auden's poetry and metrical art (Faculty of Arts of Manouba, Tunisia). She is a lecturer of English literature. She has published articles that focus on philosophical, aesthetic theories of poetic rhythm. She published her first poetry collection, *Fractal Reflections,* in 2015. She has also several poems published in poetry journals like the quarterly journal the *Cannon's Mouth* and in several poetry anthologies.

Jessica Lawrence studied under the MFA program at Longwood University, participates in paid writing workshops, and has presented her poetry at the Southern Humanities Conference.

Cade Leebron is a writer living in Columbus, Ohio. She holds an MFA from the Ohio State University, where she served as an editor at *The Journal.* Her work has appeared in *Brevity, Electric Literature, American Literary Review,* and elsewhere.

Cathy Cultice Lentes is a poet, essayist, and children's writer. She has been writing and publishing since the age of eight, when her first poem appeared in a small-town Ohio newspaper. She was born in Xenia, Ohio, and grew up near

Springfield, Ohio. Since 1987, she has lived and worked in the Appalachian foothills near the big bend of the Ohio River, halfway between Cincinnati and Pittsburgh. She received her MFA from the Solstice Program of Pine Manor College in 2013. Her work appears in literary journals, magazines, and anthologies including *Every River on Earth: Writings from Appalachian Ohio* (Ohio University Press, 2015). She is the winner of a 2014 Work-in-Progress Grant from the Society of Children's Book Writers and Illustrators and the author of a poetry chapbook, *Getting the Mail* (Finishing Line Press, 2016).

Lynda Levy is a retired psychologist and life coach. She has been preoccupied with women's voices all her life. She took her first writing class at the Woman's Building, a feminist art center in downtown Los Angeles. She has lived in Chicago and Los Angeles, with brief sojourns in Israel and Boston. She now resides in Phoenix, Arizona, where she's pursuing her writing full-time, focusing on creative nonfiction and occasional poetry.

Kali Lightfoot grew up in Michigan and currently lives in Salem, Massachusetts. Her poetry has appeared in journals including *Illuminations 29, Lavender Review,* and *Poetry South* (poem nominated for a Pushcart Prize). Kali holds an MFA in writing from the Vermont College of Fine Arts.

Katharyn Howd Machan, author of thirty-eight collections of poetry (most recently, in 2018, *What the Piper Promised* from New Alexandria Press [national chapbook competition winner], her *Selected Poems* from FutureCycle Press, and *Secret Music: Voices from Redwing, 1888* from Cayuga Lake Books), has lived in Ithaca, New York, since 1975 and, now as a full professor, has taught writing at Ithaca College since 1977. After many years of coordinating the Ithaca Community Poets and directing the national Feminist Women's Writing Workshops, Inc., she was selected to be Tompkins County's first poet laureate. Her poems have appeared in numerous magazines, anthologies, and textbooks, and she has edited three thematic anthologies, most recently a tribute collection celebrating the inspiration of Adrienne Rich.

Eileen McDermott is an editorial consultant and journalist living in Brewster, New York, with her wife and dog, Colby. She enjoys hiking, snowboarding, traveling, reading, and taking her dog to the woods. Her love affair with Manhattan is over.

Llewellyn McKernan is a poet, children's book writer, and teacher who has lived and worked in Huntington, West Virginia, for more than thirty years. She has an MA in creative writing from Brown University and an MA in English from the University of Arkansas. Among her eleven writing grants are ones from the American Association of University Women, the West Virginia Commission on the Arts, and the West Virginia Humanities Council. Her work has won ninety-six prizes, awards, and honors in state, regional, and national contests. Her poetry has appeared in forty-three anthologies and in such journals as the *Kenyon Review, Appalachian Journal, Southern Poetry Review, Antietam Review, Appalachian Heritage, Now & Then,* and others. Her published poetry books for adults are *Getting Ready to Travel, Short and Simple Annals, Many Waters, Llewellyn McKernan's Greatest Hits, Pencil Memory,* and *The Sound of One Tree Falling.* Four of her poetry books for children have also been published: *More Songs of Gladness, Bird Alphabet, This Is the Day,* and *This Is the Night.* Almost all these achievements occurred in West Virginia, where she still lives with her husband on a rural route. "If home is where the heart is," she says, "writing poetry is always home to me, and I've written more poems in West Virginia than anywhere else on earth."

Lisa Minney lives on a secluded farm on Memory Lane in central West Virginia with her husband, a spoiled beagle, a yellow tabby cat, and several hens. Formerly an award-winning news reporter, Lisa is now director of a public library and a college professor. She received her MFA in creative nonfiction at West Virginia Wesleyan College.

Bonnie J. Morris is a professor emerita of women's studies at George Washington University and now is a women's history lecturer at the University of California, Berkeley. She is the author of sixteen books, including *Women's History for Beginners, Revenge of the Women's Studies Professor, Eden Built by Eves, The Disappearing L,* and, most recently, *The Feminist Revolution, Sappho's Bar and Grill,* and *Sappho's Overhead Projector.* She is now the archivist at Olivia Records and may be heard on C-Span Book TV as well as Olivia Cruises and Semester at Sea.

Maggie Thach Morshed is a former award-winning sports journalist whose byline has appeared in multiple news outlets across the country. She has an MFA in creative nonfiction from the University of California, Riverside, Palm Desert. She is currently working a memoir about living and teaching in South Korea. Much of her writing revolves around the themes of immigration, identity, and assimilation.

Rashida Murphy, PhD, lives in Perth, Western Australia. She is the author of the novel *The Historian's Daughter* (UWA). Her work is forthcoming in several anthologies from Orient Blackswan, Exisle, and Ethos Books. She is currently finishing her second novel.

Frances Nicholson's poetry has been published in *Soundings Review, Evening Street Review, MARGIE, Paper Street,* and *Pearl* and anthologized in *Touching: Poems of Love, Longing & Desire,* and *In the Telling.* Her chapbook *Smoke and*

Mirrors has been twice a semifinalist for the Robin Becker Chapbook Series. She is the author of two published collections of poetry.

Mary Heather Noble is an environmental scientist, writer, and mother whose work is inspired by social and environmental issues and informed by her former career as an environmental regulator. Her writing has been recently honored with two Pushcart Prize nominations, the Editor's Prize in *Creative Nonfiction*'s Learning from Nature issue, and as a finalist in *Bellingham Review*'s 2016 Annie Dillard Award in Creative Nonfiction. She is a contributing editor with the *Longridge Review* online journal and has recently published work in *AboutPlace Journal, Barrelhouse, Hippocampus Magazine,* and *Orion,* among others. Noble is a graduate of the Stonecoast MFA in Creative Writing Program at the University of Southern Maine. She lives with her family in Vermont.

Renée Olander is the author of *American Dangerous* (Backlash Press, 2018) and the chapbooks *A Few Spells* (Finishing Line Press, 2010) and *Wild Flights* (Black Bird Press, 2000). Recipient of a Kate Smith Award for Poetry from *Amelia Magazine* and a Pushcart Prize nomination for *Sistersong: Women~across~Cultures,* her poems, essays, reviews, and interviews with writers have appeared widely in anthologies, journals, blogs, and podcasts.

Lucy Palmer is from Cornwall in England but now lives in the United States. Her poetry has appeared in *By&By Poetry, The Pickled Body,* and others. Her flash fiction has appeared in *Cherry Tree,* the *Radvocate,* and the *Matador Review.*

Ann Pancake is the author of two short story collections, *Given Ground* and *Me and My Daddy Listen to Bob Marley,* and a novel, *Strange as This Weather Has Been,* which was one of *Kirkus Reviews*'s Top Ten Fiction Books of the year; won the 2007 Weatherford Award; and was a finalist for the 2008 Orion Book Award and the 2008 Washington State Book Award. She has also received a Whiting Award, an NEA grant, the Bakeless Prize, and a Pushcart Prize. Her fiction and essays have appeared in journals and anthologies like *Orion,* the *Georgia Review, Poets and Writers,* and *New Stories from the South, the Year's Best.* She's currently serving as writer-in-residence in the Humanities Center at West Virginia University.

Penny Perkins holds an MFA in creative writing from the Institute of American Indian Arts in Santa Fe, New Mexico. Recent short stories and poems have been published in the *Pine Hills Review, Rocky Mountain Revival, Waxwing,* the *New Verse News, Entropy/Enclave, Beecher's Magazine,* and *HOAX.* Other publication credits include *Salon, Conditions, The Portable Lower East Side, Curves, Girlfriend No. 1,* and *Book,* among others. She currently lives in upstate New York and is working on a novel.

~DREAMA PRITT is a native West Virginian who was cradled by mountains and is still delighted by lightning bugs. Her publishing credits include *Biostories, Et Cetera,* and the *Boys Will Be Boys* and *All about the Girls* anthologies. She's received awards and publications in multiple genres, including poetry, fiction, and creative nonfiction.

SUSAN RICHARDSON has published poems, stories, and articles in various magazines and anthologies. In 2014, *California Quarterly* nominated one of her poems for a Pushcart Prize. In 2015, Susan won first place in the *MacGuffin* Poet Hunt. She works as a writer, editor, artist, and crossword puzzle maker in Boise, Idaho.

LOIS ROMA-DEELEY's poetry collection *The Short List of Certainties* (Franciscan University Press, 2017) won the Jacopone da Todi Book Prize. Her previous collections are *Rules of Hunger, northSight,* and *High Notes*—a Paterson Poetry Prize finalist. Roma-Deeley's poems are featured in numerous literary journals and anthologies. Currently she serves as the associate editor of *Presence.*

RUTH SABATH ROSENTHAL, a New York poet, is well published in the United States and internationally. She is a Pushcart Prize nominee and author of five books of poetry: *Facing Home; Facing Home and Beyond; Little, but by No Means Small; Food: Nature vs Nurture;* and *Gone, but Not Easily Forgotten.*

SARAH SADIE is the founder/owner of Odonata Creative. She writes, coaches other creatives, and teaches Qoya dance. Her poems and books have won multiple prizes, including a Pushcart. Her second full-length collection, *We Are Traveling through Dark at Tremendous Speeds,* was published by LitFest Press. She attempts to bloom in the shape of a poem every day.

SHLOKA SHANKAR is a freelance writer, editor, and visual artist from Bangalore, India. She enjoys experimenting with Japanese short forms and found poetry techniques from time to time. A Best of the Net nominee, her work has appeared in more than two hundred print and online venues of repute. Shloka is the founding editor of the literary and arts journal *Sonic Boom* and its affiliated press, Yavanika.

ANNETTE SNYCKERS is a visual artist and poet living in Cape Town, South Africa. She studied literature (English, French, and German) at the University of Pretoria and, later, fine art at the University of South Africa. She was a high school teacher and translator before dedicating herself to the visual arts. Her poems have been selected for several anthologies and are published in literary magazines. Annette writes in English, Afrikaans, and German. Her multilingual collection *Remnants Restante Reste* was published in 2018 by the feminist press Modjaji Books.

JESSICA SPRUILL is an assistant professor of English at Alderson Broaddus University in Philippi, West Virginia, and a graduate of the low-residency MFA program at West Virginia Wesleyan College. She is a poetry editor for *Heart-Wood,* a literary magazine in association with the MFA at West Virginia Wesleyan College. Jessica is a Pushcart nominee whose poetry has appeared in *Burnt Pine Magazine,* the *Pikeville Review, Still: The Journal,* and the *Travelin' Appalachians Revue.* She is the founder and curator of the Wordstock Wednesday reading series.

Tuesday Taylor is an author, educator, and public speaker. Recipient of the Robert F. Kennedy Visionary Award, Ms. Tuesday, as her students call her, established and facilitates youth programs specializing in behavioral management, summer enrichment, and visual and performing arts throughout West Virginia and Ohio. She earned her degree in communications from West Virginia State University and is creator and host of the multimedia show *What's Real West Virginia.* Her poetry collection, *A Dandy Lion Dreams,* is available online.

Terry Ann Thaxton has published three collections of poetry, *Getaway Girl* (Salt, 2011), *The Terrible Wife* (Salt, 2013), and *Mud Song* (Salt, 2017), as well as a textbook, *Creative Writing in the Community: A Guide* (Bloomsbury, 2014). Her essay "Delusions of Grandeur" won the *Missouri Review*'s 2012 Jeffrey E. Smith Editors' Prize. She has also published essays and poetry in the *Chattahoochee Review, Pithead Chapel, Defunct, Gulf Coast, Cimarron Review, Flyway, Sou'wester, Lullwater Review, Teaching Artist Journal,* and other journals. She holds an MFA from Vermont College and teaches creative writing at the University of Central Florida, where she also directs the MFA program.

Barbara Ungar's fifth full-length collection, *Save Our Ship,* won the Richard Snyder Memorial Prize and is forthcoming in 2019 from Ashland Poetry Press. Prior books include *Immortal Medusa,* one of *Kirkus Reviews*'s Best Indie Books of 2015 and cowinner of the Adirondack Center for Writing Poetry Award; *Charlotte Brontë, You Ruined My Life; The Origin of the Milky Way,* winner of the Gival Prize, a Silver IPPY, and a Hoffer Award; and *Thrift.* An English professor at the College of Saint Rose in Albany, New York, she has published in the *Southern Indiana Review, Rattle, Salmagundi,* and many other journals; she has been nominated for five Pushcarts and a Best of the Net.

Gina Valdés's poetry has been widely published in journals and anthologies in the United States, Mexico, and Europe. She has recent or forthcoming work in *Spillway, Huizache, Adanna, Full Bleed,* and *50/50: Poetry and Translations by Women over Fifty.*

Jamie Wendt is the author of the poetry collection *Fruit of the Earth* (Main Street Rag, 2018). She is a graduate of the University of Nebraska Omaha MFA program. She received a BA in English from Drake University. Her poetry has been published in various literary journals, including *Lilith, Raleigh Review, Minerva*

Rising, Third Wednesday, and *Saranac Review.* Her essays and book reviews have been published in *Green Mountains Review, Forward, Literary Mama,* and others. She teaches high school English and lives in Chicago with her husband and two children.

Anne Harding Woodworth is the author of six books of poetry and four chapbooks. Her most recent book is *The Eyes Have It* (2018). An excerpt from her most recent chapbook, *The Last Gun*, won the 2016 COG Poetry Award, judged by A. Van Jordan. It has subsequently been animated by Cogswell College. Harding Woodworth is cochair of the Poetry Board at the Folger Shakespeare Library, Washington, D.C., where she lives when she isn't at a cabin in the mountains of Western North Carolina. Her work is published widely in the United States and abroad, in print and online

Marianne Worthington is a poet, editor, and cofounder of *Still: The Journal,* an online literary magazine publishing literary, visual, and musical artists with ties to the Appalachian region since 2009. She received the Al Smith Fellowship from the Kentucky Arts Council and the Appalachian Book of the Year Award for her poetry collection *Larger Bodies than Mine.* She was awarded grants from the Kentucky Foundation for Women and the Appalachian Sound Archives Fellowship at Berea College. She has edited four literary anthologies, most recently *Piano in a Sycamore: Writing Lessons from the Appalachian Writers' Workshop,* coedited with Silas House. Her work has appeared in *Oxford American, CALYX, Grist, Shenandoah,* the *Louisville Review, Southern Poetry Anthology,* and *Vinegar and Char: Verse from the Southern Foodways Alliance,* among other places. She lives, writes, and teaches in southeast Kentucky.

Müesser Yeniay was born in İzmir, 1984, and has won several prizes in Turkey. She has written books on poetry and poetry criticism and has translated the books of many world poets. Her poetry books have been translated and published in the United States, Hungary, France, India, Colombia, Spain, and Vietnam. She is studying for her PhD in Turkish poetry at Bilkent University, Ankara.

Andrena Zawinski has three poetry collections: *Landings* (Kelsay Books, 2017), her most recent; *Something About* (Blue Light Press, 2002), a PEN Oakland Josephine Miles Literary Award recipient; and *Traveling in Reflected Light* (Pig Iron Press, 1995), a Kenneth Patchen Poetry Prize winner. She has also authored four chapbooks and compiled and edited *Turning a Train of Thought Upside Down: An Anthology of Women's Poetry* (Scarlet Tanager Books, 2012). A longtime teacher of writing and an avid feminist, she founded and runs the Women's Poetry Salon in the San Francisco Bay Area and is the features editor at PoetryMagazine.com.

About the Editors

Andrea Fekete is a native West Virginian and granddaughter to Mexican and Hungarian immigrants. She is author of the historical fiction novel *Waters Run Wild* (2018). She has one poetry chapbook, *I Held a Morning* (Finishing Line Press, 2012). Her poetry and fiction have appeared in *Chiron Review, Borderlands: Texas Poetry Review,* the *Kentucky Review,* the *Montucky Review,* the *Smithville Journal,* the *Adirondack Review,* and *ABZ* and in *Eyes Glowing on the Edge of the Woods: Fiction & Poetry from West Virginia* (WVU Press, 2017), among other anthologies. An excerpt from her newest novel, *Native Trees,* was a finalist in *Still: The Journal*'s 2019 Fiction Contest. She earned her MFA in creative writing from West Virginia Wesleyan College and her MA in English from Marshall University.

Lara Lillibridge is the author of *Mama, Mama, Only Mama* (Skyhorse, 2019) and Girl*ish: Growing Up in a Lesbian Home* (Skyhorse, 2018). She is a graduate of West Virginia Wesleyan College's MFA program in creative nonfiction. In 2016 she won the *Slippery Elm Literary Journal*'s Prose Contest and the *American Literary Review*'s Contest in Nonfiction. You can read some of her work in *Ms.,* the *Guardian,* the *Washington Post,* the *Advocate, Hippocampus Magazine, Luna Luna,* and *Huffington Post.*

Publication History

"1888–1988" by Marianne Worthington first appeared in *Larger Bodies Than Mine* (Finishing Line Press, 2007).

"Acts of Protest" by Gina Valdés first appeared in *Pilgrimage* 38, no. 2 (2014).

"All I Know of Death" by Pauletta Hansel first appeared in *Tangle* (Dos Madres Press, 2015).

"Apologizing for the Rain" by Lois Roma-Deeley first appeared in *northSight* (Singularity Press, 2006).

"The Apparatus of the Dark" by Renée Olander appeared in *A Few Spells* (Finishing Line Press, 2010), *Hawai'i Pacific Review Best of the Decade: 1997–2007,* and *American Dangerous* (Backlash Press, 2018).

"Between Worlds" by Gina Valdés first appeared in *Spillway* (2016).

"A Box, Full" by Ruth Sabath Rosenthal first appeared in *Facing Home and Beyond* (Paragon Poetry Press, 2011).

"Brown" by Shobhana Kumar first appeared in *Conditions Apply, Writers Workshop* (Calcutta, 2014).

"Butterfly Woman" by Gina Valdés first appeared in *SageWoman* (Spring 2016).

"Dear Torso, Stone Carved" by Renée Olander first appeared in *American Dangerous* (Backlash Press, 2018).

"Failed Meal" by Marianne Worthington first appeared in *Grist: The Journal for Writers,* no. 8 (2015).

"Fe-Male" by Boutheina Laarif first appeared in *Cannon's Mouth Magazine* (2015).

"For Want of Red" by Ruth Sabath Rosenthal first appeared in *Facing Home and Beyond* (Paragon Poetry Press, 2011).

"Fuck Us Harder" by Cade Leebron first appeared in *The Manifest-Station* (2015).

"Girl Villanelle" by Pauletta Hansel first appeared in *Tangle* (Dos Madres Press, 2015).

"God (According to Pastor Smucker)" by Cheryl Denise first appeared in *I Saw God Dancing* (DreamSeeker Books, 2005).

"Gravidity" by Melissa Helton first appeared in *Motif* 4 (2014).

"Harvard in the Sixties: (Un)Speakable Memories" by Ellen Cantarow first appeared in *The Family Track: Keeping Your Faculties While You Mentor, Nurture, Teach, and Serve* (University of Illinois Press, 1998).

"Ice Fight" by Ann Pancake previously appeared as "Our Own Kind" in *Willow Springs* 71 (April 15, 2016).

"I've Spent My Life" by Jessica Lawrence first appeared in *The Lake* (United Kingdom, 2015).

"Journey through the Door into Always-Always Land: 1966" by Katharyn Howd Machan first appeared in *Amazon* (1979).

"Keel" by Shobhana Kumar first appeared in *The Voices Project* (2014).

"Les-Salles-du-Gardon" by Katharyn Howd Machan first appeared in *ByLine* (2002).

"Mirrors and Reflections" by Jacqueline Doyle first appeared in *Hippocampus Magazine* (August 2013).

"Moments in Sand: Fragments between Sea and Sky" by Michelle Elvy is an excerpt from a poem that first appeared in full in *Ika* (New Zealand, 2015). The opening first appeared in slightly different form in *Room* (Canada, 2014).

"Mother and Child" by Susan Richardson first appeared in *The Dos Passos Review* (June 2008).

"My Brother" by Katharyn Howd Machan first appeared in *Negative Capability* (1983).

"Natalie on Men," "Natalie in the Dirt," and "Natalie Land-Locked" by Michele K. Johnson Huffman originally appeared in *The Avenue*, no. 3 (2016).

"On Faith" by Pauletta Hansel first appeared in *Tangle* (Dos Madres Press, 2015).

"On Motherhood" by Frances Nicholson first appeared in *Margie* (2009).

"The Orange-and-White High-Heeled Shoes" by Ellen Bass first appeared in the *New Yorker* (March 30, 2015).

"Pins and Rope" by Jamie Wendt first appeared in *Fruit of the Earth* (2018).

"The Poison Our Mothers and Grandmothers Drank" by Michele Tracy Berger first appeared in *Trivia: Voices of Feminism* (Spring 2013).

"Porcelain" and "1888–1988" by Marianne Worthington first appeared in *Larger Bodies Than Mine* (Finishing Line Press, 2007).

"Post-Natal" by Lucy Palmer first appeared in *By&By* (2017).

"Postscript" by Mary Hutchins Harris first appeared in *A Tongue Full of Yeses* (Stepping Stones Press, 2008).

"Somewhere with Cows" by Meridian Johnson first appeared in *Esme* (Winter 2015).

"The Stain" by Mary Imo-Stike first appeared in *Antietam Review* (Spring 2003).

"Swallowing" by Cheryl Denise first appeared in *Fluent Magazine* (Winter 2015).

"Tackle Box" by Elizabeth Johnston previously appeared in *Lunch Ticket* (Summer 2015).

"The Tear" by Lynda Levy first appeared in *Feminine Collective* (2016).

"Things I (Shouldn't) Have to Tell My Daughters" by Mary Heather Noble first appeared in *The Fem* (June 2016).

"The Women's Gown" by Melissa Helton first appeared in *Still: The Journal* (Summer 2014).

"Working" by Carol Gloor first appeared in *Broad Ideas* (May 2018).